T0247849

CHAOS
COMES
CALLING

ALSO BY SASHA ABRAMSKY

Little Wonder: The Fabulous Story of Lottie Dod, the World's First Female Sports Superstar

Jumping at Shadows: The Triumph of Fear and the End of the American Dream

The House of Twenty Thousand Books

The American Way of Poverty: How the Other Half Still Lives

Inside Obama's Brain

Breadline USA: The Hidden Scandal of American Hunger and How to Fix It

American Furies: Crime, Punishment, and Vengeance in the Age of Mass Imprisonment

Hard Time Blues: How Politics Built a Prison Nation

Conned: How Millions Went to Prison, Lost the Vote, and Helped Send George W. Bush to the White House

CHAOS COMES CALLING

The Battle Against the Far-Right Takeover of Small-Town America

SASHA ABRAMSKY

 BOLD TYPE BOOKS

New York

Bold Type Books

Hachette Book Group

1290 Avenue of the Americas, New York, NY 10104

www.boldtypebooks.org

@BoldTypeBooks

Printed in the United States of America

First Edition: September 2024

Published by Bold Type Books, an imprint of Hachette Book Group, Inc. Bold Type Books is a co-publishing venture of the Type Media Center and Perseus Books.

The Hachette Speakers Bureau provides a wide range of authors for speaking events. To find out more, go to hachettespeakersbureau.com or email HachetteSpeakers@hbgusa.com.

Bold Type books may be purchased in bulk for business, educational, or promotional use. For more information, please contact your local bookseller or the Hachette Book Group Special Markets Department at special.markets@hbgusa.com.

The publisher is not responsible for websites (or their content) that are not owned by the publisher.

Print book interior design by Amy Quinn.

Library of Congress Cataloging-in-Publication Data

Names: Abramsky, Sasha, author.

Title: Chaos comes calling : two small counties and the epic battle for America's soul / Sasha Abramsky.

Description: First edition. | New York : Bold Type Books, 2024. | Includes index.

Identifiers: LCCN 2024000153 | ISBN 9781645030430 (hardcover) | ISBN 9781645030454 (ebook)

Subjects: LCSH: Radicalism—California—Shasta County. | Radicalism—Washington (State)—Sequim. | Right-wing extremists—California—Shasta County. | Right-wing extremists—Washington (State)—Sequim. | Political culture—California—Shasta County. | Political culture—Washington (State)—Sequim. | Political culture—United States.

Classification: LCC HN79.C22 S533 2024 | DDC 320.53/30979424—dc23/eng/20240410

LC record available at https://lccn.loc.gov/2024000153

ISBNs: 9781645030430 (hardcover), 9781645030454 (e-book)

LSC-C

Printing 1, 2024

To my darling Marissa, who makes me laugh
and keeps me even-keeled. I look forward
to our endless adventures together.

And to my wonderful children, Sofia and Leo, who
fill my days with pride and joy. May you always
keep your fine-tuned sense of right and wrong.

"For every action there is an equal and opposite reaction."

—Isaac Newton

"Don't talk unless you can improve the silence."

—Jorge Luis Borges

"The vulgar proclaims and imposes the rights of vulgarity, or vulgarity as a right."

—José Ortega y Gasset

CONTENTS

Introduction

FLOODING THE ZONE WITH SHIT

D R. ALLISON BERRY, PUBLIC HEALTH OFFICER FOR CLALLAM COUNTY, WASHINGTON, SAT AT A table at the Rainshadow Café in downtown Sequim (pronounced "Squim"), a town of 8,000 residents on the Olympic Peninsula, 110 miles northwest of Seattle. She readied herself to tell me about the tsunami of hatred that had come her way during the COVID-19 crisis.

Since the pandemic began and she had introduced local mitigation measures to slow the spread of the deadly virus, Berry had been receiving threats on a near-daily basis. It was December 2021, eighteen months into the calamity, and the young doctor still had a target on her back. "Hundreds of hate mails," she said. "It was mostly in a really misogynistic direction. Think of your most color-ful misogynistic language, and that's what came my way."

Six months earlier, in June 2021, with the COVID vaccine cam-paign well under way and with most elderly and immunocompro-mised residents double-vaccinated, Washington's governor, Jay Inslee, had reopened the state, allowing "nonessential" businesses to function again and people to congregate without limitations on number or setting. New variants of the virus were starting to pick up steam, however, and—as public health officials had predicted would be the case—despite the widespread vaccination effort, the number of COVID infections immediately surged. "We just couldn't hold it back," Berry recalled. "People were indoors regardless of vaccination status, with masks off. People were traveling. The message had been sent that the pandemic was over."

Just like that, in Clallam County the caseload shot up to 1,300 per 100,000 residents over a two-week period. The contact-tracing system that Berry and her team of tracers, which had grown from three people to roughly twenty as the pandemic ground on, had operated so effectively for the first year of the pandemic—speedily shutting down local outbreaks through a rigid regimen of tracing and concentric testing—broke down under the stress. The local hospitals were overwhelmed: every bed was full, and so many staff were out sick that the facilities were having to call in trainee EMTs to work in the emergency rooms. Doctors were putting together makeshift negative-pressure breathing rooms in which they could house the growing number of intubated patients, and the county's few respiratory therapists were working virtually around the clock. Local residents were so scared of getting infected while in the hos-pital that some stayed away, even when they were experiencing life-threatening medical emergencies such as strokes. And even if they weren't scared off, many had no way of getting to the hospi-tal: ambulance crews were so busy that critically ill patients were forced to wait hours for the vehicles to arrive to transport them. And then, once they arrived, they would have to wait ungodly long times to be seen by the frantically busy doctors. Stroke victims were languishing up to eight hours in the emergency room, their brains accumulating more and more permanent damage. Seriously ill COVID patients, their oximeter readings showing dangerously low oxygen levels, likewise had to wait hours before they were admitted.

"I was getting calls from doctors in tears, saying, 'Everyone's dying,'" Berry said. "One told me, 'I've intubated five people today.' The health system's on fire, and everything else is normal. The bars are open, people are partying. The disconnect was incredible."

Knowing that putting in place another local shutdown order just after the state had officially reopened would create a firestorm, Berry, along with two public health officials in neighboring counties on the peninsula, scrambled to find a solution. At first, she chose to reinstate mask mandates. Given the message coming out of the state capital, Olympia, that everything should reopen and that people could get on with their normal lives, it seemed the least draconian response. But it soon became clear that restaurants and bars—the venues in which diners and drinkers were still allowed to congregate maskless—were epicenters of the rampaging COVID surge. Contact tracers estimated that in one bar alone a trivia night had resulted in two hundred new cases and at least two deaths. When Washington State as a whole followed Clallam County's lead and introduced a mask mandate, its public health teams also found that it wasn't putting the brakes on the surge.

After two weeks in which, despite the new masking mandate, COVID rates continued to spiral upward, Berry contacted the county's lawyers. Labor Day was fast approaching, and she knew that tourists would soon be swarming onto the peninsula. The new school year was about to begin, and there were rumblings of having to return to Zoom classes if the county's surge couldn't be rapidly tamed. For the public health officer, it seemed madness to keep bars functioning as normal at the cost of having to remove kids from the classroom for another school year. She wanted to implement what she thought was the next-least-bad option, certainly less of an economic ball and chain than restricting eateries to 50 percent capacity: an order mandating that to be allowed to enter a local eatery or bar, patrons would have to produce proof of vaccination. The lawyers set to work drafting language that they believed would stand up in court, and Berry got to work preparing to issue the new regulations. "I was nervous about it; I knew I was going out on a limb," she recollected. "But I felt really confident it was the right thing to do. I was thinking: this is *my* responsibility. There's not many other people who can do it. I have to do my job. And so I did."

Within days, with most restaurants and bars complying with the orders—only four anti-vaccination owners took preliminary steps to sue Berry, litigation that they would ultimately abandon after she promised to lift the mandate by March 2022—the COVID infection rate began to fall, and within a couple of weeks the hospitalization and death rates in the county also plummeted. After about a month, the new case rate had dropped not just marginally but like a stone, retreating from a high, at the time Berry put in place the mandate, of more than 1,300 new cases per 100,000 residents in a given two-week period down to 207. Berry's instincts had been proven right. A month later, officials in Olympia acknowledged the success of the strategy and extended the proof-of-vaccination mandate to include the entire state of Washington.

By then, however, Berry had attracted the venomous interventions of anti-vaxxers not just in Sequim, not just in Clallam County, not just in Washington, but around the world. "I knew there'd be push-back [to the vaccine mandate]," Berry later recalled. "But I had no idea what was coming."

The morning after she posted about the mandate on her office's Facebook page, she woke up to find that the post had been shared thousands of times and that people from around the world were registering their disgust at the vaccine requirement. "People saying they knew where I was," people threatening to hunt her down and kill her. "I didn't anticipate that level of animosity. It was scary. I was living alone with my toddler in a studio in farmland without lights. I knew people were trying to find us, and I heard people were narrowing in on where I lived. I couldn't let my toddler play outside. I was like, 'What have I done? Am I going to get killed? I'm her only mom. Am I going to get my daughter killed?'"

Recently separated from her husband and raising her toddler daughter as a single mom, Berry suddenly found herself front-center stage in a bitter conflict that risked tearing the country apart. Armed mobs began showing up outside her public health offices, threatening to lynch the doctor and her colleagues. When the phones rang in her office, her colleagues girded themselves, knowing that there was a pretty good chance the person on the other end of the line would begin hurling obscenities at them as soon as they answered. When Berry opened her emails, she steeled herself for the barrage of hateful, frequently obscene messages that would flood her inbox.

Generally, Berry felt, with a justifiable pride, that she was hard to scare. But as she admitted, "I was scared here. I was absolutely scared here. I'm definitely scared of white supremacists and misogynists who want me dead." The emails, especially, gave her the chills.

"You're a brazen hypocrite who gets off on torturing children, much like your creepy Nazi pope gets off on torturing puppies. Moreover, you, and anyone going along with your mass, coerced medical experiment and the prolonged torture of children, will face judgement," went a fairly typical one, dated October 28, 2021.

After a few more venomous paragraphs, the author signed off with a "Happy Halloween." It was, to say the least, creepy, but when Berry forwarded it to the sheriff's office, the sheriff determined that it didn't rise to the level of a specific criminal threat.

On Facebook, one outraged anti-vaxxer waxed that "it is my religious freedom to not get vaccinated." And then, using most unreligious language, he waned, "Fuck every single one of you cunts."

Hundreds of miles to the south, in California's sparsely populated Shasta County, public health officer Karen Ramstrom, along with her supporters in county government, were facing a similar set of terrors.

As COVID spread, and as local public health officials desperately tried to craft regulations to keep the populace safe, talk-radio hosts would go on their shows and tell their audience of anti-vaxxers, anti-maskers, anti-RINOs (Republicans in Name Only), and anti–Black Lives Matters that it was time for blood to flow in the streets. "Communists only recognize the limits of their power when their necks are stretched," opined one shock jock on the Redding-based KCNR 1460 AM radio station, whose shows were subsequently scrubbed from the radio station's archives after he veered too far into the language of violence. A Facebook group called Open Shasta put up a posting about "taking out Dr. Ramstrom." A flood of other online threats soon followed. Anti-vaxxers picketed the public health offices. Fearing violence, the Redding Police Department ramped up patrols of Ramstrom's neighborhood.

So intimidating were the threats that, for a short time, Ramstrom even had a security team stationed outside her house. She put up cameras around her home; after a slew of particularly horrifying threats, she had to give statements to investigators from the DA's office.

When she looked to the county's elected officials for support, Ramstrom was rebuffed. Several hard-right members of the county board of supervisors pointedly refused to meet with the public health officer to show their support for her in light of the threats that she was facing. Instead, they urged their colleagues to go to bat against the county's and the state's public health responses, and to refuse to enforce the lockdown, nonessential business closings, and masking mandates. When the more moderate members balked at this, the hard-right contingent, backed by local militia members, "parents' rights" advocates, and a bevy of fundamentalist churches, pushed a recall campaign against them and, in doing so, turned Shasta County into an epicenter for the burgeoning anti-vaccine and anti-masking movements building to a head across America.

By 2022, most of the moderates had been driven out of county government. Ramstrom herself, after enduring months of protests against her, had been fired, as had many of the other top officials in public health and community services in the county. And the new hard-right majority on the board of supervisors, perhaps having realized the political potency of a heavily armed crowd, was pushing to make the rural locale a "Second Amendment sanctuary county."

On some levels Clallam County's and Shasta County's travails were hardly new. Pick pretty much any period in US history, and one can find a goodly assortment of demagogues and political hustlers, snake-oil salesmen and apostles of violent confrontation. Father Coughlin used his radio platform to blame Jews for the ills of the Great Depression. Senator Joe McCarthy used televised congressional hearings and stump speeches to bandy about fictitious lists of supposed Communist infiltrators in the army, in the civil service, in universities, and in Hollywood to raise his profile as America's ultimate Cold War Warrior. There have been know-nothings who blamed the country's ills on immigrants and religious diversity; populists such as President Andrew Jackson and Louisiana governor Huey Long who promised salvation to their followers and destructions of their enemies, real and imagined; military figures who gloried in the particularly creative torture and execution of resistance fighters in the Philippines; and newspaper editors and owners who used their platforms to sell to the public everything from eugenics to racially based immigration restrictions to patent medicines and elixirs of youth. There have been Hitler-sympathizing demagogues who riled up crowds of a few thousand here, a few thousand there. There have, of course, been those in positions of power who embraced the wave of lynching that swept the Jim Crow South in the century following the end of the Civil War, and men such as President Woodrow Wilson, who viewed the Ku Klux Klan as necessary defenders of southern virtue and white womanhood. And there have been those, like Jim Jones, who founded death cults to ensnare the emotionally vulnerable.

What is different about today's cast of characters selling their snake oil and their conspiracy theories isn't their irrationality per se, or even the violence that they preach, but their reach: the fact that, largely via social media and right-wing TV and talk radio in an era of 24/7 news and lightning-fast communications, their desire to burn down the pillars holding up the US democratic experiment can so rapidly percolate through all levels of society. Their disinformation isn't necessarily more toxic to individual users; it's just being distributed far more effectively. In consequence, it is adopted by a lot more people, who are posing a larger stress test for key political institutions and cultural norms than did most previous waves of conspiracists and ideologues. And when other disrupters, other black-swan moments, are added into the mix—Donald Trump's election to the presidency, the pandemic, the vast racial-justice protests of 2020, say—those snake-oil salesmen simply crank up the volume and ramp up their destructive sales pitch, urging Americans at both the local and the national level not to coalesce around common goals but to retreat into their echo chambers, into their real or figurative bunkers, to regard their opponents as enemies to be eradicated. And by the tens of millions, that is what Americans are now doing.

That's something qualitatively different from most other key moments in US history, with the singular, deadly exception of the Civil War. During the Spanish flu pandemic of 1919–1920, despite the enormous death rate—675,000 deaths out of a population of roughly 106,000,000—and the almost unendurable fear and lockdown conditions of those months, the country didn't fissure at the seams. During the McCarthy years, for all of the demagoguery and hysteria both unleashed and channeled by the junior senator from Wisconsin, at the end of the day neither major political party chose to actively discourage confidence in the electoral system. The John Birch Society might have denounced the fluoridation of water as a Communist conspiracy to poison Americans, but the vast majority of citizens, even those who didn't particularly like the idea of fluoride being added to their drinking water, weren't willing to take up arms to overturn the fluoridators. Nor did the Birchers' outlandish theories ever acquire the sort of mass currency that the even more outlandish QAnon has in the 2020s. Even during years of profound political upheaval and violence—the Great Depression, to take one example, the turbulent 1960s, to take another—the numbers, from either the Left or the Right, agitating to bring down support pillars of American democracy such as the judicial process and electoral system remained relatively small.

That's not to turn a blind eye to the raw power of violence in shaping US history. The deadly *attentats* that speckle the American story, the individual assassinations, the lone-wolf bombings—from the anarchist assault on Wall Street in 1920 to the militia-inspired attack on the Oklahoma City Federal Building in 1995—and the racial pogroms and riots have undeniably cost thousands of lives and caused vast pain. They have also brutalized entire groups and sought to inflict racial and class terror throughout entire regions. And that violence has often escalated in spectacular fashion. The four years of civil war resulted in more than 620,000 deaths. In the mid-1920s, millions of Americans were members of the Ku Klux Klan—by some estimates, one in six adult Protestant males were KKKers at the time—and its noxious influence extended far along the corridors of power in city halls, in statehouses, and in Congress. In the 1950s and 1960s, with the civil rights movement pushing for economic and voting rights for African Americans, proponents of eternal racial segregation made sure that the Old South was a hotbed of lynchings, bombings, and political noncooperation with the federal government. In 1968 the segregationist presidential candidate George Wallace won 13.5 percent of the vote—and carried five southern states. Young white men, in particular, flocked to his racist banner.

Locally, strongman leaders and their supporters have, at times, taken over individual city halls or frog-marched enemies over the county line, but the country as a whole, the checks and balances embedded into the federal system, have largely survived intact. That durability, that sense of the broad invulnerability of the Republic, is, however, no longer a given, especially in the wake of the January 6, 2021, attempted putsch and the antigovernment conspiracy theories metastasizing throughout the culture.

Throughout the 2010s and 2020s, polls have shown that an increasing percentage of Americans believe that political violence is justified. By 2022, according to polling by the *Washington Post* and the University of Maryland, that number had risen to well over 30 percent. Among white voters, the number was nearer 40 percent. Similarly, more than four in ten Republican voters expressed some level of comfort with the idea of turning toward political violence, a far higher percentage than the proportion of Democrats or independents saying that they could imagine turning to violence to realize their political ends. Taken as a whole, the percentage of Americans willing to countenance political violence had more than doubled since 2010 and had gone up more than threefold since the 1990s.

By 2022, two-thirds of those polled about the durability of American democracy answered that they viewed the democratic system as being under threat, and more than six out of ten voters now thought it likely that the losing side would turn to violence in future presidential elections. It was a pessimism that risked becoming self-fulfilling. "We're caught in an arms race between civility and incivility, fact and fake, unity and division, and it's not clear that America's better angels are winning," Harvard professor of government and the press Thomas Patterson wrote in *How America Lost Its Mind*. "Mature democracies don't collapse with a bang. They do it slowly, as expediency, anxiety, and miscalculation erode them a piece at a time."

Perhaps not coincidentally, during those three decades Americans had been on a gun-buying spree unprecedented in US history. By 2023, more than one-third of American adults owned at least one gun, with most of those individuals owning multiple weapons. There were, in total, well over 400 million privately owned guns in the country. Since 2020, when the pandemic hit, racial-justice protests spread across the country, and the country's political divisions came to a head around the presidential election that Trump refused to concede, Americans have purchased between 16 and 20 million new guns per year. That is two and a half times the quantity bought annually in the early 2000s. Of the 857 million guns estimated by the Small Arms Survey to be in private hands around the world, nearly half of them are in the United States, a country with only 4.4 percent of the world's population.

———

The advent of social media, initially marketed as an untram-
meled good, as a historic expansion and democratizing of the
information-delivery process, has instead helped to spread propaganda, to break down trust in traditional news sources, and to trap
consumers within ever-more-powerful echo chambers. The rise of
Donald Trump, with his extraordinary skills as a demagogue, and
the emergence of a personality cult around him—a cult that survived, largely intact, in the post-2020 years, even as Trump was ultimately indicted multiple times on serious criminal charges that could
land him in prison for decades—has made rational governance seem
almost a quaint throwback to a calmer, saner past. The proliferation
of powerful racial-, sexual-, and gender-justice movements—and
the fierce cultural backlash against these movements—have fundamentally and rapidly reshaped the country's cultural terrain. Throw
into the mix unprecedented environmental degradation and weather
calamities, from apocalyptic wildfires that leave thousands of people
homeless to once-in-a-thousand-year storms and floods; the emergence of an increasingly conservative federal judiciary; the horrific
proliferation of semiautomatic weapons on America's streets and an
extraordinary number of mass shootings; escalating chaos around
abortion access; cascading levels of homelessness; the fentanyl epidemic; the after-effects of a half century of mass-incarceration
policies; and then, to cap it all, a once-in-a-century pandemic and
more than a year of punishing lockdowns and quarantines, and you
have all the ingredients for a time of startling political upheaval and
chaos.

It is out of this petri dish that the violent mobs confronting
Dr. Berry at the height of the pandemic grew. Absent the intoxicat-
ing power of social media—where, veiled by anonymity, users can
and do lean into conspiracy thinking and insults—it's unlikely that
these mobs would have coalesced in such a manner. Absent, too,
the political demagoguery of the Trump era and Trump's efforts to

politicize the pandemic lockdowns and mask mandates for his own short-term advantage, and it's unlikely that the rage would have been so intense. After all, Sequim, with its picturesque bungalows, its pretty little steepled churches, its 1950s diner in pride of place halfway along Washington Street, its cafés advertising locally roasted coffee, its arts-and-crafts stores, and its abundance of well-heeled retirees, wasn't exactly a hotbed of social despair. Sure, it had its fair share of problems, from drug addiction to young folks struggling to make the rent—but no more so than most other small towns dotting the peninsula, and far less so than many larger cities. Absent the furies and fears, the *you're-with-us-or-against-us* absolutisms unleashed by America's endless culture wars, and it's hard to see how Dr. Berry would have come to be seen by so many of her neighbors as an enemy of the people.

Put all these different factors together, however, mix them up, and sprinkle the resulting political fairy dust over a community—even a community as seemingly anodyne as Sequim—and, unsurprisingly, bad things start to happen. By the time that the COVID pandemic arrived on America's shores, the country was a tinderbox, with incivility and intolerance spreading throughout the body politic, with yelling and social media insults replacing genuine political discourse, and with feeling replacing fact in all too many debates.

On January 19, 2021, the day before Trump left office, the *New York Times* published a compendium of all of his Twitter insults from the time he was a candidate in 2015 until a few days before his presidency's end, when the social media platform suspended his account for its incitement of violence. The *Times* article contained thousands of entries, which collectively showed the power that he wielded in shaping his followers' perceptions of the world. The insults ranged from accusing Black Lives Matter protesters of being treasonous to attacking the comedian Samantha Bee for having "no talent." He attacked investigative journalist Carl Bernstein, of Watergate fame, for thinking "like a degenerate fool," and the rock star Neil Young as a "total hypocrite." The tweeter-in-chief called out others as dopey, as losers, anarchists, terrorists, thugs, fools. Some were "dumb as a rock"; others were simply "low energy." Many of the attacks, which were lapped up by Trump's nearly ninety million Twitter followers, were crude and vulgar, others designed to focus mass anger on one individual or organization.

As the discourse at the top of the country's political totem pole degenerated, so conditions on the ground also grew more perilous. Heavily armed men and women were routinely taking to the streets to protest—or to counterprotest—something or someone. Pluralism, that ability to listen to one's opponents, maybe even to learn from them, was increasingly being tested by absolutism, the willingness to compromise being corroded by an authoritarianism that both trickled down from the top and bubbled up from the grass roots. The result was chaos, an endless rupturing of the fabric of Americans' daily lives.

All of this is presenting a vast challenge to the country's stability. And, regardless of individual election outcomes, regardless of who the next president is, or the next one after that, or, for that matter, who the next mayor is in one's hometown, these forces will continue to present a stress test for the foreseeable future.

How individual communities respond to these challenges, whether or not the forces of reason and of moderation can be marshaled to push back against extremism and irrationalism, will shape the next chapters in America's history. For America has truly reached a critical fork in the road. Will it continue along a path that promises only more division, more irrationality, or will it, at the eleventh hour, shift its trajectory, opting instead to rein in its darkest impulses?

This is a story about the forces tearing at America's twenty-first-century fabric. It is about a country that, pushed to the emotional and political limits by Trump, by COVID, and by the endless misinformation and echo chambers of social media, has found itself on the edge of a precipice, with political violence normalized and with wild conspiracy theories too often framing public discussions. It is about what occurs when mistrust and fury, extremism and irrationality, replace dialogue and the daily compromises that make a vibrant pluralist democracy possible. It is about the damage done when small-town newspapers vanish and are replaced by rumor mills and social media mobs, and when political opponents come to be seen as political enemies—as people with whom no discourse is possible and no concordance desired. The Trump and COVID era has not gone quietly into the night. In ways little and large, that moment continues to define who we are, what we debate and fight about, how we communicate, and how communities across this vast land function. Siren songs are, by their definition, seductive. They are also dangerous, dulling critical faculties and substituting simple bromides for complexity. They affect people at a national level, but at least as significantly, they lure people in at the local level as well, often pitting neighbor against neighbor. In so doing, they rend community bonds and fracture vital local institutions.

What happens when the residents of a small town or county look in the mirror and realize that everything is cracked, that their own sense of self is being eviscerated by the sharp edges of the broken glass? Does the destructive, take-no-prisoners drift of modern politics and the rightward lurch of regions such as Shasta accelerate, or does the chaos eventually trigger a reckoning, one that ultimately recalibrates politics back toward the center?

Over the coming years, which of these two forks in the road will America take? Will the scorched-earth visions of Donald Trump, of Steve Bannon, of Marjorie Taylor Greene, of Tucker Carlson, and of Alex Jones become the new norm, fundamentally reshaping the Republic into something more closely resembling Viktor Orban's Hungary and his experiment in "illiberal democracy"? Will the world vision of QAnon win out?

In 2018 Steve Bannon, the Rasputin of the Right, the Svengali of MAGAism, stated that "the real opposition is the media. And the way to deal with them is to flood the zone with shit." Disorient the public, convince them to distrust established sources of information, muddy the waters when it comes to filtering out truth from falsehood, and, Bannon believed, a slide rightward would naturally follow. Break down confidence in government institutions, and it would be only a matter of time before a movement like MAGA could "deconstruct the administrative state." Bannon once teased his audience that he viewed himself as a Leninist, not because he supported Vladimir Lenin's ends, not because he wanted to create a Soviet Union of the United States, but because he recognized the destabilizing force of Lenin's take-no-prisoners revolutionary means.

Will the alt-right fever dream of a pure, nationalist state, unfettered by global alliances and treaties, its members freed of any obligations outside of their immediate community, conquer us? Will the nativism and the xenophobia, the distrust of sexual and cultural and racial minorities, draw in ever more foot soldiers to the alt-right cause? Or will these corrosive forces burn out in the face of growing public unease—and even repugnance—at all that is lost when extremists seize the helm? It is in local communities throughout America, in ordinary places such as Sequim, Washington, and Shasta County, California, that this challenge will be met, and it is in those same locales, and in the actions of residents in response to political chaos, that the answers to the above questions will over the coming years be found.

Part One

SEQUIM, WASHINGTON

Chapter One

THE GOOD DOCTOR

THE RAINSHADOW CAFÉ WAS A PICTURESQUE LITTLE PLACE ON A SIDE STREET ON THE NORTH SIDE of town, its walls lined with paintings from local artists, its outside patio filled with tables for customers. From its grounds, one could look out at the peninsula's mountains off to the south. It was the sort of hangout where laptop-toting locals would sit and work for several hours while drinking locally roasted coffee and eating fresh-out-of-the-oven pastries. The Rainshadow was, for Allison Berry, also something of a sanctuary—a spot where she knew, from experience, that she was more likely than not to encounter people who would thank her for her work rather than unleash a slew of insults in her direction. She might meet there some of the people who in April 2020, in the early days of the COVID pandemic, had responded to her urgent requests for more N-95 masks to be delivered to frontline medical workers by donating their own precious supplies of masks: stevedores from the nearby docks who had long worked with hazardous cargoes and kept masks on hand, firefighters, and others who had access to personal protective equipment. She had never forgotten their generosity in the face of danger.

———

Berry was young, smiled a lot, wore knitted woolen sweaters and scarves, and had worked in the city's small public health department since 2016. Before that, she had been a doctor at a local clinic run by the nearby Jamestown S'Klallam tribe. And prior to that job, she had worked with refugees and homeless people while doing her medical residency at Seattle's prestigious Harborview Hospital. Harborview was a level-one trauma center, meaning that it catered to those with particularly serious injuries; it was also a county hospital, so it didn't turn away those who came through the hospital doors without insurance. If you were poor and seriously ill in Seattle, there was a better-than-even chance you'd end up being treated there.

Many of Berry's Harborview patients had overlapping health crises, including brain trauma, addiction, and serious mental illness; deeply impoverished and often aggressive or uncooperative, they were, in consequence, frequently seen as somehow disposable by those in positions of authority who interacted with them. In her recollection, "They didn't have a lot of places where people treated them as full human beings." Some of those she had worked with were violent—one, she remembered, tried to choke her while she was examining him. *Why did she continue treating him after that episode?* She paused for a long time, then laughed self-deprecatingly. "Well, somebody had to. He was a little scary, but I also cared about him and wanted him to do well." Berry and her colleagues set up safety protocols so that doctors were never left alone with him, and then they continued to assist the man with his medical needs. Another of her patients was a Somali refugee who had tried to commit suicide by jumping off a bridge. He hadn't succeeded in killing himself but had shattered both legs in the attempt, and he subsequently became addicted to the painkillers that he was given to treat his pain. When he arrived on Berry's rostrum, months later, he was heavily addicted, confined to a wheelchair, and unable to hold down a job. Over the course of three years, Berry worked with him, gently weaning him off the painkillers, helping him rehab, and finally assisting him in learning to walk again. By the time she left her residency, he was drug-free and had a job. This was the sort of success story that made her long days and difficult working environment worth it. "We stayed with it and built trust," she recalled. "It felt good. He did great."

Allison Berry had known practically her whole life that caring for the vulnerable was her calling. She had first decided she wanted to be a doctor when she was only eleven years old, in 1996, and witnessed her beloved grandmother, Violet Hoar, die an agonizing death from colon cancer in Tacoma, Washington. Low-income and on Medicaid, Violet was denied treatment at many private hospitals. In her final death agonies, she developed peritonitis—a catastrophic infection of the abdomen and the surrounding organs—and was rushed to one of those private facilities in an ambulance. There, the intake staff warned Berry's mother that because Violet lacked private insurance, the dying woman would soon have to be moved to the county hospital—despite the fact that moving a patient with acute peritonitis was guaranteed to cause her agony. "Thankfully," Berry says, "she died within twenty-four hours," before she could be moved.

The experience scarred the young girl, but it also gave her a passion for medicine—and, as she grew older, specifically for public health and working with those on society's margins. During her college years at Lawrence University, a small liberal arts college in Appleton, Wisconsin, she double-majored in biochemistry and music, playing the French horn in the college conservatory and specializing in works by Russian composers such as Tchaikovsky, Reinhold Glière, and Shostakovich. But she knew that her passion lay with the healing arts. "My colleagues in the conservatory woke up every day thinking about music. And I woke up thinking about medicine and social injustice."

Summers, Berry would return home to Washington State and work in a biomedical engineering research lab on a project aimed at developing the scaffolding for esophageal tissues that could someday be used to replace the esophagi of cancer patients. She also volunteered at the Free Clinic in the Beacon Hill neighborhood of Seattle, working with poor patients who couldn't even afford the common prescription drugs used to treat the forms of heartburn that, if left untreated, could lead to the very cancer that the lab was seeking to help cure. "We would see people facing shockingly difficult circumstances, based on poverty and racism," she remembered. Esophageal cancer was only part of it. "Kids with asthma living in vacant row houses. The primary driver of their problem was terrible housing." Yet she never gave up hope.

With housing very much on her mind, Berry graduated in 2007 and moved to New Orleans for a year to work with Habitat for Humanity, helping to rebuild the poorer parts of the city that had been shattered by Hurricane Katrina two years earlier. "You'd see sewage on the streets, blackouts. The trauma was still very fresh for most of the folks. I interviewed a family living in the scraps of their own home," she recalled.

When her year with Habitat for Humanity was up, she enrolled in medical school at Johns Hopkins University. The aspiring doctor would spend the next four years there, and after that another year studying for a master's degree in public health.

Time upon time, the divides between the haves and the have-nots, between those with opportunity and those without, got up into her face. In Baltimore many of her patients, most of them poor and

African American, came to the hospital with debilitating chronic diseases that, had those patients been more affluent, would likely have been treated effectively years earlier. She started working on a syringe-exchange program, driving an old RV around town and giving out safe syringes and birth control, treating open wounds, and doing outreach with sex workers in the city's adult-entertainment clubs. Late nights, after the rounds were over, she would bicycle back to her house in Charles Village. The work honed her sense of empathy: "They're interesting folks, and the more you talk to them—they have the same worries: worried about their kids, stress about their relationships; they care about what they're going to eat, where they're going to sleep." "Hey, Doc!" the sex workers and the addicts would shout out to her in greeting. In caring for them, and showing them respect, she had become their confidante, their friend: "It was really nice to have that sense of community," she said. "I really liked the work; I liked the community. It was a wonderful place to be."

———

Like Port Angeles, Port Townsend, and the other picturesque, historic port cities of the northern Olympic Peninsula, Sequim had a cute, intact old downtown complete with boutique stores, high-end eateries and galleries, and clusters of houses—surprisingly affordable despite recent appreciations in real estate values—built into the windswept, rainy hills surrounding the center of the city. It was, in short, the sort of place where retirees and tourists alike came to calm down after years of high-stress urban living. Sell a small apartment or condo in Seattle, and with the proceeds one could buy a large house with copious grounds in Sequim. Those valuable coastal-city real estate dollars allowed a person to trade in all the hassles of urban living for the tranquility of existence in the small towns and rural enclaves of the peninsula.

On the surface, Sequim hardly seemed the kind of place that would play host to a hard-right political upheaval. Underneath that surface, however, tensions had been building to a head for years.

Doctor Berry's hardscrabble childhood in Tacoma, her experiences in New Orleans, her realizations about Baltimore's divides, and her work with the homeless and refugee communities in Seattle had all taught her to stay calm under pressure. She prided herself on knowing that she could wake up from a deep sleep in the middle of the night and instantly be able to click into gear, to make good decisions in what could be life-or-death situations. She had learned, especially through her work with mentally ill homeless patients, to project calm even when someone was screaming at her or trying to do her physical harm. Yet none of this was enough to fully prepare her for what came her way in the first two years of the COVID pandemic.

"I knew there'd be push-back [to the vaccine mandate]," Berry later recalled, "but I had no idea what was coming." What was coming was a barrage of hate: much of the county, including several of its elected officials, turned on her during the darkest months of the pandemic, wishing her various ugly permutations of ill as if, in acknowledging the seriousness of the COVID crisis, she was herself responsible for bringing the consequences of a pandemic down upon local residents. The conservative majority on Sequim's city council even passed a resolution condemning the vaccine mandate, giving cover to many local restaurants wanting to simply ignore the rules that Berry's office had put in place. But that was the least of it. More worryingly, the longer the pandemic went on, the less seriously Sequim's mayor, William Armacost, seemed to take the crisis. Some days, he seemed to dismiss the dangers entirely.

———

After being appointed to replace an outgoing council member, Armacost had subsequently been elected unopposed, in a low-turnout election, to a four-year term on the city council in November 2019. Two months later, the hair-salon owner and motorcycle aficionado was elevated by his colleagues to the position of mayor. At the time, most residents of the sleepy little town probably didn't even notice. Yet once he became mayor, he seemed to crave controversy as his own peculiar form of oxygen.

In the wake of Black Lives Matter protests, Mayor Armacost began showing up at official city functions wearing a Blue Lives Matter, Marvel Comics Punisher skull pinned to his lapel. His critics saw this as a vaguely coded shout-out to vigilantism; after all, the Punisher respected no legal boundaries in his war against organized crime and evil gangsters. In recent years the Punisher decal had been embraced by returning Iraq War veterans as well as police officers around the country. Armacost claimed that the elongated skull imagery simply demonstrated his support for law enforcement, that he wasn't embracing vigilantism. On the national stage, other right-wing figures would make similar claims: *Fox News*'s Sean Hannity also began wearing a Punisher stars-and-stripes skull lapel pin to work. Early in his tenure, the mayor was caught on camera pushing a shopping cart at a local Costco while wearing a T-shirt emblazoned with a stars-and-stripes–dyed skull and reading "This is the USA. We eat meat. We drink beer. We own guns. We speak English. We love freedom. If you do not like that, get the fuck out." In another instance he was photographed at the self-checkout line of the local Safeway wearing khaki camo pants and a shirt with an image of a James Dean–like Donald Trump in a leather jacket and holding the large steering wheel of a car in one hand, a semiautomatic rifle in the other. Atop the image were the words "USA #1," and at the bottom of the shirt was the pledge "I Support Making America Great Again."

Armacost didn't like liberals, he didn't like racial-justice advocates, he didn't like undocumented immigrants, he didn't like people who spoke strange foreign tongues, and he certainly didn't like public health officials like Allison Berry. The hairdresser had long fashioned himself as a right-wing provocateur, engaging in local versions of the *attentat*—the political spectacle—as often as possible, frequently, it seemed, just to piss off his opponents. His voice may have been soft, almost velveteen, but the words that he ushered forth were filled with fire and fury. Like Donald Trump, he had crafted a political career—albeit on a dramatically smaller stage than that the real estate mogul bestrode—premised on bombast. Much of the time, he seemed to positively thrive on conflict. Like so many on the alt-right, he gave the appearance of reveling in "owning the libs" in deeds and in words guaranteed to provoke a reaction.[*]

But perhaps Armacost's most egregious act was orchestrating the forced resignation of the popular and extremely competent city manager, Charlie Bush, in the winter of 2021, after Bush pushed back against Armacost's decision to go on a local radio show on August 27, 2020, at the height of the pandemic and in his official capacity as mayor, and urge his listeners to check out QAnon theories.

———

For the past few months, Sequim had been lit up with stories about how the mayor's personal Facebook page was adorned with QAnon logos and links to QAnon videos. He seemed to have bought lock,

---

[*] He also didn't like journalists. He ignored my phone calls and email messages, and when I caught up with him at his hair salon, Changes, late one afternoon in mid-December 2021, he flatly stated that he had no time and wouldn't agree to an interview either then or any other time. When I left, I could see him whisper something to the man whose hair he was cutting, and they both looked out the window in my direction and laughed. Over the next two years, he ignored, or in other cases turned down, numerous additional requests to talk for this book. All his allies on the council from the 2020–2021 period and his friends in local conservative organizations either ignored my interview requests or, when reached by phone, likewise declined to comment, to tell their side of this story.

stock, and barrel into QAnon's ideas about malfeasance and criminality in high places, into the idea that Trump had essentially received a mandate from God to take down the "deep state" and to expose and bring to justice the pedophiles and human traffickers who had wormed their way into positions of power in the political, financial, and media realms. Armacost's postings (screenshot by outraged locals before he ultimately deleted them) were tagged with the logo "WWG1WGA," which, for those in the QAnon-know, stands for "Where We Go One We Go All," a secret slogan intended to convey, like a nod and a wink, to initiates that Armacost was one of them.

On his Facebook feed the hair-salon owner denounced Lord Jacob Rothschild, whose "banking clan" owns "nearly every central bank in the world." Armacost claimed that climate-change activists had deliberately started massive wildfires in Australia to highlight their green cause. In late 2019 he posted a YouTube video announcing that, after thousands of years, "the Luciferian Reign is over—The Healing of Nations has begun." He posted a picture of a smirking Trump against a large US flag, and the words "Pro-God, Pro-Life, Pro-Gun, Pro-American, That's Our President!"

Armacost had no qualms about pushing the QAnon agenda. On a local radio program, a weekly *Coffee with the Mayor* morning show on KSQM FM radio—a pandemic-era substitute for the in-person coffee sessions that the Sequim mayor had traditionally hosted—he explained that "QAnon is a truth movement that encourages you to think for yourself. It's patriots from all over the world fighting for humanity, truth, freedom, and saving children and others from human trafficking—exposing the evil and corruption of the last century in hopes of leaving a better future for our children and grandchildren."

Armacost continued, musing aloud about why the media spent so much time attacking QAnon as a cult and a purveyor of violence, and why the FBI had labeled the cult a domestic terrorist risk, when there were genuine threats out there like Black Lives Matter.

A few days later, on September 3, Armacost gave another interview about QAnon, telling a local newspaper that "the sad part is, it doesn't seem to be what the item is, whenever you have an organization that is inclined to expose evil things to humanity, there's going to be a push-back. It [QAnon] is an opportunity to . . . dig up the information, maybe look at a different channel."

Such was the sort of devil fighting that QAnoners specialized in. A storm was coming, they believed, and when that storm was through, America would have been purged of political evil. Unfortunately, there were no guarantees that the upheaval would be peaceful; adherents, who defined themselves as a vanguard of "true patriots," might have to turn to violence. Indeed, given the messianic paranoia that ran through the QAnon conspiracy, violence seemed inevitable. Public Religion Research Institute (PRRI) polling data in the early 2020s found that roughly one in five Americans adhered to at least some of the QAnon belief system's central tenets and that a quarter of Republicans identified with QAnon's ideas. Astoundingly, fully 16 percent of American adults who were polled by the PRRI researchers believed that the commanding heights of power were controlled by Satan-worshipping pedophiles.

Not surprisingly, Mayor Armacost's comments attracted an outsized amount of attention. Suddenly, the little retirement hub on the Olympic Peninsula was on the national news. After a false calm in the days immediately after the broadcast, by early September journalists began descending on the little town, a community that until a few days earlier would only have been on anyone's radar for winning a series of awards for encouraging community engagement, investing in neighborhood revitalization, and promoting local businesses. City staff took particular pride in having been recognized for their work with a coalition of nonprofits to help address the housing needs of local families at risk of homelessness. Out of all the cities in Washington with a population of under ten thousand, it had been picking up quite a reputation for effective governance. Now, with Armacost's off-the-cuff remarks on QAnon, it was about to become the focus of some very different attention. In the blink of an eye, seemingly everyone wanted a piece of the story. Over the coming weeks and months, a reporter for Bloomberg's "Citylab" podcast would hit the peninsula to interview locals, national magazine writers (myself included) would journey out to Sequim to see what was going on, newspapers would dispatch teams to get a handle on the story. There was something of the pursuit of a Holy Grail here: it was, after all, one of the first documented instances of what would, over the coming years, become a disconcertingly common phenomenon in locales around the country—an elected official explicitly allying with the QAnon death cult and using his public platform to promote a bizarre web of conspiracy theories to his constituents.

The *Washington Post* had recently reported that eleven congressional candidates hoping to win election to the US House of Representatives that coming November, including one Marjorie Taylor Greene, of Georgia, were QAnon supporters. In public speeches, Donald Trump, as well as his sons Eric and Don Junior, tested out just how many nods and winks to QAnon they could get away with. Trusted advisers to the president, such as General Michael Flynn, actively spread QAnon ideas online and from their speaker platforms, Flynn touring the country to recruit what he called an "Army of God," a modern-day crusade to recapture the country from people such as Nancy Pelosi, whom he decried as "demons"; to rescue a fallen nation from schools that peddled pornography; and to reestablish the country as a proudly Christian nation. The United States was, Flynn argued, embroiled in a "5G war," in which social media, the law, and the news media had all been taken over by an assortment of socialists and Communists who were now busily using these tools to wage psychological war against ordinary, God-fearing Americans. The controversial general's views overlapped well with the fundamentalist worldview of the Dominionists, with those who believed in the Seven Mountains Mandate, a theory increasingly adhered to among those on the Christian Right that spelled out how, separation of church and state be damned, Christians could— and should—organize to capture the commanding heights of society and of government.

———

After Armacost's public embrace of QAnon, City Manager Charlie Bush, whose even-keeled managerial style had kept Sequim on a firm footing for the past six years, felt that he had no choice but to intervene.

Bush had just returned from a hiking and backpacking trip with his brother-in-law Zev along the Timberline Trail, deep within the Mount Hood National Forest, in Oregon. An avid hiker, during the pandemic he would frequently hike fifteen to twenty miles per day, sometimes more, shouldering a large orange backpack containing food, water, super-lightweight camping gear, and other necessities for backcountry expeditions, communicating via text with his wife on a satellite gizmo named the Garmin Mini. On these trips he would often film and narrate his excursions, posting vlogs that frequently got upward of a thousand views.

This time around, the weather was hot, the sky only slightly discolored by smoke from massive fires that had been raging in California to the south for the previous couple of weeks, and he hiked out in shorts and T-shirt, a large white floppy-brimmed hat and reflector sunglasses protecting him from the sun. The forty-mile trail, circling Mount Hood, ascended at times above the tree line and through bare, rocky, sometimes sandy terrain, with little shade to offer respite from the heat. Elsewhere, it descended into the lush forest. There, on fallen tree branches, Zev and Charlie carefully forded the rapidly flowing Zigzag River and passed the cascading Ramona Falls. Overnight, that first night, the fogs rolled in, the temperature cooled, and when they dismantled their camp and began walking early the next morning, for the first few hours they were trekking through the clouds and mist.

It was a hard hike, and on their return to Sequim, Zev and Charlie were looking forward to some good food and drink, to showering, to doing not very much for a few hours as they recuperated. Instead, immediately on their return on September 6, the city manager was suddenly presented with a rush of information about Armacost's comments on the *Coffee with the Mayor* radio show two Thursdays previously, comments that he had been unaware of before he left on his hiking trip.

The forty-four-year-old city manager, his beard just starting to fleck with gray, realized that the city was facing a crisis. He felt that it was unacceptable for the mayor, ostensibly a nonpartisan who was selected by his fellow council members to focus on the nitty-gritty of local governance, to have used his official role—and a radio show intended to link the mayor up with his constituents, no less—to put the seal of approval on QAnon's noxious theories.

Bush went into crisis mode. He contacted the mayor, with whom he felt he had always had "a cordial, respectful relationship," to try to work out how to quell the growing firestorm. With all the vast pressures of the pandemic, Armacost's comments on QAnon were, Bush felt, simply adding fuel to an already volatile situation: "There was just a lot of pressure. People in the community were more heated than they would have been if there wasn't a pandemic. Everyone had time to isolate and to reflect and to get way deep into social media. Issues that had been there for years got magnified. It felt like the volume was turned up on everything. There was no sport, nothing to help people cope with life. For people's mental health, it's not a bad thing to have distractions."

By Tuesday afternoon, the city manager had drawn up a statement that the mayor reluctantly signed off on, acknowledging that the radio comments had been inappropriate. "Any responses to questions reflecting the personal opinion of the Mayor do not reflect policy positions of the Sequim City Council," the statement read. Armacost was also quoted directly, issuing something of a begrudging nonapology apology for his words: "While I believe that people should fight for truth and freedom, it was inappropriate to respond to this question as Mayor during a program designed to talk about City of Sequim issues."

It was released on Wednesday morning, and Bush dearly hoped that would do the trick and quell the furor. But perhaps to no one's surprise, the controversy continued to fester. Armacost might have signed off on the mea culpa, but in private he was seething. Already at odds with the county's public health team over pandemic-mitigation measures, he now found himself at loggerheads with the city manager. He likely resented the imputation that he was fascinated by irrational conspiracy-thinking when, he felt, QAnon was simply blaring warnings to a quiescent public about a host of clear-and-present dangers.

Armacost and his allies would never forgive the city manager for the slight. From then on, they were on a war footing, looking for any opening they could find to retaliate for Bush's humbling of the mayor.

———

Jodi Wilke lived in Port Hadlock–Irondale, a small, rural community outside of Port Townsend in neighboring Jefferson County. From the 1870s, Port Hadlock, nestled on the steep banks of a bay, had been a rough-and-ready sawmill town, complete with the sorts of seedy establishments that catered to sailors from around the world. A few years later, the area was the first in the Washington Territory to host an iron-producing blast furnace, hence the town's hyphenated name. In the relatively brief span of time that it had been in operation, the foundry employed hundreds of men who produced thousands of tons of pig iron.

Wilke was a soft-spoken nurse who looked considerably younger than her years—she was, in fact, in her early sixties—had a shock of unruly dark-brown hair, wore spectacles, and rouged the cheeks of her otherwise pale face. In her spare time, she played the guitar and piano (she loved 1970s rock anthems, but her true passion was Christian rock and old hymns) and liked to sing.

The Port Hadlock–Irondale resident's area of expertise was elder care. For much of the more than three decades that she had been a nurse, she had worked in nursing homes; she specialized in caring for Alzheimer's patients, as well as those with other forms of dementia. Not surprisingly, when she talked about the human traits that she most valued, empathy was high up on her list. Like Berry, she also had direct experience working with the homeless; Wilke had, she said, taken dozens of homeless men and women into her homes over the decades (twenty-eight was her best-guess estimate), had helped pay for their clothes, had worked with them to navigate bureaucracies as they tried to get copies of their identification documents, and had coached them in how to fill out job applications. She understood addiction intimately; indeed, the nurse had met at the AA meetings that she had been attending for thirty-plus years many of the homeless people whom she ended up temporarily housing. "What made me do that?" she asked rhetorically. "Humanity. A sense of wanting to make the world a better place one person at a time. For every homeless person, there's a different experience. Some of them are injured, damaged people. The solutions we have have to be as diverse as that population." But at the end of the day, she regarded it as a moral imperative to help the needy. "Anybody that wants help should have help available to them," she said quietly.

But none of this history and none of this sense of moral urgency that, at least on the issue of homelessness, she shared with Berry made Wilke sympathetic to the local Jamestown S'Klallam tribe's idea for a large medication-assisted treatment (MAT) clinic with wraparound social services catering to 250 drug-addicted clients being placed on a 19.5-acre site in the middle of Sequim.

For years, local tribes on the peninsula had played a critical role in providing health-care access to the community. Since 2002, the Jamestown S'Klallam tribe had run a large health clinic employing more than twenty health-care providers that saw up to 17,000 patients per year, Native American and non-Native alike. In 2017 another tribe, the Swinomish, had opened up a medication-assisted treatment clinic that used a wraparound services model created by researchers at Johns Hopkins University to help opioid addicts wean themselves from their addiction. The Swinomish's center had achieved strong results—and hadn't encountered much push-back from local residents—so soon the Jamestown S'Klallam tribe also decided that they wanted to operate a similar clinic.

That was when Wilke—a gun-rights enthusiast who had once shown up at a Second Amendment rally at the state capitol holding a sign reading "RNs for ARs" (Registered Nurses for Automatic Rifles)—decided that enough was enough. It would, she felt, bring huge numbers of mentally ill, addicted men and women, and the concomitant criminal justice and health challenges that would likely come in their wake, into the Olympic Peninsula from Seattle and other large cities to the south, and, she argued, it wouldn't even serve the addicted population well, forcing them to take daylong bus rides for treatment at this one big center. Far better for all concerned, she believed, to build a number of smaller clinics in a variety of locales around the region. That, at least, was her rationale. Her opponents felt, perhaps unfairly, that she was merely a NIMBYist, that she and her allies didn't want those less fortunate than them to live and get services in their neighborhoods.

In 2018, as the planning for the tribe's methadone clinic picked up steam, Wilke—who was an active member of a nearby county's Republican Party, who had run for (and lost) an election for public office, and who didn't herself live in Sequim—set up a group called Save Our Sequim (SOS) to organize against the tribe's proposed mega-clinic. The whole approval process was, she felt, too secretive: the city and the tribe working together in the shadows to bypass the will of the people. She and her allies began posting anti–MAT clinic messages on Facebook—messages that some supporters of the clinic viewed as veering into racist, antitribal language. They claimed that at SOS meetings and on the group's Facebook page, opposition to the tribal plans frequently degenerated into the delivery of racial slurs. Vicki Lowe, a fifty-six-year-old longtime public health worker with the Jamestown S'Klallam tribe, who was also executive director of the state's American Indian Health Commission and who traced her lineage both to tribal ancestors and to pioneer stock, recalled hearing phrases such as "Indian idiots" and "playing cowboys and Indians" during the meetings. When Lowe asked the SOS organizers to tone down the rhetoric that she and others saw as being anti-indigenous, they were simply blocked from accessing the Facebook page. When they managed to get back on anyway, they were shocked to encounter still more racially inflammatory postings. Later, after she successfully ran for and won a seat on the Sequim City Council, Lowe remembered how during those days when the anti–MAT clinic rhetoric was at its height, she called out SOS at a council meeting by holding up, and discarding one at a time, cardboard signs emblazoned with each offensive, racist phrase, à la Bob Dylan in the music video for "Subterranean Homesick Blues." It was, for Wilke, a particularly painful allegation. She had always prided herself on being color-blind. "We should love one another and be kind to one another," she believed. "And your race doesn't make any difference to me. I look in your eyes and see a human being."

SOS hired an attorney out of Seattle to file a lawsuit against the clinic, but the courts ultimately told SOS that it didn't have legal standing to bring the case. Nevertheless, the swirl of anti–MAT clinic activity only grew. Within a few months, Wilke recalled, thousands of people from across the peninsula, and across the political spectrum, had become SOS supporters.

For Charlie Bush, when he read the letter of the law and explored Sequim's zoning regulations, it was an open-and-shut case. The tribe had gone through the required process for getting the clinic approved, with it to be situated on land between a large Costco and Highway 101, and the city council really had no say in the matter. Following the letter of the law meant that Bush was obligated to sign off on the clinic once the tribe submitted its permit application in early 2020 and once opponents had run through their initial legal challenges in the months following. For Mark Ozias, the county commissioner for the Sequim region, who wrote an open letter to his constituents in support of the project, the clinic being situated in Sequim "makes great sense due to its central location, ease of access, appropriate zoning, availability of necessary services and critical mass of health care resources. As property rights advocates understand, it is the right of any individual or business entity to purchase land that has been put up for sale, and to build an allowed facility on appropriately zoned land." For an array of public health advocates, first responders, and law-enforcement officials—grown tired of responding to one overdose after another, as America's opioid epidemic raged untamed—the MAT clinic was a rare ray of light in an otherwise bleak addiction landscape. Ozias pointed out that national studies had demonstrated that in areas where MAT clinics went up, property-crime and personal-crime rates plummeted, in some instances by as much as 80 percent.

The opponents of the clinic weren't mollified. Ozias accused them of attempting to "bully and intimidate public officials through angry and aggressive threats" and of sending out "inflammatory and provocative" mailers. He finished his open letter by warning that Save Our Sequim could actually "destroy what makes us special."

In mid-2020, as the COVID pandemic raged, with the peninsula on lockdown and the city of Sequim in emergency-management mode, Bush's office finally issued the permits. Despite Ozias's efforts to calm the waters, the city manager ran into a buzz saw of opposition. Infuriated residents, many already on edge after months of pandemic-induced isolation and fear, immediately began launching more challenges: six in short succession. All were reviewed by the hearing examiner, and all failed—although the examiner *did* approve a few modifications to the initial permit.

Later, Wilke would assert that her side in the conflict was entirely peaceful—that she was sick and tired of all the fighting and shouting and crudeness that passed for political debate in contemporary America, that too often the "lizard brain" kicked in and people stopped talking with each other and instead acted as if everything could be reduced to a fight for personal survival. She said that people on her side were entirely civil in their voicing of opposition to the proposal, that it was the clinic's supporters who jumped the shark into verbal warfare. Those supporters, perhaps not surprisingly, remembered otherwise. In truth, with tensions running high, insults were likely flung on all sides.

The acrimony flowed both ways. Many on Wilke's side felt that a bunch of well-meaning but thoughtless do-gooders were working to spoil their little bit of paradise. At a city council meeting in early January 2020, one critic, Jenna Rose, argued that studies of other MAT clinics and their patients suggested that around half of the clinic's participants would likely be "homeless drug addicts." It was, she said, an appalling prospect. "Have you considered how a regional MAT facility would be the ruin of Sequim?" she asked the council members, her voice rising in agitation. "Have you thought about your legacy, city council?"

Wilke herself believed that the decision to locate the twenty-million-dollar clinic in Sequim was a betrayal of local people's freedom to choose what sort of environment they wanted to live in, yet another example of unaccountable bureaucrats stomping on fundamental liberties. "I'm very concerned about where we're going as a world," she explained. "My biggest interest is the common person. How does all this affect the average person's life? Most people love their family, want to go to work, have a nice meal in the evening, have fun with their friends on the weekends, watch movies, live a life that's kind of normal. Here in America, we have a lot of freedom to choose what this is. Americans treasure that freedom. What bothers me is when things outside of their control start to interfere in people's lives."

———

Regardless of the merits of the MAT clinic, and regardless of the soundness of the legal reasoning behind Charlie Bush's decision to approve it, Armacost and his supporters apparently believed that the controversy gave them cover to take the city manager down. The closer the clinic project came to being realized, the louder the voices of opposition got. Backed by Armacost and several other councillors, opponents descended on council meetings to vociferously air their views. Throughout the fall and early winter months of 2020, the city manager would frequently be in the verbal crosshairs during these meetings. By early 2021, Armacost's allies believed they had drummed up enough support to at last remove Bush from his job.

For Charlie Bush, the onslaught against him was a kick in the teeth, to say the least. He was a veteran of city government, having been employed by a number of cities throughout Washington since the mid-1990s, and prided himself on his professionalism. For most of that almost quarter century, his work environment had been fairly calm, his decisions made and implemented largely out of the public eye and certainly out of the way of the ideological storms sweeping the country. Although national politics was being reshaped by movements such as the Tea Party and, before that, Newt Gingrich's "Contract with America," by an often-inchoate sense of anger against expertise and against public officials and institutions, local government tended to be sleepier, more technocratic—and that suited Bush's temperament just fine. He liked simply being left alone to get on with his work, and he believed that he was good at his job. But in recent years, as the tone of national politics grew ever uglier, the Sequim city manager had noticed something that disturbed him: even at the local level, politics was becoming so polarized that the middle ground was disappearing. Constituents were getting angrier. The rough-and-tumble of local politics was becoming more unforgiving. And the decisions he made were now being filtered through the lens of social media, where his motives were routinely impugned and his values sometimes derided.

A few years earlier, members of the school board had put a measure before voters to pass a bond that would have allowed for the building of new schools in the county. A group called the Concerned Citizens of Clallam County (known to locals simply as the "Four C's"), which grew out of Tea Party organizing efforts on the peninsula early in the Obama presidency, opposed the bond. By 2015, with the refugee crisis from the Syrian civil war in full bloom, members of this group latched on to a growing wariness of refugees, especially those from Muslim countries, to hone their arguments. The bond, they argued, was a front: it wasn't about building new schools; rather, it was about opening up school buildings to house Syrian exiles. Their argument was nonsense, but it also resonated. Four times in a row the bond, which required a 60 percent supermajority to pass, got support from more than half of the electorate but nevertheless went down to defeat by failing to cross the 60 percent threshold.

───

At about the same time as the Four C's was ginning up anti-Muslim sentiments on the Olympic Peninsula, on the other side of the country Donald Trump, campaigning to be the Republican presidential candidate, was unveiling his plans to block any and all Muslims from migrating to America, or even coming for a vacation. On January 4, 2016, Trump's campaign unveiled one of the most demagogic television ads in American political history. Against a backdrop of photographic images of terrorism victims, the narrator intoned, "The politicians can pretend it's something else. But Donald Trump calls it radical Islamic terrorism. That's why he's calling for a temporary shutdown of Muslims entering the United States until we can figure out what's going on."

No matter the impracticality of this proposal—or the fact that Trump himself had myriad business contacts in Saudi Arabia, where most of the 9/11 terrorists had originated—the real estate mogul's growing legion of followers ate it up. Here, at long last, was a straight-talking politician willing to call things like he saw them. On the stump, Trump would recycle a convoluted story (one that historians doubted was even true) about how the Americans defeated Muslim independence fighters in the Philippines in the late nineteenth century by shooting them with bullets dipped in pigs' blood, a death so horrific that it sapped the enemy of their will to fight. The more he dialed up the ferocity of his rhetoric, the more he energized his crowds.

When I traveled to Sparks, Nevada, a few weeks later to talk to Republicans caucusing on his behalf, one after another they told me, without any sense of shame, that Muslims in America ought to be deported. Several went a murderous step further. They would give Muslims in the United States a choice: either they could opt to leave the country or they would face the possibility of execution. "You can't tell the good from the bad," one caucus-goer explained to me, as if it were the most self-evident thing in the world. "So you have to throw the baby out with the bathwater. I'd give them a choice—a trench on one side or a ticket out of here." I asked him to clarify: *Was he talking about mass executions?* "Absolutely. That's what they do to us in their countries. I'd give 'em a choice: get out of here, or else."

Another Trump-supporting caucus participant told me, "You fight fire with fire. The Bible says, if they don't want to conform to what society is like, get rid of them. What did God tell Joshua? Get rid of every man, woman, child and beast. If the Lord says it's OK, He has the final say-so."

When I asked one woman what she thought of the ideas of killing terrorists using bullets dipped in pigs' blood and of barring all Muslims from the country, she answered generically: "I like what he [Trump] stands for. I want us to love our country and be proud of it. I want to bring God back into our country. He loves our country so much. He loves our country."

Each time someone said something so extraordinarily dangerous that it veered into the language of genocide, I looked around, hoping against hope that the other caucus-goers would distance themselves from these sentiments. Each time, however, I saw thumbs going up in agreement.

As the political rhetoric coarsened at the national level, so the policy discourse on the ground, in places like Clallam County, Washington, also devolved. The debate around the Clallam County school bond and the xenophobic, anti-Muslim tactics of the Four C's had gone a long way toward poisoning political discourse in Sequim, toward turning neighbor against neighbor, one community against another. Then, a few years later, another wedge issue, this one around drugs, homelessness, and whether placing a MAT clinic in Sequim was appropriate, burst onto the scene with equal intensity. That issue also bitterly divided the community.

When the pandemic hit, far from everyone rallying together to meet the exceptional needs of the moment, the fracturing picked up pace. As 2019 gave way to 2020, the MAT clinic controversy was temporarily sidelined by the horrors of the new pandemic. Many of Bush's staff took to working remotely; Bush himself, who had moved into an emergency-response office co-populated by staff from the Fire Department and other emergency services, spent many of his working hours navigating Zoom meetings. Retirement parties were replaced by drive-through gatherings in which Bush and other senior staff would give out prepackaged boxes of food to staff as they drove by, with everyone masked, and would then walk alongside the slow-moving cars for a few yards, talking through the open windows with the drivers. In-person staff meetings, traditionally so important in any office environment, gave way to the occasional gathering, via Zoom, of clusters of employees. Even the outdoor meetings on the little plaza in front of the city offices, to which the employees did at times resort, had to be meticulously planned, making sure that all state protocols and requirements about social distancing, masking, and so on were carefully met.

Now, however, in the wake of the Armacost-QAnon controversy, the MAT clinic was once again serving to highlight the broader political divides in the community. It had become a homegrown, made-in-Sequim litmus test, an easy if not always precise way of working out where people stood on Armacost and QAnon, where their sympathies lay on public health restrictions in the face of COVID, and perhaps even who they were likely to support in the upcoming presidential election. Bush himself was either loved or loathed, his presence as city manager arousing the same sorts of impassioned emotions that were generated by Allison Berry.

Among Bush's most determined opponents was Mayor Armacost. The hair-salon owner was joined in this opposition to Bush and to the MAT clinic by another fiery council member elected at the same time as he was: Troy Tenneson, a young man with a chiseled jaw and an Instagram profile tagged with the words "God, good people, this country, and financial freedom in that order." At one point Tenneson had been in the military, then he had worked as a firefighter, and finally he had moved into construction. He came out of the Young Republicans, liked to throw verbal slingshots, and—critics observed—seemed to model himself on Donald Trump. He would attend right-wing street-corner rallies waving his Stars and Stripes, surrounded by a bevy of young supporters. Periodically, he would explode in anger at local and state politics, telling listeners that he wanted to move to a state with a more right-minded governor. At least one councilman recalls him having theatrically stormed out of a council meeting in which he didn't get his way.

Tenneson's had been one of the four votes cast, out of seven council members, on behalf of making the newly sworn in William Armacost mayor of the little town of Sequim. Tenneson's and Armacost's tenures had been kicked off by chaos. During the rambling two hundred-plus-minute January 13, 2020, meeting in which the new council members were sworn in, the new mayor and his acolytes seemed not to know how to follow basic rules about how council meetings would be conducted. They let their allies in the audience bust through their allotted speaker times. They made comments that could be construed as being sympathetic to QAnon—comments that so enraged some audience members that they wrote furious letters to the new council members immediately afterward.

Armacost, in his three-minute speech that day—the tone suggesting none of the anger that would come to characterize his time in charge of Sequim—urged his colleagues to vote for him as mayor: "I've had the blessing of thirty-five years of running several very successful businesses. At one point we ran five salons and had as many as sixty-five employees. . . . I have a pulse on what's the need for both the business owner and the employee . . . and the public uniting with concern around the MAT center. I have sixteen-plus years of working with alcoholics and with drug addicts; that experience is invaluable." The hairdresser concluded, grandiosely, "I'll take a quote from Winston Churchill: 'We make a living from what we get, but we make a life from what we give.'"

By day's end, Armacost would be Sequim's new mayor, Tenneson would be one of his wingmen, and the MAT-clinic–supporting Charlie Bush was about to become a punching bag for conservatives throughout the peninsula.

In hindsight, Bush would come to think that what unfolded during those months, as the city fractured around the MAT clinic, then fractured again around responses to the Black Lives Matter movement and the street protests around the country that followed the police killing of George Floyd, then tore into itself yet another time around how locals responded to Armacost embracing the QAnon conspiracy theory, was at least in part a product of all the pent-up fears and frustrations that accompanied the COVID outbreak. "I think it was a high-stress time for everybody," Bush said. "You had a lot of uncertainty in the world. And there was opportunism by a lot of individuals. There was a lot going on. It was a perfect storm for volatility."

In February 2021, all of that volatility came to a head. In a closed session, Armacost and his colleagues, still smarting over Charlie Bush's intervention in the QAnon controversy, voted to ask him for his resignation. He no longer enjoyed the confidence of the majority on the city council.

Exactly what went on in that closed session was never made public. The council members wouldn't talk, and as part of the severance deal that Bush negotiated with the city, he had to sign a nondisclosure agreement limiting what he could divulge about these events. For his supporters, however, the message was clear: Charlie Bush had enforced the letter of the law around the MAT clinic, and Charlie Bush had pushed back against Armacost's QAnon-supporting comments. Both positions had riled up the mayor and his allies. And in the end, the popular city manager had fallen victim to the take-no-prisoners timbre of modern American politics.

Over the next few years, as the debate around the clinic gave way to bigger concerns—to what the community thought about responses to the COVID pandemic; to how the region and the country responded first to the George Floyd killing, then to the November 2020 election, and after that to the January 6 assault on the US Capitol; to issues around what can and cannot be taught in the classroom and whether transgender people have a right to choose their gender identity—Jodi Wilke's grievances became broader. One fear fed into the next, and one suspicion reinforced another until, over time, a worldview was set into stone. Not trusting the experimental science behind mRNA vaccines and desperately worried that the spike protein on which the vaccine was based would both damage the human body and require an endless whack-a-mole game of booster shots every time the virus significantly mutated, she refused to take the shots. She was convinced that the major international medical journals, the public health departments, and the Centers for Disease Control and Prevention (CDC), along with Big Pharma, were imposing a system of censorship that was designed to hide evidence of the vaccine's dangers. But then, resolutely unvaccinated, she found that public health vaccine mandates for medical personnel essentially froze her out of regular employment, so she was left scrambling to find what hours she could at one of the private clinics in the region that still allowed unvaccinated nurses to attend to patients. For someone who had spent most of her adult life in the caregiving business, it was a heartbreaking denouement—enough, she said, to almost make her want to reconsider her career choices.

Later, when she saw the events of January 6, 2021, she was horrified at the mainstream media's interpretation of what had happened. Where she got her news—on YouTube, Rumble, and the gaming site DLive—she had seen not insurrectionists but peace-loving demonstrators. "We can agree it was a protest. Other people would use other words. But I would call it a protest," she would subsequently explain. "More information will come out about what happened. Tucker Carlson put out some information on it. Who was shot? Ashli Babbitt got shot. Did anybody get hit with a fire extinguisher? Riddle me this: why did they keep the video of that event under wraps for so long? They would not release it."

In her quiet voice, Wilke continued on, talking of election systems that had been compromised, of widespread voter fraud, of children being subjected to all sorts of medical treatments without their parents' knowledge or consent.

Two generations earlier, the mid-century historian and public intellectual Richard Hofstadter had coined the phrase "the paranoid style in American politics." In 2020s America, that style was, it appeared, retro chic.

Meanwhile, as Sequim's political dysfunction gathered pace, so Allison Berry's nightmare intensified. With the COVID pandemic running amok and the public health restrictions put in place to try to limit the virus's spread and minimize the number of fatalities it would cause triggering a frequently violent political backlash around the country, all of Berry's life lessons were being put to the test.

The more that Donald Trump and his team knocked public health officers for partisan advantage—the president took to publicly mocking Anthony Fauci, the infectious-disease expert in charge of crafting America's pandemic response—the more a section of Clallam County's populace responded in kind. When Trump urged people to ingest bleach to counter the effects of COVID, poison-control hotlines around the country reported increased numbers of people poisoning themselves with bleach. When he urged people to take unproven medical cures such as Ivermectin, demand for these drugs soared. The more Trump attacked lockdowns, tweeting that voters in Democratic-led states such as Virginia, Michigan, and Minnesota should rise up to "LIBERATE" themselves, the more Berry struggled to get out her public health message. When commentators on *Fox News* came out against the public health interventions, large numbers of Republican-leaning voters simply opted out of anti-COVID preventative measures. *Fox News* and other conservative media gave cover for up-and-coming GOP politicians such as Florida governor Ron DeSantis, people looking to make a name for themselves on the national stage, to try to out-Trump Trump in opposing any and all public health restrictions. Where much of the rest of the world was closed down that first pandemic summer, with parties and large social gatherings banned by law, places of worship shuttered, sports events played in empty arenas, and even funeral attendance numbers strictly limited, in Florida, with the blessing of local political leaders, tourists were still flocking to beaches and bars and theme parks.

"That was when we started to lose our footing," Berry recalled of those months of political conflict. Yet for several more months, Clallam County managed to contain the fallout. "In 2020 we really didn't have COVID deaths, but then the Delta variants and the lifting of mitigations really took us out. We had people who delayed care and then took Ivermectin," the horse medicine that Trump erroneously claimed was a COVID cure. "We had people who died, elderly people who stayed home for two weeks and took Ivermectin and came to the hospital when they couldn't breathe."

As the deaths mounted in 2021, so the deflected fury against Berry and her colleagues in public health picked up steam.

One man took to regularly emailing a slew of particularly fantastic threats to Berry, especially his claims that she was committing crimes against humanity and should be tried accordingly, as well as ever-more-picaresque insults and name-calling, and copying the messages to a slew of other public health officials, to elected politicians, and to miscellaneous journalists. After Governor Inslee shut down high school athletics, an infuriated mother, apparently believing that Dr. Berry had personally decided to penalize local teenage athletes, wrote to her to tell her she knew where Berry's young daughter went to daycare. There was no explicit threat. There didn't need to be. The menace was clearly intended to simply linger in the air.

Chapter Two

PTSD

THE STORIES OF DOCTOR BERRY, NURSE WILKE, AND MAYOR ARMACOST WERE BUT PIECES OF A complex puzzle. Over the prior few years, partly because of the pandemic and partly because of underlying political schisms, Sequim, like so many other communities around America, had spiraled into crisis. With the pandemic under way and Trump's presidency cleaving the country, it was bitterly divided politically, as was Clallam County, of which it was a part.

A majority of voters in Sequim were Democratic—and had reacted in horror to Armacost's mayorship and his homage to QAnon. But as was the case all over America, voter turnout in local elections tended to be low—the National Civic League reported in 2020 that turnout in these elections ranged from 15 percent up to a still-paltry 27 percent in cities around the country—and many of these Democratic voters, as well as moderate Republicans and independents, had sat out the election that elevated Armacost to an elected role on the city council and then to the mayorship. That was, for them, a hard lesson learned.

Going into the 2020 election, there were nineteen counties throughout the nation that had voted for the winner of every presidential election since Ronald Reagan was first elected in 1980. Yet eighteen of those nineteen counties, all rural, lost their bellwether status in 2020 after again voting for Trump in an election that Joe Biden won. Clallam County was the single holdout, going for Trump in 2016 but then narrowly supporting Biden four years later. It was the last true bellwether rural county in the United States, and for local Democrats that lent it an almost mythical quality: for Clallam to trend blue instead of red seemed, after the 2020 result, as improbable a reality as the local Sasquatch legend, the Bigfoot creature seen in the shadows of the dense rain forests of the peninsula but somehow never quite clearly captured in photographs.

The 2020 presidential election result exposed a profound ideological and cultural divide in the remote, watery region, a two-hour drive northwest of Seattle, abutting the ninety-six-mile-long, windswept Straits of Juan de Fuca, which divides the United States from Canada. Whereas most of the county's small towns trended blue and voted heavily for Joe Biden, in rural areas signs were hung among the trees with wording like "Trump won the election. Wake up sheeple." Pickup trucks could be seen with flags urging fealty to the "Trump revenge tour 2024." In more remote redoubts, places such as Whidbey Island, militias and paramilitaries, groups such as the Washington Three Percenters and the Proud Boys, began setting down roots, with the heavily armed Three Percenters—committed to fighting back against "tyrannical" government—taking over the local grange on Whidbey Island and using it as an organizing hub to first protest mask mandates and then, later on, diversity curricula in the island's schools. At the local high school, in the wake of efforts to implement the more inclusive curricula, an irate resident sprayed a simple message on the Class of 2021 banner: "Fuck Commies." Alongside it was scrawled an image of the Soviet-era hammer and sickle.

———

That sense of snarling rage at the liberals and the wokesters, the politically correct and the bureaucrats with their senseless rules, was alive and well in Sequim's city hall.

As the pandemic raged, Armacost would log on to Zoom council meetings sitting under a large cross at his home—deliberately inserting religious iconography into what by law should have been a secular setting. He would end city council meetings with the somewhat cryptic couplet "Jesus is the reason for the season." When motorcyclists gathered by the hundreds of thousands in Sturgis, South Dakota, in the summer of 2020, Armacost donned his motorcycle gear and made the pilgrimage east—and afterward pointedly refused to self-isolate, despite the event seeding major COVID outbreaks around the country. A year later, after the CDC had analyzed national data surrounding the Sturgis gathering, it was able to trace 649 cases directly to the motorcycle festival. Given the rapidity with which the virus was spreading at the time, it's likely that these cases in turn led to many additional infections around the country. The CDC's researchers, in fine bureaucratese, dryly concluded that Sturgis had "many characteristics of a superspreading event." Armacost pooh-poohed it all.

When public health officials were urging caution in the face of the Delta variant, at an October 2021 *Coffee with the Mayor* Zoom meeting Armacost opposed additional mandates and rather implausibly claimed to have access to more—and better—medical advice than did the county public health officer. At his hair salon, on a semiresidential street just off Washington Street, with a neon-pink sign on his door advertising "sexy" haircuts, the mayor, who worked ostentatiously maskless despite county requirements to the contrary, would attend to his equally unmasked clients. It was all performative, all designed to stir up a ruckus.

At a time when clear thinking was urgently needed, Armacost's stewardship of the city instead generated endless strife. During street protests, each side alleged that the other was prone to violence. The deputy mayor, the aptly named Mike Pence, and Pence's wife were caught on a hot mic at the end of an April 2021 Zoom council meeting cursing out their female opponents, including the septuagenarian Karen Hogan. Jodi Wilke even filed a police report against the seventy-two-year-old Hogan, who had a long-established local reputation as a take-no-shit progressive organizer and who was wont to joke that she had "a Celtic warrior in me; they had heads of enemies hanging off horses when they went into battle." "Think of the end of *Psycho*. That's me," the hard-edged Hogan was alleged to have told Wilke, who, not surprisingly, took umbrage and told the police that she feared she would be stabbed in her shower. Nothing ultimately came of the police report—and Hogan was keen to point out that her hyperbole was meant to be taken with a grain of salt—but the threatening interaction spoke to the increasing acrimony tearing Sequim apart.

———

By December 2021, thirteen months after the elections and nearly two years into the COVID crisis, vaccinations had been available for a year, and communities around America were starting to return to life after twenty-one months of upheaval. Yet deaths from the virus remained horrifyingly high, and wave after wave of variants, mutations of the original virus that were both more contagious and more able to evade immune responses triggered by earlier infections and by vaccines, were stymieing efforts to end the pandemic. In 2020 more than 350,000 Americans had died of COVID, making it the third-most-common cause of death in the country. That year, Americans' life expectancy declined by 1.8 years. In 2021, even as a mass-vaccination program took off, another 415,000 Americans lost their lives to the disease, and life expectancy declined by another 7 months. Globally, in those two years the World Health Organization estimated that nearly 15,000,000 more people died than would have been expected absent pandemic conditions. That was nearly as many people as the total number of soldiers and civilians killed over the four years of fighting during World War I.

Numerous countries remained locked down to overseas visitors or required weeks of quarantining after arrival, and noncitizens couldn't enter the US without proof of vaccination. According to CDC guidelines, those infected with the virus, as well as those exposed, had to quarantine for five to ten days, depending on the severity of their symptoms. Many workplaces and universities still had rigid testing regimes in place, and although most schools had reopened for in-person instruction after more than a year of studies had been given over to "remote learning," in many states students still had to wear masks to class. And as restaurants, businesses, theaters, sports arenas, and other places where people congregated and socialized gradually reopened—frequently short of staff because so many people had left the labor market or died in the months following the original lockdowns of March 2020—many carded patrons at the door to ensure that they were double-vaccinated. To visit a theater, one would likely not only have to show proof of vaccination but also wear a mask throughout the performance. Often, venues even banned the sale of drinks, worried that patrons would spread the disease by unmasking in order to take sips from their beverages. In several states around the nation, particularly states governed by Democrats, masking on public transit, at indoor entertainment venues, in restaurant waiting areas, and in doctors' offices was mandatory. In other states, however, where the legislatures and governors were Republicans, the alarm level was pitched much lower, and most mandates had long been ditched—or had never really been implemented to begin with. Meanwhile, on federal property, including airports, masking remained obligatory, with warnings blared out of the PA systems that it was against the law to not comply with these mandates.

As a result of these divergent approaches, masks, vaccines, and lockdowns all became hyper-politicized, cudgels to be wielded in an escalating culture war. Two pandemic narratives were fast being seeded: in one, a proactive public health response and an expansive use of emergency public health powers had saved countless lives and had kept America's health infrastructure from caving in under the pressure of millions of desperately sick people flooding hospitals all at once; in the other, plucky politicians and armed citizens with pioneer spirit and a strong sense of their Second Amendment rights had stood up to autocratic public health mandates and misguided officials at the CDC and had, in opposing lockdowns, protected fundamental values of liberty and individual rights.

———

Over the previous twenty months, from the first days of the pandemic, those battles over perception had taken place between Trump—who had an unerring ability to harness and manipulate and magnify rage—and his own public health officials, as well as between the president and Democratic state politicians. Trump called Anthony Fauci "a disaster" and dismissed the team of scientists advising the White House on the pandemic as "these idiots." When Trump tweeted that his supporters should "LIBERATE" a number of Democratic-led states that were on lockdown, Mary McCord, legal director of the Institute for Constitutional Advocacy and Protection, denounced the president for tweeting out what she viewed as incitements to insurrection: "It's not at all unreasonable to consider Trump's tweets about 'liberation' as at least tacit encourage-ment to citizens to take up arms against duly elected state officials of the party opposite his own, in response to sometimes unpopular but legally issued stay-at-home orders," she concluded. "The pres-ident's tweets—unabashedly using the current crisis to encourage a backlash against lawful and expert-recommended public health measures, falsely claiming a Second Amendment 'siege' and calling for insurrection against elected leaders—have no place in our public discourse and enjoy no protection under our Constitution."

Trump reveled in flouting public health orders. As the election neared, he held huge campaign rallies around the country, and his supporters would gleefully flock to these gatherings. Perhaps, they thought if only enough people flouted the social-distancing require-ments simultaneously, if only they laughed heartily enough at Trump's crude anti-Chinese jokes about the "kung flu," or if only they ostentatiously tore their masks off when they saw a photographer or reporter from the loathed "mainstream media," somehow, magically, the virus itself would lose its edge. Trump seemed to encourage this belief in the supernatural, stating dozens of times over the course of that terrible spring, summer, and fall that the virus would somehow just "go away." That it would suddenly pull up stakes and leave. That, puff, it would vanish "like magic." That, medical advice and common sense notwithstanding, you could kill it by ingesting bleach. That you could recover from it by ingesting horse medications.

The liberal outrage these outbursts provoked was, for Trump and his acolytes, simply part of the show. It was white noise. It was dis-traction. It was all about "owning the libs"—even at the cost of a fractured, often incoherent, political response to a deadly disease outbreak.

Perhaps that's why Alex Jones, the king of conspiracists, told his audiences in mid-March 2020, in the early days of the pandemic, that the toothpaste and diet supplements that he hawked on his website, each containing some colloidal silver with supposedly miraculous antiviral properties, would serve as a "stopgate" to kill off the virus "at point-blank range." Maybe it's why Jones would ludicrously claim on his InfoWars show, after the Pfizer and Moderna vaccines were approved, that many of those who were injected with the shots could no longer eat beef. Or why he would definitively announce on Twitter that the vaccine "destroys the subject's natural immune system."

In keeping with his strategy of flooding the zone with shit, Steve Bannon invited on to his War Room talk show supposed experts who told listeners that COVID was "one hundred percent treatable" via unproven drugs such as hydroxychloroquine, that the approved vaccines were filled with fetal tissue, that the virus had been bioengineered in a Chinese lab, and that Bill Gates owned a patent on an injectable cryptocurrency that was being surreptitiously inserted into patients' bodies when they got the COVID shot. Bannon was also convinced that the lockdowns were being used as cover to implement an unprecedented power grab by big governments against their civilian populations.

In early November 2020, the alt-right provocateur used his social media feeds to upload a video in which he called for the beheading of Anthony Fauci and other top public health officials. "I'd put the heads on pikes. Right. I'd put them at the two corners of the White House," he declared. "As a warning to federal bureaucrats: Either get with the program or you're gone." Shortly afterward, Bannon's lawyer resigned in disgust, and Twitter banned Bannon from the platform.

———

Sequim under Mayor Armacost was no exception to this altered regimen, to the schisms between public health officials and MAGA politicians, and to the political divides this played into with the voting public.

By the fall of 2021, diners were once again able to sit indoors at restaurants and cafés like the Rainshadow—but, as a result of Dr. Berry's mandate, only if they could show proof of vaccination.

It was an uncomfortable bargain. On the one hand, until the emergence of the vaccine-dodging Omicron variant a few months later, the mandate meant that diners in Clallam County could eat and drink in relative safety at establishments throughout the county. It also meant that workers in those restaurants, the waiters and cooks and busboys who kept the eateries running, could go to work each day knowing they had at least some protections against being infected with a potentially deadly disease. But on the other hand, no matter its success, that same mandate struck many locals as being a massive infringement on their personal liberties. As a result, Berry had become even more of a lightning rod for anti-vaxxers, antigovernment militias, and QAnon conspiracists. Unfortunately for her, these included Armacost as well as a majority of the six-member city council, three of whom had been appointed during the Armacost mayorship when sitting councillors had died or resigned. In September 2021 the council passed a nonbinding resolution condemning Berry's public health mandate and then, critics alleged, largely stayed silent as mobs, in which many participants were armed and, the doctor believed, apparently with lynching on their minds, protested outside her offices and tried to find her home.

By that second summer of the pandemic, hundreds of demonstrators were showing up outside the public health building in downtown Sequim. "People called for my public hanging," Berry said. "It was insane." On a daily basis, the doctor received hundreds of threatening phone messages and emails. One text said, "Sleep with one eye open. I'm coming for you." Young men in souped-up pickup trucks flying American flags would cruise her neighborhood—her exact address was kept private, but her enemies knew roughly which part of the county she lived in. "My daughter couldn't go outside because we didn't want people to see us," she remembered. "I was so scared I wasn't sleeping. I'd keep it together during the day and cry at night." Eventually, fearing for both her safety and her mental well-being, Berry and her young daughter *did* leave the county for a while.

Shortly afterward, though, she returned, defiant. She hired on additional staff for the county health department and accelerated her push for mass vaccinations and other pandemic-mitigation measures. Yet under the surface, the doctor knew the signs of trouble. "In all honesty, it's going to take a while to fully recover from everything that happened," she recounted three years after the first hate mail started arriving in her inbox. "Having protesters with guns show up at your office wears you out. We're all recovering. Now we [she and her staff] try to take on the regular public health work as we come out of that. I got diagnosed with PTSD [post-traumatic stress disorder], am jumpy when I hear loud sounds."

In her nightmares, Doctor Berry pictured the men who had threatened her showing up in her yard and then breaking her windows and entering her house: "My office in my home is made of glass. I picture someone coming across the lawn toward me. It was a very powerless experience being a single mother alone in a house at night with a toddler. That was very scary. I mostly sleep well now, but things bring it back up. When we have a difficult public meeting and there's angry dudes shouting about stuff, it raises my blood pressure faster than it used to." Before the pandemic, Berry had been an avid listener to public radio in the morning. These days, however, she found the news too stressful: "I've got a good counselor; that helps. I was struggling with nightly nightmares, got scared being outdoors alone—and I used to be a thru-hiker. But it really shook me."

Part Two

SHASTA COUNTY, CALIFORNIA

Chapter Three

ITEM "R2"

WITH HINDSIGHT, GIVEN THE UPHEAVALS THAT WOULD SOON FOLLOW, THE MARCH 10, 2020, four-hour-long board of supervisors meeting in Shasta County, part of northern California, more than six hundred miles to the south of Sequim, was shockingly sedate.

For the previous three months, the COVID virus had crept inexorably toward the United States. First there had been the stories in December 2019 about Wuhan, China—and the images of hospitals inundated with patients who couldn't breathe. Then there had been the shocking scenes in Italy—where the virus swept through the north of the country, killing off thousands of elderly and immunocompromised people within just a few days. In the city of Bergamo, so many people died in that opening act of the pandemic that the local crematorium was overwhelmed. Army vehicles had to be brought in to transport the sealed coffins of the victims, the bodies treated as hazardous materials, to other parts of the country for disposal. Whole regions had been placed under a rigid lockdown in a frantic effort to slow the spread of this new killer virus, and then, the day before the Shasta board meeting, the entire country had been placed under emergency pandemic restrictions. Seemingly overnight, Italy had gone from being one of the largest economies on Earth to being a frozen-in-place death zone with all nonessential businesses shuttered and the population mandated to shelter in place. Modernity had, in the blink of an eye, been replaced by the unfathomable terrors of the medieval plague years.

In February and March, a few cases began being identified in the United States, many of those early infections tied to people who had traveled to China or Italy or some other hotbed and had then returned stateside, others related to cruise ships, but some additional ones seemingly caused by community transmission. It was those cases that caused public health workers and epidemiologists the most grief. For these cases meant that the disease was already among us, a silent, stalking killer, establishing beachheads in nursing homes and hospitals, in prisons and in public gathering spots, among families and in workplaces. It was only a matter of time now before the case numbers would begin to explode and then, a few weeks later, the deaths would escalate.

Public health officials, from the CDC through local officials at the county level, were frantically scrambling to isolate new patients, to identify people who had been exposed to the virus, to set up mass testing systems for COVID, and to purchase protective gear for medical personnel. And ordinary residents were rushing to grocery stores, where the shelves were increasingly empty of basic staples, to stock up for the unthinkable—a twenty-first-century pandemic lockdown, a quarantine that would shutter businesses, mandate that people stay in their homes, and keep children away from schools for months, maybe even years, into the future.

It sounded impossible, but the impossible had already happened in China and in Italy. Borders were starting to be closed to noncitizens. Air travel was being restricted.

Six days before the March 10 meeting, California governor Gavin Newsom had declared a state of emergency in response to the developing crisis. Six days after the meeting, seven Bay Area counties would coordinate to declare a local lockdown to try to slow the spread of a disease that showed every sign of being likely to rapidly swamp health-care systems. A couple days later, Newsom would extend those lockdown restrictions to the entire state. Soon, similar restrictions would be implemented across most of the nation. By April, much of the rest of the world would be locked down, with draconian penalties imposed in many places for people who ventured into the streets without permits or did previously everyday things like hold birthday parties or attend funerals for departed friends and relatives. On television (could one bear it) one could tune in to images of once-vibrant cities from London to New York, from Shanghai to Mexico City, largely shuttered, their streets eerily empty, their skies denuded of airplanes, the noise of ambulance sirens providing an otherworldly soundtrack to an unthinkable catastrophe. In Venice, Italy, the waters in the famed canals would clear as pollution from boat traffic vanished. In Paris, Rome, Moscow, and other vast metro areas, millions of commuters would stop using public transport almost overnight, and large cities would become akin to a collection of autonomous villages, their residents hunkered down in their homes or venturing out for exercise to walk the streets only in their immediate neighborhoods. Descriptions of life on the other side of town would become as exotic as centuries-old travel journals written by adventurers exploring far-off lands.

That retreat into the hyper-local wouldn't just be a result of personal preference; it would also be official government policy. In many countries in Europe, by the mid-spring of 2020 residents would need passes to travel more than a few miles from their home, to be outdoors for more than a certain number of hours a day, or to be on the streets after curfew—passes that would generally be granted only for medical emergencies or vital work needs. These pass-based travel restrictions would be as coercive as any issued on the Continent since the end of World War II. In Australia, the states would impose rigid lockdowns, and the federal government would implement draconian, multiweek quarantine rules for anyone entering the country. By March, Hong Kong had already moved to a mandatory fourteen-day quarantine for travelers. Soon, other megacities would follow suit in locking themselves down: places that had until recently bustled with life and culture would enter deep freeze, with only "essential workers" allowed to attend their places of work. In India entire apartment complexes, in cities such as Bombay, would be locked down when a resident tested positive, sometimes with guards patrolling the streets below to ensure that residents didn't break out. Stories would emerge of millions of destitute migrant workers in India trekking back home to villages, their jobs having vanished overnight.

───────

But when the Shasta County board of supervisors met, most of that was still in the future. On March 10 few people in attendance seemed to grasp the vastness of the changes that were about to befall them.

Board chair Mary Rickert opened with a few perfunctory comments, followed by a short invocation prayer by Pastor Dave Honey, of the Good News Rescue Mission. Despite it being a government meeting and thus supposedly nondenominational, Honey, his hair graying, wearing a black shirt, the top buttons undone, and a black sports jacket, made no bones about his Christian impulses. "In Jesus's name we pray," he concluded softly. Shasta was a conservative county; it was unlikely that anyone would make a fuss about the invocation.

After Honey, several minutes were spent on giving a young female county staffer an employee-of-the-month award. Only then, only after the ordinary, everyday business of politics in a small county had been dispensed with, did the meeting swing around to COVID. Dr. Karen Ramstrom had been asked by the board to come in and provide a public health briefing on what was happening and how the county was preparing for what might come. Standing at the dais, a low-cut purple blouse exposing the three thin necklaces around her neck, the doctor looked tired, even a little gaunt. She had been working flat-out in recent days, coordinating phone calls with the CDC and with state officials, getting travel manifests so that contact tracers in Shasta could reach out to people who might have been exposed overseas, setting up from scratch a new COVID-testing system for the county. Amid all of this, she had had to schedule time to work on this PowerPoint presentation.

On the projector hung behind the five supervisors, Ramstrom's slides appeared. There was a dry, technocratic quality to the update, nothing to convey the earth-shattering enormity of what was starting to unfold. Eighty percent of COVID cases were thought to be mild or moderate, but that left 20 percent that were more serious—14 percent would likely be classified as "severe," and 6 percent would leave victims critically ill and at risk of death. Ramstrom tried to contextualize: those numbers made the new virus far less lethal than other recent coronavirus outbreaks, such as MERS (with a 35 percent mortality rate) or SARS (with a 10 percent death rate), but far more lethal than many other communicable diseases. Measles had a 0.2 percent death rate, and seasonal influenza, which affected tens of millions of Americans every year, had a 0.1 percent rate. What was more worrying, though, was that no one had immunity to the disease, so once it got embedded in a community it would likely spread extremely quickly, via respiratory droplets, from one person to the next.

Ramstrom explained how even though scientists thought that asymptomatic transmission was not a big problem—a conclusion they would have to revise over the coming weeks and months—because it *could* happen, it still made social distancing particularly important. Moreover, because older people and those with weakened immune systems were particularly vulnerable, it was crucial, she explained, even if she had to admit that it "isn't sexy," for healthy residents to take the disease seriously and not to go to work or socialize with others if they were sick and therefore contagious.

The doctor ran down some more numbers. To date there had been 3,800 COVID deaths globally and 20 fatalities in the United States. California had confirmed 133 cases, 19 of which seemed to have been acquired by community transmission, and Shasta County had identified one case: a middle-aged man who had been infected while traveling overseas.

Ramstrom rapidly explained that the public health people were at this point in the pandemic trying to contain the spread of the virus but that at some point soon they would likely have to give up on that strategy and move to "community mitigation, which really has to do with social distancing." They were strategizing how to keep hospitals functioning even as large numbers of staff got sick. And as she almost casually added toward the end of her presentation, "We are starting to have some conversations about consideration of a local emergency."

As noted, it's unlikely that many in the audience, including the board of supervisors members, fully understood either the magnitude of the situation or the import of those thirteen words. After all, a disease that had infected one person out of a county population of around two hundred thousand hardly seemed like something to fuss about. There were more immediate concerns—a spiraling epidemic of opioid drug use, homelessness, and poverty issues, not to mention all the physical, psychological, and economic impacts of years of massive wildfires throughout northern California.

One by one, the board members thanked her, and Rickert made small talk about how her own daughter had been in Milan when the outbreak there started but had come back to the United States and seemed not to have picked up the virus. Everything was calm, all the participants in the conversation civil. Less than half an hour after Ramstrom started speaking, the board meeting moved on to other, more immediate concerns: local power-grid problems, information about the county's wellness clinic, conversations about how to respond to wildfires, a speech praising the work of a local children's advocacy center, and so on. COVID had just been reduced to item "R2" on a crowded meeting agenda, on a par with all the other goings-on, all the other daily frustrations, of local governance.

Chapter Four

A PRESSURE COOKER PRIMED TO EXPLODE

IN THE COMING YEARS, THE CIVILITY THAT SURROUNDED RAMSTROM'S COVID PRESENTATION THAT March would be in increasingly short supply. Like Sequim's, the region's politics would become ever more acrimonious as the reality show that was the Trump presidency and post-presidency ran up against the actual reality of a once-in-a-century pandemic. Over time, these forces would fundamentally reshape Shasta's image, leading to an attempted recall against three supervisors, one of whom, Leonard Moty, an ex–police chief of Redding, would be booted out of office by a surging right-wing, populist movement furious at the public health restrictions implemented to slow the spread of COVID.

By 2020, with the Trump personality cult in full bloom, America was at a crossroads. Trump's relentless assault on democratic norms, his empowering of paramilitaries, his flirtation with overseas dictators such as North Korea's Kim Jong-Un and Russia's Vladimir Putin, and his nod-and-a-wink embrace of white nationalism and the alt-right—be it after the Charlottesville neo-Nazi rally of 2017 or during the presidential debates, when he doffed his cap to the Proud Boys—had exposed the fragility of many norms and institutions long thought inviolable in the United States.

In Charlottesville, neo-Nazis protesting the removal of statues commemorating Confederate leaders had rallied with tiki torches, raucously shouting that they would not "be replaced" by other races and creeds. The ghastly apogee of the event occurred when James Alex Fields, an ex-teacher fascinated by Nazi iconography, deliberately rammed his Dodge Challenger into the crowd of antifascist protesters. Thirty-two-year-old Heather Heyer died on the scene. Several others were seriously injured. Afterward, unwilling to make a complete break with the white nationalists who were increasingly a significant part of his electoral coalition, Trump had stated that there were some "very fine people" on both sides of the conflict.

Donald Trump "joked" about installing himself as president for life and openly mused about desiring the sort of absolute powers accorded Xi Jinping in China. When he withdrew the United States from the Paris climate accord, his language and phrasing about how the world once laughed at America but no one was laughing now was eerily redolent of some of the passages from Adolf Hitler's wartime speeches. Trump's willingness to push whatever big lie was convenient to meet the political needs of the moment, his overt racism, his misogyny, his labeling of the press and his political opponents as "enemies of the people," and his extraordinarily effective use of Twitter and other social media outlets, as well as right-wing television and radio networks, to build up a strongman's propaganda machine were fundamentally reshaping not only American politics but also the broader culture. It was creating a cult of personality based around loyalty to one man and that man's ever-shifting whims.

"Gaslighting forces subordinates to agree that the person in charge gets to determine what reality is. Victims must surrender either their integrity or their ownership of their own perceptions," the historian Heather Cox Richardson wrote in *Democracy Awakening: Notes on the State of America.* "In either case, having once agreed to a deliberate lie, it becomes harder to challenge later ones because that means acknowledging the other times they caved." In Richardson's telling, adherence to the Big Lie thus became a loyalty test used by Trump and his advisers to deliberately shatter democratic norms. "Big Lies are springboards for authoritarians," Richardson wrote. "They enable a leader to convince followers that they were unfairly cheated of power by those the leader demonizes."

Onto that authoritarian fire, two accelerants were thrown: first, in the winter of 2020 came COVID and the resulting lockdowns and prolonged enforced isolation, the move to remote schooling, and the shuttering of "nonessential" businesses. Hundreds of thousands died in those brutal first months of the pandemic.

The psychic trauma that built up, the continual stress—both of not knowing who would be infected and who would die next, and not knowing when the bone-crushing isolation would end—were sledgehammers turning to powder the world that we thought we knew. As psychologists began studying the neurological impact of the disease itself, the stress generated by fear of the disease, and the collateral damage caused by the lockdowns and isolation, they chronicled increases in suicide, in divorce, in domestic violence, in depression, in anxiety, and in PTSD.

Those who were already psychologically fragile were made more so, and a number of studies showed that people infected with COVID-19 were more likely to subsequently receive a diagnosis of schizophrenia and that those who went into the pandemic psychologically healthy ran through more of their reserves just trying to maintain their well-being. Meanwhile, the availability of in-person psychiatric and counseling assistance plummeted, and those on the edge, struggling to hold it all together, were left trying to navigate a new world of Zoom medical appointments and distance diagnoses. Continuity of care, so vital for the effective treatment of serious mental health disorders, largely fell by the wayside. And drug and alcohol use increased as desperate people sought whatever coping mechanisms they could find to manage the loneliness and fear.

It's hard to imagine a scenario more tailor-made for social explosions. And, sure enough, those explosions came hard and fast: armed uprisings against the lockdowns in several states, plots to kidnap and execute the governor of Michigan, lynch mobs lined up against public health officers, school board and county board of supervisors meetings that degenerated into screaming matches, parents attempting to carry out citizen's arrests against officials who were keeping the schools closed, supermarket cashiers being violently attacked for asking customers to don masks.

In Fort Worth, Texas, a woman at a 7-Eleven store was filmed screaming at a cashier after he asked her to put on a mask. As she left the store, she turned around and spat on the counter. In Wayne County, Pennsylvania, a man spat in the face of another shopper, a sixty-nine-year-old woman who had approached him and asked him to put on a mask. In Harrisburg, Pennsylvania, a woman shopping at the local Kline Village Giant store spat in the face of a young female employee.

The violence picked up steam. Numerous store employees around the country reported being punched or kicked for asking customers to mask up. Flight attendants were pushed, slapped, and punched by passengers infuriated at mask requirements on planes.

Finally, the anti-mask tantrums turned lethal. In Flint, Michigan, forty-three-year-old Calvin Munerlyn, a Dollar Store employee, was fatally shot in the back of the head by a relative of a shopper whom Munerlyn had told couldn't stay in the store without a mask. At the Big Bear Supermarket in Decatur, Georgia, forty-one-year-old Laquitta Willis was murdered after asking a customer to pull up his mask when he approached her cash register to pay for his groceries.

———

As the winter of 2020 gave way to spring, COVID became an extraordinary political football. At Trump rallies—gatherings that broke every public health recommendation of both the CDC and the states and cities where the events were held—tens of thousands of unmasked participants screamed obscenities at public health figures such as Anthony Fauci.

The country had become a pressure cooker, primed to explode.

And then, a few months after the initial outbreak, the lid blew off the pressure cooker following the police murder of George Floyd in Minneapolis, as well as the renewed emphasis on teaching about America's brutal racial history that grew out of this traumatic event.

Millions of Americans, pent up and isolated for months, desperate to find an issue larger than COVID to focus on, poured out into the streets that May and June in what would rapidly become the largest racial-justice protests in US history. All of this contributed to the general political swirl around COVID. Those who had objected to masking and isolation mandates from the start of the emergency responses back in March noted that many of these protesters were themselves violating regulations but that they were doing so without arousing the censorious voices of liberal figures who had been so scathing of the Trump rallies held that spring.

Most of the protests that took place in the wake of Floyd's killing were peaceful, but some, especially in the country's largest cities, *did* degenerate into violence and looting. And when they did, Trump was ready, urging the military to get involved in quashing the protests.

On May 29 he tweeted out an extraordinarily inflammatory saying from 1960s Miami police chief Walter Headley: "When the looting starts, the shooting starts." It was almost as if the president of the United States, far from trying to calm the situation, was egging on his supporters to themselves take to the streets; it was almost as if the commander in chief *wanted* to see an explosion of violence on those streets. Three days later, Trump amped up the rhetoric further. At a Rose Garden address on June 1, with protesters filling the streets leading up to the White House and police firing volley after volley of tear gas into the crowd, the beleaguered president promised that "if a city or state refuses to take the actions necessary to defend the life and property of their residents, then I will deploy the United States military and quickly solve the problem for them." On a call with governors that same day, Trump repeatedly urged them to "dominate" protesters and, again, repeatedly promised—or threatened, depending on how one heard the president's words—to send in the troops to restore order. He backed off only when the army chiefs made it clear they would balk at any such orders.

Around the country, however, in the last days of May and the first days of June, as protests and rioting spread from coast to coast, state governors took their own decisions to deploy National Guard troops in many of America's major cities. And in several communities right-wing militias activated their members to patrol the streets as a vigilante add-on to overstretched law enforcement. Over the course of that month, at least nine protesters were killed, according to information compiled by the nonprofit Armed Conflict Location and Event Data (ACLED). More than two thousand cities saw protests, many of them on numerous occasions, throughout that summer—polling from later in the year found that as many as 26 million Americans took part in the racial-justice demonstrations, making it the largest protest movement in US history. And although the vast majority of those protests did not turn deadly, and the vast majority of the demonstrators remained nonviolent, the 5 percent of protests that ACLED researchers estimated *did* turn violent resulted in a huge amount of property damage and numerous injuries to police officers and to protesters alike. In Minneapolis alone, more than one thousand buildings were burned or otherwise damaged. In New York City, 450 buildings were attacked. In Atlanta, several buildings and vehicles in the Centennial Olympic Park area were vandalized, the interior of the CNN headquarters among them. Looters emptied out stores in Santa Monica and hit two federal buildings in Los Angeles. Nationwide, the Department of Homeland Security estimated that more than 200 federal buildings were damaged. The Associated Press calculated that in the first week of protests alone, more than 10,000 people around the United States were arrested for their role in the demonstrations and unrest. Upward of a quarter of those arrests were in Los Angeles, a city with a strong collective memory of the protests and violence that had followed the Rodney King beating nearly thirty years earlier.

When, two months after the initial protests, a seventeen-year-old white vigilante, Kyle Rittenhouse, shot dead two protesters in Kenosha, Wisconsin, Trump and his conservative media allies jumped to his defense. The president announced, even before the teenager's trial, it appeared to him that Rittenhouse had acted in self-defense. Tucker Carlson claimed that the teenager was "attempting to maintain order when no one else would." Ann Coulter quipped that she wanted the young man "as my president." Later on, after Rittenhouse was acquitted by a jury of the charges against him of reckless and intentional homicide, Congressman Matt Gaetz would reach out to him about an internship, and Trump would invite him to come and meet with him at Mar-a-Lago, later pronouncing him a "really nice young man."

76

Two weeks before Rittenhouse fired his fatal shots, with California five months into pandemic lockdowns, with large parts of the economy still shuttered and many residents financially desperate, with most school districts in the state about to enter a new school year of remote learning and no real road map to rapidly reopening schools, and with masking mandatory in public places, Carlos Zapata, who lived on the edge of the small farming town of Palo Cedro, attended the weekly board of supervisors meeting unmasked. Normally, this meeting would have been held in the morning; that day, it was scheduled for six o'clock in the evening.

By then, five months into the pandemic, many of Shasta's residents were at a breaking point. The lockdown policies, implemented at speed by the governor, using emergency powers, had been haphazardly designed—as they had been by desperate governments all over the world as the pandemic threatened to swamp health-care systems and the COVID death count skyrocketed. Federal relief measures had been passed, but it was taking time to process all the applications for loans and unemployment benefits. Meanwhile, laid-off workers and small-business owners were scrambling to make ends meet, to pay the mortgage or rent, and to put food on the table. That spring and summer, food banks saw huge spikes in the numbers of hungry people coming to them for help. In Las Vegas miles-long lines of cars snaked down the fabled Strip toward food pantries distributing emergency relief to casino workers and entertainers who had been laid off as the tourism industry shut down. It was a particularly stark image of a reality turned upside down. In New York and other large East Coast cities, pedestrians waited in line for hours to get what little food the charity centers could provide them. Food-bank workers reported that the scale of need was surpassing that seen even at the height of the Great Recession in 2008–2009. In April 2020, as the country ground to a halt, unemployment suddenly spiked at nearly 15 percent. By the summer, millions of Americans were running through what little savings they had, and millions feared that, unable to pay their rent or mortgages, they might lose their homes. (Not until September would the CDC use its emergency public health powers to declare a national eviction moratorium.) Even as Congress passed a series of relief acts that rapidly threw trillions of dollars into supporting the economy, in the short term, before the money started flowing, the economic damage caused to individuals was immense, and the political fallout that resulted from this situation grew increasingly dangerous.

As the pandemic ground on that first spring and summer, so the profound levels of fear and anxiety in communities around the country escalated. Increasingly, how one believed that the public authorities should respond to COVID was determined by one's political allegiances. In this fissuring, nuance and empathy for one's political opponents were lost. Progressives overwhelmingly embraced the precautionary principles that animated the lockdowns, and they denounced conservatives as know-nothings; conservatives overwhelmingly came to oppose the COVID restrictions and denounced progressives and public health experts as fearmongering, liberty-shredding, wannabe tyrants. What had started off as simply a once-in-a-lifetime public health emergency was rapidly becoming a stark political litmus test, with both sides talking past each other in increasingly loud and angry terms.

At Shasta County's board of supervisors meetings, representatives from the county Democratic Party would show up to petition the county to "recognize the COVID-19 reality" and to require the "simple compliance of wearing a mask and practicing social distancing." Meanwhile, conservatives—of whom there were many more in Shasta—would denounce the whole affair as being simply un-American, the emphasis on public health as somehow unpatriotic. Some would show up in costume—one local anti-vaxxer, ex-supervisor Leonard Moty remembers, would turn up dressed as a syringe—while others would come ostentatiously packing weapons. At the height of the pandemic, when the supervisors themselves were sectioned off behind Plexiglas, each in their own bizarre cubicle, one outspoken local supporter of the idea that rural counties should secede from California and form the State of Jefferson turned up at meetings wearing a mask over his eyes, instead of one over his mouth and nose, to theatrically lambaste the supervisors for what he called their "shameful" defense of mask wearing.

The early August meeting, which would ultimately last nearly six hours, was full of acrimony—young children denouncing masks for making them feel claustrophobic (one twelve-year-old recited an anti-mask poem), adults screaming at the supervisors for making the speakers stand far back from the dais as a social-distancing measure and denouncing the masked supervisors for not looking them directly in their eyes. "Move the desks aside, come outside, and look at the people. Shake our hands. We're not sick," one young mother shouted, her voice dripping with sarcasm. "We're not criminals. But if you make the wrong decisions for too long, you *will* make the most law-abiding citizens into criminals. And you *do not* want to do that."

Some people spoke calmly, respectfully—one local doctor, for example, fully accepted the gruesome reality of COVID but, with great dignity and with a powerful sadness at the mental health damage and loss of education that school shutdowns were imposing on poorer, more vulnerable children, pushed back against the continued closing of schools. Later on, the doctor would become a prominent voice in the local anti-lockdown movement that was bubbling up from the grassroots. But, whether loudly or softly, in these meetings the rejection of California's statewide mandates was nearly unanimous. Locals paraded to the dais to compare COVID to the flu, notwithstanding the vast difference in mortality rates between the two diseases; to denounce masks as being un-American; to demand the county push back against the mandates originating out of

Sacramento. Some implored the supervisors to unshutter churches. Others pled for small businesses to be reopened so that the owners could make payroll and also feed their children. One impassioned small-business owner told them, "I employ fifteen employees, not minimum wage. . . . We are the people that donate to your Little League team, church, every school function, organization, sports team imaginable, Carr Fire victims,* the mission, adopt-a-family, and more." She continued, pivoting to a more general political critique: "We are tired of carrying the load of a welfare state, tired of being told we can't open our business after doing what was asked of us, tired of early-release criminals roaming our neighborhoods . . . we are just tired of being tired. The damage of being shut down will be far-reaching and long-term."

A Cottonwood resident, whose father had died fighting in Korea, told the supervisors that they were "complicit" in destroying American liberties and needed to open up the churches "immediately, immediately. It really is tyranny. You need to consider your place, and your responsibility, in this lockdown. You need to open up, search your heart. You need to stop obeying Fauci and the so-called medical experts who are forcing this country into the disaster we are headed into."

"I'm a God-fearing, patriotic, flag-loving, tax-paying citizen here. It's time for us to go back to work," one local woman implored the board. "My seventy-five-year-old mother is contemplating bankruptcy. My twenty-three-year-old daughter just had a baby and hasn't had a paycheck in seventeen weeks. My house is on the chopping block because I deferred my payments so I could help my kids eat. I don't understand what is going on."

But none of the speakers were a patch on Carlos Zapata. The ex-marine strode to the speakers' podium and launched a broadside

---

* The Carr Fire had torn through the county a few years earlier, leaving charred hillsides and ashes where homes once stood.

against the political leaders around the state who had signed off on the public health measures. He was wearing a black baseball cap and a white T-shirt, his muscular arms bulging out of the sleeves. He looked a bundle of pent-up energy, his arms folded in front of his chest, his torso hunched slightly forward as he leaned into the mic. There was something undeniably charismatic about him, something almost hypnotizing in the way he could conjure up the fury and angst that so many people were feeling when confronted by a poorly understood new disease and emergency public health measures of open-ended duration.

Zapata was a natural-born crowd-pleaser, a skilled orator who knew how to gin up the crowd, how to pace his words, how to adjust his volume to play to the emotions of the audience, how to build to a magnificent climax. In some ways he was a right-wing version of Mario Savio, the University of California at Berkeley graduate student who had lit the flame of the free-speech movement nearly sixty years earlier when he stood atop the steps at Sproul Hall and announced that there came a time when the system proved itself so corrupt, so rotten, that you had no real choice but to stand in its way, to gum up the works of the machine until it was forced to a stop. There was a magnetism to his presence, a rock-star quality to his stagecraft, and when he got into his rhythm, he simply owned the meeting.

"It's absolutely horrendous what you're doing to people," Zapata shouted. "I'm a business owner; I tell you, our families are starving. Right now, we're being peaceful," but, he continued, "it's not going to be peaceful much longer. Good citizens are going to turn into revolutionary citizens real soon." And when that happened, Zapata promised, they would become an unstoppable force. "If you don't hear this in my voice, then open your ears and listen to what I'm saying, because this is a warning."

Directly addressing the five members of the board of supervisors, who, by now, four months into the pandemic, were sitting socially spaced and wearing masks, Zapata demanded that they "open the county. Let us citizens do what we need to do. Let owners of businesses do what they need to do to feed their families. Take the masks off. Quit masking and muzzling your children. The psychological damage you're doing to them is horrible. I've had six friends kill themselves since this happened; veterans who lost their jobs. How do you feel about being complicit in perpetuating that? The greatest hoax ever perpetrated on the American people—and you're part of it by wearing your masks. In Shasta County we're supposed to be a red county up here. Not a blue county. You guys know that; you claim to be conservatives, maybe you're not, maybe you're *liberals*." The way the word "liberals" came out of his mouth, it might as well have been "pedophiles" or "devil worshippers." Each sentence was a rhetorical gunshot, a sharp, explosive detonation: "I don't know, but by God we're Americans, and remember that! Take your masks off! Quit muzzling yourselves! Join us! Fight what's going on in Sacramento!"

Within hours of Zapata's short screed being posted online, it had gone viral, and the previously unknown ex-marine had become a lodestar for the anti-lockdown movement that was coalescing in many countries around the world. Later, Zapata would estimate that, posted and reposted around the internet, his broadside had been viewed roughly 30 million times.

In the era of Trump, COVID, the echoing chambers of social media, catastrophic fires, and the collapse of life's certainties for so many of its residents, Shasta County, centered around the gold-rush–era city of Redding, had embraced vitriol—and miracle seeking—with at least as much gusto as any other locale in the country. In consequence, it was beset by increasingly acrimonious and often irrational and even violent turmoil. Many of its political leaders would be hounded out of office during the pandemic, and graphic death threats against election officials, public health officers, and moderate political leaders would become a dime a dozen.

Yet it was, at the same time, undeniably a genuinely warm and extraordinarily generous place. In 2018, after the Carr Fire, thousands of residents, many of them too poor to afford insurance or who were homeless, had to fall back on local largesse. Their neighbors lived up to the challenge: Go Fund Me's year-end report listed Redding, with its population of roughly ninety thousand, in the top ten of the most generous cities in America. It had an active philanthropic culture, historically centered around the McConnell Foundation, its assets originating with a McConnell ancestor's lucky investment, nearly a century ago, in the Farmers' Insurance Company. Redding's residents took pride in volunteering long hours with the homeless, the victims of domestic violence, and others.

Much of this charitable impulse was channeled through the Bethel megachurch, one of the largest fundamentalist churches in the country, with eleven thousand members and a Dominionist mandate to create a local version of Heaven on Earth. The church had been founded more than a half century earlier, in the 1950s, and after Pastor Bill Johnson's hiring in 1996, it had morphed into what believers termed an "ecstatic" church.

Johnson was an imposing figure, with a weathered face and a shock of wavy gray hair, brushed backward off his forehead and hanging down toward his shoulders. When he gave speeches, he wore natty sports jackets and polo shirts or, sometimes, a buttoned shirt open at the neck. He came from a long line of charismatic pastors, and observers noted that he adhered to the tenets of the New Apostolic Reformation, a hands-on ideology that promoted the nuts and bolts of miracle work over abstract readings of Scriptures, believed in near-continual spiritual warfare, and sought to take cultural and political control over the broader society.

A quarter century after his hiring, Johnson was now a fervent MAGA supporter, and he argued that, at least in part through elections such as the one that had brought Trump to power in 2016, America stood on the edge of the greatest religious revival in its history. His book, *Invading Babylon: The Seven Mountain Mandate*, was cowritten with Lance Wallnau, who was described in an article by Tim Dickinson in *Rolling Stone* magazine as a "self-styled 'prophet'" who argued that Jesus wanted his followers to take over nations, not just churches, and that America had a special historical mission to spread Christianity over the face of the Earth. In December 2020, Wallnau was one of the main voices in the "Jericho March" in Washington, DC, in which participants prayed for divine intervention to keep Donald Trump in office. Participants in the New Apostolic Reformation movement, of which Wallnau was a leading figure, believed, according to Dickinson, that "the physical world is enveloped by a supernatural dimension, featuring warring angels and demons, and are convinced that demons afflict their enemies on behalf of the devil."

Looked at locally, Pastor Johnson's goal of earthly conquest in the name of the church wasn't doing half badly. By some counts, in fact, as of the early 2020s a majority of the members of the city council were Bethel adherents.

Bethel's worshippers came from around the world, many to study at the church's School of Supernatural Ministry, one of five schools that it ran in the county. Students would live in local houses, sometimes as many as a dozen in a single small building, and devote their days to studying the mysteries of Bethel, to tales of angel sightings and stories of pastors communicating with the dead ensconced in their roosts in Heaven. At Bethel gatherings they might discuss the Prosperity Gospel, a school of thought, adhered to by some of the church's pastors, that preaches the value of acquiring material possessions and wealth. They would participate in healing services, in which the sick were miraculously cured. Some Bethel pastors also praised the benefits of gay-conversion therapy.

In a normal year, the school, which taught students how to attain "intimacy with God," "intercession" (the act of intervening with God on behalf of others), life coaching, and miscellaneous additional skills, enrolled 2,300 students. In the fall semester of the pandemic year of 2020, in concession to the power of the virus to spread rapidly among crowds in indoor spaces, it limited its enrollment to 1,600 students, each of whom was paying the school more than $5,000 per year, for three years, to attend. The reduced numbers, combined with a mandatory fourteen-day quarantine for new arrivals, didn't have the desired effect. Within weeks of in-person classes commencing, the school had reported 137 infections, a large proportion of the students and staff had been ordered to quarantine in their homes, and the School of Supernatural Ministry had been temporarily forced by the virus to beat a hasty and ignominious retreat into online classes. That didn't, however, stop one of its pastors, Sean Feucht, from holding massive rallies on the steps of the California capitol in Sacramento, in Washington, DC, and elsewhere against what the demonstrators argued were unnecessary restrictions on the freedom of worship. On his website, Feucht railed against bans on in-person worship that he saw as being about "silencing the faithful." Another senior figure in the church posted videos arguing that the wearing of masks was a waste of time.

But Bethel wasn't just about the school and the communion with God, about the faith healing and the miracles that, for a hefty fee, it taught students to be a part of. It wasn't just about the speaking in tongues that worshippers practiced or the possibility of the raising of the dead that its leaders preached. And it certainly wasn't just about opposition to state public health orders. It was also about charity as a religious mandate and about making sure that the megachurch's clout was felt in venues large and small around the county and points beyond. That was why Johnson's crew founded a nonprofit, Advance Redding, to generate funds to save the civic auditorium, the city's largest performing-arts venue. It was why they raised half a million dollars to pay the salaries of four Redding police officers who, after a sales-tax initiative failed, were about to be laid off because of lack of funds, and why they launched a huge fund-raising effort to stop several firefighters' jobs from also being eliminated. It was why the church gave one thousand dollars to every family in the region that had lost its home during the Carr Fire. It was why, too, the church established a global disaster-response team. "Bethel's success in assisting Redding suggests a broader lesson," wrote the columnist Joe Mathews in the *Redding Searchlight* in 2019. "Stop overthinking, and throw yourself, heart and soul, into addressing your neighbors' needs."

The buzz-cut Patrick Jones wasn't a Bethel member, but his religious and charitable impulses did run in similar directions to those of the megachurch members. Sitting under a huge stuffed buffalo head and an almost equally impressive preserved stag's head, mounted in his gun store on the opposite wall from the high-velocity rifles and next to a cardboard shooting target, its chest riddled with bullet holes, Jones—who would eventually become the hard-right chair of the county board of supervisors—recalled the time that a bear hunter from the area got badly burned. The man had ended up in the UC Davis Medical Center's specialty burn unit in Sacramento, and Jones, smiling fondly at the memory, proudly recounted how fellow hunters held an auction to raise funds for him that ultimately collected tens of thousands of dollars. Fund-raisers held for local hunting clubs, sports associations, and other community groups also routinely netted tens if not hundreds of thousands of dollars. The Second Amendment Banquet, held to help fund a lawsuit against

California's restrictions against the open carrying of guns, was a guaranteed barn raiser, at which everything from flintlocks to loads of gravel were auctioned off. At other events, Jones would emcee while his board of supervisors colleague Chris Kelstrom would put up for sale goats, puppies, hogs, even chainsaws—"Whatever we get donated," Jones explained.

To boosters, these were golden days for Redding. The center of the town, flush with Bethel donations and an array of other charitable contributions, was undergoing something of a renaissance, with hip new cafés and galleries opening, new condos being built, and new health-care and other service facilities slated for construction. The stunning Sundial Bridge, which had spanned the Sacramento River for the past couple of decades, attracted huge numbers of visitors, with annual winter light shows that drew impressive crowds from throughout the region. Performance artists and climbers came from around the world to hang off the steel cables of the suspension bridge. To celebrate the bridge's tenth anniversary, in 2014 the Bandaloop Dance Company's members created a "vertical dance" that took the troupe up and down the entirety of the soaring 217-feet-high mast from which those hundreds of tons of steel cables hung. Outré performance art notwithstanding, the modernizing impulse had its limits. At its core, Redding remained a rigidly traditionalist place, a spot far from California's big cities—both in terms of miles and in terms of worldviews—where conservatives tended to cluster to avoid the interference of big-city bureaucrats and where libertarians and back-to-landers and gun freaks and Bible thumpers came to live their vision of the mythical State of Jefferson, a sort of Idaho-writ-large, far removed from the hippie-liberal-Communist wing nuts down in Sacramento and the Bay Area.

Jones, who was unabashedly nostalgic for an America that resembled something out of a 1950s TV sitcom, spoke with pride about how he hewed to a Southern Baptist "fire and brimstone" worldview, one that believed in the curative power of the rod. He talked nostalgically of how his father "wooped" him with a leather strap when he was a boy and how such parental whippings helped ensure a respect for morality and a broader societal tilt toward law and order that since the 1960s had, he intuited, been in increasingly short supply: "A little bit of fear from your father, you respect your father." As for homosexuality, although he wouldn't go so far as to advocate corporal punishment for gays—they did, after all, have constitutional protections, he grudgingly admitted—he was clear that he "look[ed] down on those things; it's the destruction of morals in society." For Jones, the world was black and white, the gray zones of ambiguity places to shy away from: "There's right and wrong. When you do wrong, you will be punished. I believe in a very simple world; you try to be honest, be fair, be respectful. And you gotta believe in Jesus Christ."

The county was a segue region linking the picturesque orchards and farmlands of the Central Valley—which stretches from Redding in the north nearly five hundred miles south to the dusty oil town of Bakersfield—to the wild mountain lands of the northernmost part of the state, exclamation-pointed by the volcanic and glacial vastness of Mount Shasta. It had long been ultraconservative, its Democratic and trade-union heritage buried, in recent decades, by a blizzard of God-and-guns politics. And it was getting more conservative by the day. Now, the "God" and "guns" components often overlapped, with Second Amendment absolutists talking of war against the gun controllers in Sacramento, defending their "God-given" right to carry any weapon they damn well pleased, and arguing that all the rights delineated in the founding documents originated, quite literally, from God himself. One could almost see, in this worldview, Saint Peter, AK-47 strapped over his shoulder, patrolling the Pearly Gates to make sure that only the armed faithful got admitted.

Shasta County was, in other words, a paradox: a place of great beauty and generosity but also of growing intolerance and incivility, a place where, like so many other spots in modern America, a half-century-plus of social change was being litigated and litigated again on a daily basis. It was a place where those in search of miracles placed their faith in snake-oil salesmen and where those snake-oil salesmen in turn placed their faith in Donald J. Trump.

The visible presence of weapons in public spaces wasn't anything new in this part of the country. Shasta County had an active militia, widely known as the Cottonwood Militia, although to supporters it was simply a chapter of the California State Militia. On podcasts, militia members joked about doling out "Cottonwood justice" to vagrants, criminals, and other undesirables. Those militia members had been joined by local bikers, cowboys, and miscellaneous self-described "patriots," all heavily armed, in a show of force to patrol the region's towns and hamlets during the protests that erupted after George Floyd's murder in late May 2020. When a local sheriff discovered an abandoned van filled with bricks, the militias were convinced that an orchestrated Black Lives Matter effort to sow the seeds of riot in Redding and the smaller communities surrounding it had been narrowly averted. From one Facebook post to the next, rumors of the impending BLM assault grew. And as they did so, more men and women strapped on their weapons and took to the streets to patrol against the expected arrival of these outside agitators. To the militia members' immense pride, Tucker Carlson singled them out for praise on his nightly Fox show.

Shasta also had more than its fair share of provocateurs. There were far-right "citizen journalists" such as Rich Gallardo, who attempted to enact citizen's arrests of the moderate supervisors back during the lockdowns—Supervisor Leonard Moty simply laughed when Gallardo tried to arrest him during a board meeting, and Gallardo was, shortly afterward, escorted out by a local sheriff's deputy.[*]

Then there was Zapata, whose call-to-arms public appearances had riled up anti-lockdown supporters not only in Shasta County but also globally, and who had gone on to coproduce *The Red White and Blueprint*, a slick, eight-episode documentary series, accompanied by dozens of podcasts, narrating, from Zapata's perspective, the political upheavals rocking the county and the country as the pandemic played out.

In addition to the soapbox orators, there were plenty of other right-wing activists, many of them small-business owners. Chief among these was the Cottonwood barber Woody Clendenen, in his mid-fifties, with salt-and-pepper hair and a gray goatee, originally from the little Central Valley town of Turlock, 240 miles to the south. Clendenen and several friends had set up the local militia back in 2010, two years after Barack Obama's election and shortly after the passage of the Affordable Care Act. In the spring of 2020, as the COVID lockdowns took hold and as violent opposition to both Governor Newsom and local county officials grew, Clendenen had posted a cover photo on his Facebook page showing five men in a forest, their faces painted like special-forces operatives, their bodies clad in camo, each holding a high-velocity rifle. The public health response, Clendenen explained to me, "came down to tyranny. People realized 'this government is way out of control.'" Implied in the Facebook image was a not-so-subtle message of armed resistance.

Clendenen's boxy wooden barbershop—perhaps, at a stretch, 60 feet square—was on the corner of Olive and Main Streets, in the

---

[*] When I contacted Gallardo to request an interview, he wrote back, "Your writings show as an extreme leftist, almost statist, and facistic [*sic*]. I don't think anything I would have to say would be fairly reported by someone of your mindset."

tiny town of Cottonwood—opposite the headquarters of the California State Militia, the door of which was adorned with a poster helpfully telling visitors that "socialism has no home here." Some days, particularly in the late afternoon, the barbershop's floor was coated with a carpet of what appeared to be weeks' worth of shorn hair. On the wall just to the left of the door upon entering, a large rifle hung. Also on the walls were bumper stickers with decals such as "Build El Wall," "Not a Liberal," and "Liberty or Death. Don't tread on me." Behind the two barber chairs was tacked up a price list: $15 haircuts for men/boys, $12 for seniors, retired military $11, families of two or more $13, buzz cuts $8, complaints $20, Liberals $40. Months after the first list went up, he added a second one, a "Biden Price List." On that list, liberals were charged $100, and "Vaccinated" were charged an additional $5 on top of that. When clients came in, he sat them down in one of his old swivel chairs, draped them in a huge Stars and Stripes flag sheet to protect their clothes from the trimmings, and quickly set to work with his razor.

Clendenen ran his little business as a neighborhood meeting place—an old-school barbershop, like the one his father, the child of Dust Bowl migrants from Oklahoma, had operated for more than fifty years—a place where people came to shoot the breeze, to gossip, to trade neighborhood stories about crime, about love, about intrigue, even on occasion to debate. He was a homespun philosopher, entertaining, raw, full of homilies, charming at times, willing to talk for hours with anyone who walked through his door.

The barber and his coworker, Jennifer, a middle-aged woman with seven grandchildren, made no bones about their worldview. When customers came in, they had on hand for those who were interested piles of anti-COVID vaccination literature, including Vaccine Adverse Effects Reporting System data—raw data that hadn't been vetted by scientists and that often leaped to conclusions that were way out beyond where the experts in the field were willing to go—purporting to show huge numbers of serious and often fatal reactions to COVID vaccines. They discussed their strong antiabortion views, bemoaning California's supposed abortion-on-demand-until-birth policy (the state has no such policy). They whipped each other up to paroxysms of anger about transgender people playing women's sports and about doctors performing gender-reassignment surgeries on young children.

Every so often, a crime victim would come into the shop and say that so-and-so had told them to seek out Woody for help. He would listen attentively and take notes on one of the legal pads that he kept on hand among his barber's tools, would find out details about who had beaten the person or robbed them, and would then promise to take action—though what action that would be, he left deliberately vague. He wasn't accredited law enforcement, but apparently locals knew that if Woody and his militia members got involved, as well as their friends in the huge local Community Watch network, there was a pretty good chance that the offenders—the local homeless, drug addicts, the mentally ill—would take the hint and quickly get out of town.

Woody himself somewhat improbably claimed never to have heard the phrase "Cottonwood justice," although members of the militia had joked about it on local right-wing radio shows and podcasts. But when I asked about it, his customers didn't seem terribly surprised. One, a retired construction worker and paper-mill laborer named Sergio, smiled as he recalled a story that he had read in a local history book about a notorious late nineteenth-century bully who had ended up facedown and dead in the local irrigation district's canal waters. "What happened to him?" Sergio asked, and then he answered his own question: "Use your imagination. Cottonwood justice." He laughed heartily and sat down under the flag for his haircut, content in his knowledge the bully had simply gotten what was coming to him. *How common was the doling out of informal summary justice in Cottonwood?* I asked Sergio. "A little more common than most places, but not common enough."

Clendenen had to reside in a small, conservative town, he said, because he simply couldn't abide the prospect of living surrounded by people with a Marxist worldview, and his definition of who was a Marxist and what ideas were beyond the pale was suitably broad. Supporting the Affordable Care Act qualified. So did support for Black Lives Matter. So did antipathy to organized religion—he himself was a fundamentalist Christian, steeped in evangelical beliefs, a member of a small church in town that, when the pandemic hit, moved its in-person services outdoors to grasslands on Woody's ranch. So did belief in public health restrictions to slow the spread of COVID. "A lot of the COVID deaths they wrote down as COVID deaths weren't really COVID deaths," he explained authoritatively. "It's a bunch of horseshit. And they're totally hiding the damage the vaccine's done to people."

When customers used the barbershop's small bathroom, off to the side of the cluttered storage closet next to the main haircutting area, they were presented with a choice of toilet paper: they could wipe their rear ends with either Barack Obama's image or Hillary Clinton's.

From the 1960s onward, and most especially in the years following Obama's election, the culture had, the barber feared, swung way too far from the center. In so doing, it had led to the empowerment of faux conservatives, "RINOs," like Supervisor Leonard Moty. These were people, Clendenen argued, who proceeded to treat Ordinary Joes with grievous disrespect and pushed a "woke" agenda down the throats of residents who had no patience for it.

"Moty has never been a real conservative," he explained testily, "but it was never really on full display until COVID. In the end, his arrogance got him. He had a flippant attitude toward his constituents. They'd go and talk, and he'd look at his phone. He really needed a butt stomping most of his life. He was an arrogant rich kid. He needed more spankings when he was a kid. He was just a disrespectful guy."

As for the woke worldview, "We're not going to put up with that here. Critical race theory, talking about seventy genders. We're not going to lie to our kids. The middle ground up here is probably between conservatives and RINOs. The Far Left really has no say up here."

Chapter Five

THE RED WHITE
AND BLUEPRINT

Mary Rickert opened her iPad, clicked on her hate-mail folder, and started scrolling down some of the screeds she had received over the three years since the COVID pandemic first hit. One read, "I'd like to fuck Mary Rickert in the face with a brick." Another had the subject line, "Going, going, gone, dead woman walking." She closed the folder, shuddered, and said, "I have PTSD because of this, just from the insanity of it all. I have nightmares all the time. Watching the county just crumble is absolutely devastating for me, watching it being taken over by a far-right group."

Rickert was seventy years old, with a long and storied local history in Redding. A prizewinning rancher with a degree in dairy science from Cal Poly, San Luis Obispo, she had served on the State

Board of Forestry Fire Protection, spent ten years on the local mental health board, and was currently a member of the Shasta County Board of Supervisors. She and her husband owned several ranches with free-range cattle, along with hay and rice production, throughout the county, and they managed tens of thousands of additional acres for absentee landlords from the Bay Area. Rickert lived during the workweek at the ranch that was closest to the county seat of Redding: a comfortable, spacious white wooden bungalow four miles outside of the little town of Anderson and just under a half-hour's drive from the county supervisors' offices. The 2,200 acres of the ranch ran alongside the Sacramento River for two and a half miles, had thousands of squat white oak trees under which their cattle herds sought shade in the spring before they were trucked north for their summer pastures, and had meadows speckled with stunning displays of yellow wildflowers. In the spring, beekeepers came to those meadows with boxes of bees to pollinate the trees. Deer roamed the land, ducking under the barbed-wire fence line of the property—designed to stop the cows from escaping onto the roads on the edge of their land—which the Rickerts had elevated just enough to let smaller wildlife sneak under. She liked nothing more, she said, than to explore her acres, looking for downed tree limbs to stack or dead trees to mark for removal. She was at her calmest when she could take a sandwich out to the meadows, sit under a tree with some of her cows, and eat her lunch. It was, Mary confided, the "happy place" that she retreated to in her mind's eye when the going got particularly rough during a board of supervisors meeting.

The Rickerts' main ranch was eighty miles northeast of Anderson, in the tiny hamlet of McArthur—population 334, at the time of the 2020 census—in the Fall River Valley. It was in the northeasternmost corner of District Three, the vast expanse of sparsely populated land that Rickert represented as supervisor. There, practically under the shadow of the fourteen-thousand-foot-high slopes of Mount Shasta, the county supervisor retreated on weekends, to the 1960s-era ranch house she had lived in for decades, thirty miles from the nearest stoplight, to watch the waterfowl that visited her land and to marvel at the landscape she called home.

Mary and her husband knew many of the political leaders of the state. And her family, going back three generations, had been important figures in the crafting of agricultural policy in California; her maternal grandfather, she recalled with pride, had established the state's chapter of the Future Farmers of America.

Rickert, whose office walls in the county building were filled with commendations and certificates, as well as family photos and ranching memorabilia, had until recently been considered by the public to be a rock-solid conservative, a woman who had cut her teeth in the Reagan years and voted for Trump twice, someone who could be trusted to come up with cogent arguments against government regulation and who was a proud gun owner, more than familiar with the ways of pistols and hunting rifles. She had long watched *Fox News* as her default cable network, growing disillusioned with the channel only after its commentators defended the January 6 rioters, among whom were many who had made their way from Shasta County, several of them personal friends of county supervisors.

Rickert was a feisty woman with a thick head of mouse-brown curls, a rouged face, and almost theatrically large spectacles. Everything about her was over the top, from her plaid jackets to her big chain bracelets—yet by the winter of 2023 she felt herself to be the sober personality in the room, a voice of reason in a moment in which her beloved county was going crazy. For three long years, because she, along with a majority of her colleagues on the five-person board, agreed to abide by Governor Newsom's emergency pandemic mandates from the spring of 2020, including shuttering the board's chambers and meetings to the public and moving interactions with constituents to Zoom, Rickert had been derided as a RINO. It was a label that offered no way back, a scarlet letter, and there was nothing she could do to convince those who had so labeled her that her conservative bona fides remained intact. The septuagenarian was routinely subjected to death threats and other intimidations and harassment. She was frequently denounced during overheated meetings as a "Communist"—even though it would be hard to imagine someone less likely to fit the profile of a revolutionary Marxist.

On the day of the January 6 uprising in Washington, DC, newly emboldened far-right members of the board, led by Supervisors Les Baugh and the newly elected Patrick Jones, boisterously made their way into the county building and dramatically opened the board offices. At 9 a.m. California time, as Trump began speaking to his crowd of supporters in Washington—many of whom were armed and determined to prevent the certification of the Electoral College vote by any means necessary—urging them to march down Pennsylvania Avenue to the Capitol to show their anger at the efforts to certify the presidential vote, telling them that only through strength would they retake their country, in Redding, California, their compatriots jostled their way into the county building. By the time Trump's supporters began tearing down the security perimeter around the Capitol, pepper-spraying and otherwise assaulting Capitol Police officers, and then storming into the building on the hunt for Vice President Pence, Speaker Pelosi, and others, the anti-lockdown protesters in Redding had liberated the county offices. No matter that the building was largely empty and that the board had, months earlier, in the face of spiraling infection numbers and rowdy meeting attendees who refused to wear masks or to socially distance inside the chambers, voted to take their meetings online. What mattered, according to Jones, was that a point had been made. "I said if I was elected—which I was—on Day One, January 6th, 2021, I'd open the building. And I did. It was packed. Hundred and something people," Jones said proudly, a little more than two years after that momentous day.

Did he think, with hindsight, that the events in Redding on January 6 bore some resemblance to the storming of the Capitol, three thousand miles to the east, that same day? Chairman Jones demurred. Redding, he asserted, wasn't about people storming anything; it was just about reestablishing freedom and opening a public building that ought never to have been closed to the voting public in the first place: "I told the public I was going to open up the building and people were going to come in, and I did. There wasn't no rush. It's just lies."

Then he paused and thought about the analogy to the Capitol, pondered how uncomfortable he was with the notion that the God-fearing conservatives in that Trump-inspired crowd could have acted violently. "It didn't happen here, so I'm wondering if it happened there in DC. They opened the door and let people in; they wanted to create that environment. The door just didn't magically open on its own. The national media says they were trying to overthrow the government. They opened the doors and let people in; let down the barriers. The national media says the Capitol was breached. It wasn't."

For Jones's friend Woody Clendenen, the whole January 6 thing was a big brouhaha over nothing. He knew people, he claimed, who had been stationed overseas during genuine insurrections, who had experienced the full fire and fury of a roused populace determined to overthrow their government. January 6, he felt, didn't come remotely close to meeting those terrifying standards. "It wasn't an insurrection; that's for damn sure," he opined. "If the American people insurrected, there wouldn't be a building left standing in Washington. That's not what they [the people attending the January 6 protests] were there to do. They were there to peacefully protest." The violence against the police? "Turns out none of those cops got killed. They lied about everything that happened there. It was inspired by the feds. Just like the Governor Whitmer kidnapping attempt turned out to be totally planned by the feds."

In other words, a federal government still ostensibly controlled by the Trump administration planned a massive false-flag operation designed to make Trump and his supporters look bad in order to enable a roundup of conservative patriots and ease Biden into power.

———

Board of supervisors meetings in early 2021 were dispiriting, eerie affairs. Only one member of the public at a time was allowed into the chamber to give a three-minute speech, and all the board members were masked and partitioned off from each other by Plexiglas in front of them and to their sides, making them look something like freaks in a freak-show cage. Or like prisoners, talking to visitors through bulletproof windows, their voices piped to each other over intercoms or phones. There was in that room nothing but sterility, none of the vibrancy and human interplay, none of the spontaneity, that is normally associated with local government meetings. Outside the chamber, frustrated anti-lockdown advocates, almost all unmasked, gathered with bullhorns, shouting out their demands to the five board members.

Had a time traveler somehow made the leap from early 2020 to mid-2021, they would have been utterly flummoxed at the change. Multi-hundred-million-dollar county budgets that used to be perused for hours at a time in painstaking detail by board members before votes were taken on them were now hurriedly approved with only a minimum of debate, the supervisors desperate to retreat once more into the safety of their homes, each additional minute in a group setting an added risk to their well-being.

Behind the Plexiglas dividers, a smaller, less ambitious version of public governance, and of the interplay between those doing the governing and those being governed, was taking shape. The dividers may have been only an improvised and temporary response to a raging pandemic, but in the eyes of Carlos Zapata and the other leaders of the local anti-lockdown movement, they were symbols of a yawning gap, of a cavalier disregard for democratic processes.

Later on, in June 2021, Patrick Jones would pull a savvy publicity stunt to capitalize on this growing resentment, showing up with a power screwdriver and theatrically unscrewing the Plexiglas surrounding his desk from its moorings, and then, to raucous cheers from the audience, picking up and removing the dividers that separated him both from his colleagues and from the public. Jones sat down again behind his computer screen, raised his eyebrows, and said, simply, "Much better." His audience ate it up; if this wasn't owning the libs, it was hard to know what was.

At the time, the majority of the supervisors were just trying to keep themselves and the public as safe as possible, and to do so they were abiding by state health mandates. To the unmasked attendees, however, who gathered inside the rooms when they were permitted, and outside the meeting room with bullhorns and anger when restrictions meant they had to filter in one at a time to make their comments, it was a grotesque assault on their right to participate in the democratic institutions of local governance. The thing is, they weren't entirely wrong about this—the emergency powers that democratic governments assumed all over the world and the breakdown of participatory processes during this time showed how fragile were the democratic bonds. Liberties that had long been seen as sacrosanct were, during the emergency, suddenly put on the chopping block. Parliamentary methods of decision making that had evolved over centuries were cast to one side in an instant in order to respond swiftly to the unprecedented public health dangers of the moment. There were, both at the time and certainly with hindsight, legitimate objections to the way these democratic processes were allowed to buckle, but the protesters in Shasta didn't stop at that. They turned a legitimate objection to some public health emergency measures into an across-the-board critique of public health, of the CDC, of local government, and of state government, tying everything together into a meta-conspiracy intended to deprive Americans of their God-given liberties.

———

The long tail of that resentment would impact the county for years to come.

A little more than twelve months after those strange, Plexiglas-fronted meetings, in February 2022 Rickert would survive the recall effort against her, as did a colleague, Joe Chimenti. But then–board chair Leonard Moty, like Rickert a Reagan Republican, blamed by many residents for not going to war with the state against its COVID public health mandates, wouldn't be so lucky. Even though, compared to most other counties, Shasta went light on its lockdown enforcement, tending to turn a blind eye when small businesses reopened or when mask mandates were ignored, and even though many of its schools either never shut or, if they did, reopened for in-person classes months before schools in any of the state's big cities did so, for the anti-mandate faction Moty was doing too little too late.

"COVID, when it came out, was a very distant thing," Moty said, as he thought through the two years leading up to his recall. "We were like six months behind [in terms of local infection rates]. So a lot of people 'round here saw it as Sacramento and the Democratic governor trying to tell us what to do, big government trying to take over, the New World Order. We're a hotbed for the State of Jefferson thing. It became an easy rallying point."

Moty had favored a form of "voluntary compliance" with the mandates, a go-soft approach that meant when local businesses refused to shut down, the county generally didn't issue citations. He had no problems with restaurants keeping up outdoor dining; he recognized that rural counties had different pandemic needs than did the densely populated big cities to the south.

But when the infection rates spiked late in 2020 and the local hospitals were overwhelmed, Moty and his colleagues leaned into further restrictions and tighter lockdowns. By then, however, their enemies were circling. Because most of those who supported the mask mandates and other health measures had long stopped going to these public meetings, where they knew they would bump up against unmasked and nonsocially spaced attendees, by default Zapata and his crowd were able to take center stage. In the months after Zapata's barn-raising speech went viral, they would pack the meetings, maskless, crammed next to each other, jeering the Palo Cedro resident's opponents and cheering on their homespun hero.

When Zapata, wearing a white T-shirt and a blue-and-white baseball cap, stepped to the podium in one particularly tense meeting in the summer of 2021 and went after a progressive local journalist, Doni Chamberlain, the enthused crowd members could barely contain themselves.

As Zapata raised his voice to denounce masking and to lambaste anyone who favored public health restrictions as unpatriotic and willing to inflict deliberate violence on children, he homed in on Chamberlain, who had been writing increasingly personal ad hominem attacks on him in her online publication *A News Café* over the course of the year since he had demanded the county immediately reopen. Chamberlain, a one-time print newspaper journalist who had run her online publication since 2007, first under the name *Food for Thought* and then as *A News Café*, didn't write concisely. In long screeds, often pages long, the diminutive grandmother mocked her perceived enemies, people whose rhetoric she held responsible for the escalating threats that she and her news colleagues faced. She wrote that Zapata was "unhinged," that he was "abusive," that he "embraces fighting and violence." He was, she told readers, an "unstable, out-of-control bully with an inflated ego in dire need of anger-management help."

Now the ex-marine responded in kind. He denounced the journalist as "the only person in this room covering her coward face"; mocked her for having had an unpleasant divorce, in which her and her husband's personal dirty laundry was aired in public; and, addressing her directly, hollered that "this is *our* county, Doni. We're fighting to take it back from people like you." And then he continued: "We are up against people who will say anything and do anything to hurt our children. We have to stand up." To the audience, both in the room and in the vast, amorphous expanses of the internet, he exhorted them to "take a side. Hot or cold." The unmasked crowd lapped it up. As Zapata's voice crescendoed and as he built to a climax of performative rage against Chamberlain and her ilk, a chorus of heckling, men's and women's voices mixed in about equal measure, began against the publisher of *A News Café*. There was something almost cartoonish about it: "Coward!" "Go to hell!" "Slander!" "Pussy!" "Her people are smearing people online!" "Communist!" "Fake news!"

Zapata triumphantly walked away from the dais. Chamberlain took a deep breath and returned home to write yet another article on what she viewed as the climate of rage that had taken over her county.

"We do have a pretty big population of extremists; their rhetoric is violent, very antigovernment," said Jennifer Arnold, a self-employed copywriter who had joined an online group that was called Things You Should Know—Shasta County and that had been established to track the region's slide toward extremism. But, she continued, their message was amplified less by their raw numbers than by their volume: "They seem like a bigger group because they're a loud minority. The politics went from right to far-right, but there's only a little section of extreme far-right people." Once that loud minority had established its dominance at the board meetings, the attacks against Rickert, Chimenti, and Moty, as well as any other person who was seen as being on the side of Big Government, came fast and furious. At every meeting, they were heckled and insulted. At every meeting, they were accused of having abandoned county residents, many of whom journeyed in from small out-of-the-way rural communities with names like Happy Valley, Igo, and French Gulch, to the predations of a liberal, out-of-control Sacramento administration and its public health foot soldiers.

Boosted by a huge infusion of cash from an eccentric Greenwich, Connecticut-based right-wing heir to a billionaire's fortune named Reverge Anselmo, the recall effort picked up steam through 2021.

Anselmo, whose father had made his fortune setting up the Spanish-language television station that is now known as Univision, and whose mother, Mary, had previously made it onto the *Forbes* list of the 400 wealthiest Americans, was tall and lean. His sartorial taste tended toward black suits, formal shirts, and expensive black ties. His face was creased, his gray hair cropped short. He was, as he told the producers of *The Red White and Blueprint*, infuriated by the board's actions against his business holdings. He had, he remembered, chosen Shasta County for the site of his 1,200-acre vineyard precisely because it was known to be conservative. It was, he said, 67 percent Republican, "so at least I'm not going to catch any craziness there." And then, to his disgust, he had indeed caught the craziness. Instead of greeting with favor his plans to build a winery, a restaurant, and a ranch house on his land, the county had had the temerity to demand that he go through a time-consuming permitting process. When he sued the county rather than abide by its permitting request, claiming that his property rights were being violated, the county leaned into the court proceedings instead of backing down. When the wealthy landowner then decided to add a chapel onto his property, also without a permit, the county again ordered him to stop construction. As the legal fight picked up steam, Anselmo became something of a minor celebrity on the right-wing political circuit. *Fox News* picked up his story, commentators such as Ann Coulter excoriated the board of supervisors, and local Tea Party activists made Anselmo a poster boy for their "Don't Tread on Me" antigovernment campaigns. Ultimately, however, none of this support mattered. In 2013 a federal judge sided with the county, and Anselmo was ordered to pay more than a million dollars in legal fees and fines.

Now, eight years on, Anselmo was determined to flex his financial muscle from his splashy estate on the other side of the continent to influence the recall election. Over the course of the campaign, Anselmo reputedly ponied up hundreds of thousands of dollars— close to half a million dollars, Bloomberg's "Citylab" podcaster Laura Bliss calculated—donated to local activists and political action committees, turning what could have been a sleepy local race into a spectacle that assumed global implications for the alt-right. *If* Moty were recalled, and *if* the permitting process in the county were reformed, Anselmo might, he said, consider bringing his businesses back to Shasta.

Through the spring and summer of 2021, events were held to gather the required number of signatures to qualify the recalls for the ballot. They took place in local churches such as Grace Presbyterian, where congregants were encouraged to pray and fast for the success of the recall; in gun stores; and in local restaurants such as Dill's Deli, a barbecue joint three miles north of Redding, with a sign conspicuously placed in the window: "Freedom of Choice, Not Mandates." There were drive-throughs for signature gathering. There were auctions to raise money for the campaign in local Veterans of Foreign

Wars (VFW) halls. And through it all—through the hellish months of smoke from local forest fires and through the months of growing numbers of pandemic illnesses and deaths—there were increasingly acrimonious, loud confrontations at board meetings and increasingly ugly internet campaigns against the targeted supervisors.

Zapata posted frequently on Facebook and other social media sites. He argued that killing one's opponents was, in theory, justified in the fight against tyranny. And articles published by Doni Chamberlain in August and November 2021 in *A News Café* referenced Zapata posts declaring that he had "never relinquished my kill option" and stating that given the exigencies of the moment it was necessary to teach one's children to be "wildly ruthless." When celebrity conspiracy buff Alex Jones invited Zapata to be on his InfoWars show, the ex-marine leaped at the chance to explain his ideas to a broader audience. "You don't vote your way out of socialism," he opined. "Once it's taken root, the only way to eradicate it is to fight it with arms, to have a violent, violent confrontation, have blood in the streets. And I hate to say it, but that's the reality of where we are at, Alex. And if the mechanism for fixing it is broken, then we need to fix that. You don't fix that by talking, by rallying, by even voting. You fix that mechanism by violent overthrow. You fix it by storming the chambers and forcibly removing those people that are oppressing you. You change things by rallying the troops to take up arms."

Yet even though Zapata didn't have much confidence in the electoral system, once the petition drive against the moderate supervisors took off, he was all too happy to lend his support to the campaign via memes and pithy comments directed against Moty, Chimenti, and Rickert. Nor did he object when his fellow Palo Cedro residents voted in conservative members of the local school board. This was, after all, the sort of political change, nudged from below by outraged citizens, that Zapata had dreamed of in *The Red White and Blueprint*.

"The *Blueprint* is citizens taking responsibility for our government," Elissa McEuen, one of the stay-at-home mothers who had gotten most involved in the county fights over the COVID lockdowns and school closings, told the documentary's interviewers. As far back as May 2020, barely two months into the pandemic, she had excoriated the board of supervisors for abiding by state mandates that, she argued, would result in her children growing up enslaved. Standing outside the board chambers, because the supervisors had voted to hold their meetings in closed session, the young mother grabbed a bullhorn and screamed into the chamber demands that the board members stand up to Gavin Newsom's administration and fully reopen the county. She had since gotten increasingly involved in local efforts to bring down the existing majority on the board, helping to coordinate a sprawling coalition of various libertarian and far-right groupings, all of whom were being further radicalized by the restrictions on everyday life put in place to slow down the spread of the new and deadly virus.

McEuen had been the one, at an absolutely packed board of supervisors meeting in early April 2021, a year into the pandemic, to present the three supervisors with the notices of intent to recall them. In doing so, she had spoken fluently, with passion and with conviction, about broken government, mismanagement, and even corruption. And with her long curly hair and her black pantsuit, she looked every bit the professional—not, by any stretch, an extremist, just a concerned mom. In a metered tone, she told the supervisors that the campaign was designed to "secure our rights to operate our schools, businesses, and churches as we see fit." And she also told them that "this is not personal; this is responsible citizenship." Like Zapata, McEuen had a natural gift for speaking, knew how to build to a crescendo, knew when to taper off and go for the soft, slow timbre.

Later, on episode 2 of *The Red White and Blueprint*, McEuen would elaborate on her ideas, telling the audience that she and her allies were engaged in a grand project intended to protect the Republic down through the generations. That episode also featured footage of the March 2021 Cottonwood Rodeo, complete with martial mood music and a voice-over from a speaker addressing the rodeo attendees about the American flag: "If somebody stomps on it, you put 'em in their place, and if somebody tries to take it away from us, well, you build *The Red White and Blueprint*. Don't let 'em tell us what to do. Don't let 'em take it away. I hope you will stand with us when the time comes to be true Americans." Rounding out that episode was a bizarre illustrated graphic-novel–style segment showing soldiers/avatars continuously firing off their guns. It depicted the county government and its various departments as a series of armies, the heads of the departments as generals, all of whom had maliciously decided to turn their guns on the people of Shasta County, "thereby making us slaves of the state."

By the summer of 2021, with the recall in full swing, the moderate supervisors knew that they would now face months of relentless attacks, their records impugned, and the full force of a well-funded and savvy social media campaign turned against them.

A few years earlier, Moty had gone behind the Carr Fire evacuation lines to check up on families that hadn't left and on homes that had been left behind. He brought with him gas for home generators. While behind the lines, he stopped by the large house, in a rural, hilly subdivision west of Redding, that he and his wife, Tracy, had lived in for more than a quarter of a century and added gas to his own generator. That act, that appearance of using his official position to illegitimately access his evacuated home, would eventually land him a grand jury investigation. Although he wasn't prosecuted for or found guilty of any crimes, the grand jury report *did* state that he had committed an act of "mis-feasance," essentially suggesting that he had shown poor judgment. He wasn't convicted of a crime, wasn't fined, but in early June 2021 did face a vote of censure from his colleagues on the board. Sitting in their Plexiglas cubicles, one after the other they announced their support for censure. The most conservative of them, Les Baugh, declared it "purely 100 percent malfeasance of office" and called on Moty to resign. Mary Rickert got so angry at Baugh's onslaught against her friend that she eventually screamed at him that she was "sick and tired of listening to your bullshit. I don't lose my temper very often, but you flipped that switch." Yet Rickert also voted in favor of the censure motion. Even Moty endorsed the vote, hoping that in acknowledging he had been wrong to refuel his home generator he could put the episode behind him. It didn't work. Over the coming months, his opponents would wield the censure motion like a sledgehammer to beat into the heads of the undecideds the notion that Moty was unfit to hold public office. Not surprisingly, Moty's numbers among the voting public in Shasta County took a hit.

When, in early January 2022, Moty won a 3–2 vote to become chairman of the board of supervisors, his opponents, laced throughout the audience, audibly snickered. In his first act as chair, Moty moved to limit the public comment period to forty-five minutes total at the start of each meeting, with further comments being pushed back to the end of the meeting in order to allow board members to have time to vote on the issues before them; in response, the crowd erupted in a righteous fury. From then on, the chairman seemed to be in a state of nearly permanent confrontation with his constituents. When they refused to abide by the three-minute limit on individual comments, he would repeatedly request that they stop talking; if they didn't, he ordered them removed from the room. There was, at times, something of the martinet in his persona. When the activists heckled him, he gave as good as he got, repeatedly telling them to be quiet, to abide by the time limits, to sit down, to shut up. The longer the confrontations went on, the more a barely concealed fury could be heard in the chairman's voice. It was as if he could see the writing on the wall, knew that his days as supervisor were numbered, and wanted to vent while he still had a public platform.

Sure enough, on February 1, 2022, in a low-turnout election participated in by fewer than half the total who had voted in the presidential election fifteen months earlier, Moty was booted off the board of supervisors, with 56 percent of the nearly 9,000 people who voted casting their ballots in favor of recalling him. His replacement, the basso-voiced, gray-haired Happy Valley school board chairman Tim Garman—elected with 1,600 fewer votes than Moty himself had received in the recall vote—was a MAGA loyalist, an anti-vaxxer, and a sympathizer with the local militia. His chief selling point, as he regularly reminded supporters during stump speeches, was that in his capacity as school board chair, he had taken actions to ignore the state's COVID vaccine mandates for schoolkids.

———

The election confirmed to Shasta observers what had been apparent for more than a year: riven by battles over the correct response to the COVID crisis, in thrall to Trumpism and the MAGA rhetoric of the nation's forty-fifth president, the county was spiraling rightward, its moderate Republicans sidelined by a radicalized, infuriated, take-no-prisoners populist Right. In such an atmosphere, Jones and his allies thrived, taking symbolic actions against state public health mandates that they didn't actually have the legal authority to reject. The point wasn't necessarily to actually get the board to do something; rather, it was to score political points. It was, in the words of the "Citylab" podcaster Laura Bliss, "government theater," or "basically symbolic actions" intended simply to rally the political troops. If that was Jones's goal, he more than succeeded. Pointless, threatening letters to Governor Newsom would be entered into the record while the unmasked, unsocially distanced crowd stood and whooped aloud, as if they were the audience in an episode of *The Jerry Springer Show*. After one such letter had been read out to the crowd, Jones and his colleague Les Baugh screamed at Rickert and Moty (Chimenti, sitting in the middle, looked like there was nowhere he would rather less be). Rickert, her voice breaking with frustration, talked of the numbers of memorial services she had recently attended for COVID victims; with the crowd haranguing and mocking her, she seemed, at times, on the verge of tears.

Nine months after the recall, the shift rightward accelerated: following Joe Chimenti's decision that running for reelection in such a toxic environment was more trouble than it was worth, in the November 2022 elections two more supervisors aligned with Jones and Garman were elected.

What had been a four–one moderate-right majority on the county board of supervisors in 2020 was, by early 2023, a four–one hard-right majority. Patrick Jones, Kevin Crye, Chris Kelstrom, and Tim Garman were now arrayed against the lone surviving moderate, Mary Rickert. Even when, a few months later, Garman began to tone down his positions and more frequently ally with Rickert, that hard-right majority remained. At a minimum, on most issues Jones could drum up another two colleagues to support his policy stances.

Part Three

FAKE FACTS AND CULTURE WARS

Chapter Six

THE MEN WITH
LONG GUNS

CLALLAM COUNTY'S FISSURES HAD BEEN A LONG TIME IN THE MAKING. THE REGION CONTAINED some of the most beautiful, dramatic landscape in the United States. Its mountains—inhabited by large numbers of bears and cougars—and coastline drew retirees from around the country, as well as a constant stream of day tourists and backcountry hikers looking to explore Olympic National Park. At the same time, it was home to many impoverished families, blue-collar residents who used to work in the thriving timber industry of the Northwest until a combination of overharvesting and stricter environmental protections, especially around protecting the habitat of the spotted owl, drove the industry into the ground in the 1990s. In the years since, unemployment and low wages had replaced affluence and security in a number of the smaller hamlets around the peninsula, and many residents, disillusioned by the way they had been sidelined during the environmental battles, had quite simply abandoned any sense that government could ever do right by the people. They harked back to a comment made in 1991, at the start of the spotted owl fight, by Clallam County commissioner Dorothy Duncan at a large protest organized by loggers against the regulations. "If owls deserve food, shelter, and protection from harassment," the commissioner told the crowd, "so do our contributing citizens, and they are being treated as villains."

Sure, the county's small cities all had charming old downtowns, like Sequim's, that drew in tourists from around the country and the world, and those tourist dollars had at least in part replaced the income lost when the timber industry imploded. New arrivals also looked to set down roots in a place where it might rain nearly every day but where there was, behind the misty cold veneer, natural beauty in abundance. Many of the ranch houses were huge, their living rooms proudly sporting large glass walls with picture-postcard views of the often-snow-covered Olympic Mountains. It was no wonder that so many retirees—many of them bringing with them liberal political priorities from states like California, though, truth be told, many also likely seeking lower tax bills than those they faced in the Golden State—had moved into the region over the past decade.

But at the same time as it remained a tourist hub, in recent years Clallam County, its facade of affluence concealing all of the heartache and economic pain triggered by the collapse of the logging industry, had had the unenviable reputation of having some of the highest rates of opioid use and overdoses in the state, on a par with the hardest-hit counties in Appalachia. In 2019 the *Washington Post* crunched the numbers and found that between 2006 and 2012, Clallam County residents popped 37,838,060 pain pills, which translated to a staggering 76.6 pills per county resident per year, a number far higher than in most counties in the country. Between 2012 and 2016, the yearly opioid overdose rate in the county was 16.5 people per 100,000 residents, measurably higher than most regions of the country outside of Appalachia and some particularly hard-hit areas of the Southwest. In the years since, it had only grown. State data showed that in the four years leading up to 2020, the opioid death rate in Clallam was 17.7, and the total death rate from all forms of drugs was 28.3, about 80 percent higher than the Washington State average. Even Kings County, the home of Seattle—a place the opponents of the medication-assisted treatment clinic would portray as being a den of homeless addicts just waiting to descend on the peninsula—was experiencing lower overdose death rates than was Clallam.

———

By the late spring of 2020, all the county's subterranean social tensions were bubbling up to the surface. Its local politics were already convulsed by the MAT clinic and by Armacost's rise, its populace now besieged by COVID, its residents divided on how to respond to Trump's chaotic presidency. Then came the police killing of George Floyd in Minneapolis and the outpouring of revulsion that followed in its wake.

With protesters taking to Sequim's streets, a local gun-store manager by the name of Seth Larson tried to pour as much lighter fluid as he could on the pyre. Over the previous days, Larson had become convinced that Antifa—an amorphous group of self-described anti-fascists that opponents claimed was a front for violent anarchists—was on the march, that an infuriated mob, as fearsome as any medieval head-on-a-pike peasant horde, was about to erupt out of Seattle and onto the peninsula. *Wired* magazine and other media outlets would subsequently report that over live-streamed video Larson urged residents to grab their guns and join him in defense of their towns. And many of them did, first in Sequim and later in the deeply conservative town of Forks, a little more than an hour's drive to the southwest. They were terrified—after all, Larson had told them that Antifa had promised to maraud down the peninsula, burning towns and wreaking bloody, racially motivated havoc.

A septuagenarian blueberry farmer named Dave Howat, who had lived in town for more than thirty years, recalls hearing from a "reliable source, an individual I listen to," that Antifa was on the way into town to burn buildings down. Part of him was inclined to disbelieve the story; after all, it made precious little sense for a group of big-city anarchists to trek all the way out to what was, after all, "a one-horse town" simply to prove some obscure point. But after months of living under increasingly strict pandemic regulations, after seeing every aspect of his life regulated by new dictums and new limitations, he no longer quite knew what was real and what wasn't. "Common sense took a vacation, that's for sure," he recalled of those strange months at the onset of the pandemic, "and a lot of people felt threatened when they didn't need to." Add into that sense of unmooring the images that were coming in from around the country in late May and early June, the "chaos in the streets," the mass rioting, the scenes of Seattle in crisis; add in too the fact that in recent years Sequim seemed to have changed, with more vocal activists making the town their home, and maybe it wasn't such a stretch to believe that armed gangs were about to attack the peninsula. "I wasn't sure," the farmer remembered, "if we were going to have unfriendly, unsafe, possibly dangerous circumstances in our town."

Howat called his neighbor, Patrice Johnston, one of the leading critics of the Armacost mayorship, to warn her there might be trouble ahead. She responded incredulously, practically shouting into her phone, "That is *not* happening!" Howat wasn't so sure and decided to check things out for himself. He was, he said, instinctually cautious, liked using his mind to analyze unfamiliar situations rather than relying on hearsay, tried to evaluate things firsthand whenever possible. And so the old blueberry farmer, who had moved to the small town when his kids were young because it was a place he and his wife felt had good schools and good churches, headed toward Sequim's downtown, on the lookout for anything resembling Antifa.

Jodi Wilke also happened to be downtown that day. She parked her car and got out to see what was going on. George Floyd's killing had appalled her. It was, she felt, "a tragedy. Somebody should not be killed like that. Never. Regardless of whether they're wasted on fentanyl." But she had also seen on TV all the chaos unfolding around the country that week, and she feared that the looting and the violence would soon reach the peninsula. When she got there, she saw the crowd—including many people whom she knew—marching in the center of town. It looked peaceful in the main, and she took the time to wave to some of her friends who were demonstrating for racial justice. "It was fun," she recalled thinking. "There was no vandalism or threats."

At the same time, Wilke saw the men with long guns. She didn't feel there was anything wrong with this—she was a gun enthusiast, after all—although she did wonder if maybe they were being just a tad too dramatic. On the whole, however, they were, she thought, just there to make a visual statement, to warn people who might be thinking of causing trouble, who might be thinking of copycatting what had gone down in Seattle and other large cities, not to bother. "If you have multiple people trying to break into your house, and there's a pattern, is it the right thing to do something to protect yourself or your neighbors? You don't go into something like this looking for a fight. But if somebody attacks you . . . ," she trailed off. The men weren't brandishing their weapons directly at protesters, and they certainly hadn't fired any shots. Given that, it was unclear to her what all the fuss was about. Moreover, Wilke knew Seth Larson, at whose urging at least some of these gun-toting locals had come downtown—she had once bought a Glock 22 from his store, a weapon that she kept on her person for self-defense and occasionally took out to the shooting range for target practice—and didn't consider him a racist.

Wilke went home. Meanwhile, on the streets of Sequim, despite her somewhat sunny analysis, tensions were indeed running high: most of the four hundred people in the crowd were calm, but some were calling out the police, using more intemperate language, including shouting out the confrontational slogan of the moment that "All Cops Are Bastards." The acronym ACAB had been spray-painted on buildings around the country over the past days, infuriating the police and riling up many ordinary civilians—people who may have felt revulsion at the footage of the Minneapolis police officer with his knee on George Floyd's neck but who generally respected and looked up to the local policemen and policewomen on the beat. Meanwhile, the gun-toters continued to close in on the demonstration, goaded on by Larson's ominous promise, delivered over Facebook Live, that "we will fuck anybody up who breaks our windows or burns our cities."

Dave Howat made it downtown. He looked around warily, but despite the sometimes intimidating chanting and the placards, he didn't see any Antifa-looking mob. These were locals, people whom he knew. So, with a sense of relief, he headed back home again.

Others, however, with Seth Larson in the lead, weren't so ready to concede that they had let rumors get ahead of reality. They grabbed their guns and headed downtown. Their presence infuriated the protesters, as did their gullibility, their willingness to believe Larson's outlandish warnings.

Courtney Thomas, a thirty-two-year-old local orthopedic massage therapist and mother of three, who had organized the racial-justice protest after watching on Facebook yet another video showing young black men being attacked by the police—this time a car full of teenagers in Atlanta, out past curfew, who were pulled over by the police and tasered—was one of those who doubted Larson's version of events. The day before, as she watched the video out of Atlanta and heard the tasered teenagers screaming in pain and fear and asking for their mothers, her heart had broken, she later recalled. She turned to her husband and told him she wanted to plan a racial-justice protest in their hometown. *When did she want to do it?* he asked. Courtney, who had grown up in Sequim and knew the city inside out—as a child, she had gotten her hair cut by William Armacost, and more recently she had been in conversation with the mayor about renting one of his rooms to host her orthopedic massage business—answered, "As soon as possible." So the pair began organizing, via social media, for an event the next day. They also contacted the local police department to give them a heads-up that they were planning a demonstration and to tell them where that demonstration would be—hardly the preemptive actions one would expect of a radical anarchist mob intent on burning down the city. That night, Courtney stayed up late making placards that she could give out to her friends in the demonstration. She didn't know how many would show up; all she knew was that she felt morally compelled to make the effort. And that effort was local, as homegrown a statement of horror at what was going on in the country as was imaginable. That was why Larson's allegations so rankled her.

How did Larson know about Antifa coming to town and about threats to kill white babies? Thomas asked him that afternoon when she encountered him at the protest. And then she asked him again. Loudly. *How did he know about Antifa coming in to kill white babies?* Thomas shouted, her hair pulled back in a ponytail, a small nose ring through her left nostril, her face flushed with righteous indignation, as the crowd chanted racial-justice slogans all around them.

His "intel," Larson said, in response to her question, intimating that he had hidden sources of knowledge, sources so sensitive that he couldn't possibly share them with the general public, that opened up the whole foul world of Antifa and Black Lives Matter and every other nefarious plot against God-fearing Americans. *Where did that intel come from?* Thomas probed, enraged beyond measure that Larson had brought a gun-toting mob out to her protest and that those gunmen were scaring off the families and the young children who had come out to condemn racial intolerance. "The internet," he replied to her definitively.

At times during the confrontation, Larson was apologetic, saying that he recognized Thomas was there in good faith, even claiming at one point that his gunmen were there to support the idea of racial justice; then, moments later, his tone would change again. The big man with the baseball cap and trim white beard, his sunglasses hanging off of his blue shirt, told her she was "absolutely full of hate. Look at your eyes!" As far as Thomas was concerned, it was all a manufactured spectacle. "He knew what he was doing," she said dismissively. "Knew it was a small event and came to scream fire in a theater. For show."

Given the tensions coursing through America that week, Larson's stunt was a dangerous one. Had the local police, under Chief Sheri Crain, not acted quickly, separating out the opposing factions and moving some of the gun-toters off to the side, bringing in Larson for a voluntary debriefing in which they told him, in no uncertain terms, that he was wrong about Antifa being in town, things could have gotten very ugly, very fast. Later that afternoon, the city's social media site informed readers that "at no point at today's event, was there any factual evidence suggesting violent or bad actors. Members of the community are reminded that rumors that get out of control can make people nervous and panic unnecessarily." Somewhat chastened, Larson backed off—although he did, according to denizens of the local rumor mill, bring in armed guards to patrol outside his gun store every night for the succeeding several weeks, convinced that Black Lives Matter and Antifa would single him out for vengeance because of what he saw as his good-faith efforts to secure the safety of Sequim when anarchists were burning down all of America's large cities. For the next several weeks, while Larson was worrying about being assaulted or robbed, Thomas and her husband would routinely come back to their home to find carloads of masked gunmen parked outside, scoping the house out. They never explicitly threatened the couple, but it was, Thomas said, disconcerting, to say the least.

———

Throughout the rest of that pandemic summer, episodic racial-justice protests developed in Sequim. For Dr. Allison Berry, consumed with the minutiae of COVID—the contact tracing, the constant phone calls with politicians and with medical staff, the hospitalization and death numbers that she would provide at her daily briefings with the county sheriff and Sequim's chief of police—the explosion of activism was a breath of fresh air. After all the work she had done in poor neighborhoods of New Orleans, Baltimore, and Seattle, after all the needless violence she had witnessed, including police in Baltimore routinely dropping off at the hospital suspects whom they had beaten, here, finally, was evidence that Americans could be moved to action against these systemic injustices. She took her young daughter with her one day to a protest in Port Angeles, strapping the toddler onto her chest in a little front-pack carrier. Many local medics joined her at the event. She'd wanted to attend the demonstration in Sequim, too, but that morning her daughter woke up with a cold. When critics, taking a leaf out of the book of liberals who had opposed Trump's large rallies on public health grounds, said that the Black Lives Matter protests were irresponsible in the middle of a pandemic, she took heart from a large-scale Seattle–Kings County epidemiological survey that found no increased incidence of COVID spread among those who had participated in the demonstrations: "It was part of how we came to understand that COVID doesn't really spread outside." That the racial-justice protesters tended to be masked, and many protesters and vigil participants were making at least some effort at social distancing, whereas those at Trump's rallies flaunted their unmasked status and spurned all notions of distancing, also likely made a difference. Whatever the reasons, the racial-justice protests that spring did not seem to seed new COVID outbreaks.

Despite ongoing rumors that Antifa was about to descend on the peninsula, no violence was unleashed by the demonstrators in downtown Sequim, either then or in subsequent protests. However, many conservative locals remained on edge, waiting uneasily for the explosion they thought must soon come. Later that summer, when Jacob Blake was shot dead by a police officer in Kenosha, Wisconsin, in August—an event that would lead to the riots in Kenosha where Kyle Rittenhouse would emerge as a hero of the Far Right after killing two protesters—more than a hundred locals took to the streets of downtown Sequim in protest. Once again, the predictions of violence on the Olympic Peninsula proved unfounded.

Jodi Wilke was ambivalent. She didn't like violence, and she sincerely wished that people could just learn to listen to each other once again; on the other hand, she felt sorry for Rittenhouse. He was a young man who had gotten in deeper than he realized and had ended up being stalked and threatened in an increasingly chaotic and confrontational environment out in Kenosha. "These people who attacked him, they had little to no regard for his life," she felt. "When it's us or them, me or you, most of us would rather it's not us."

Up and down the Olympic Peninsula, similar sentiments could be heard. Increasingly that summer, America was dividing into intractable camps. Was Rittenhouse a hero or a villain? Was George Floyd a victim or a perp? Was Trump a savior or a dangerous charlatan? Was Antifa a bloodthirsty outfit or a protector of democracy? Was Dr. Berry a hero or a tyrant?

For Wilke in 2023, looking back on the events with several years of hindsight, that divide was the stuff of nightmares, a product of magical thinking on all sides. Wilke might have rejected the mainstream media and might have believed that Trump had gotten a raw deal from Congress and from the despised cultural elites, but that didn't mean she bought into everything the alt-right threw her way. She thought the QAnon crowd was entirely lunatic, its view of "Trump riding in on a white horse to rescue the country, with help from the military" simply too bizarre to be worth engaging with, its ideology based on a smorgasbord of irrational notions that she could only roll her eyes at. She viewed Antifa and other groups on the left with equal disdain, and she believed that the public health officials who had taken so prominent a role during the pandemic were pulling the wool over the public's eyes. She looked at what was happening in the country, and, taken as a whole, thought it was nothing short of tragic. Too many people were "so heavenly oriented they're no earthly good. Sometimes people become so self-righteous that they make really bad errors of judgment. This happens on both the left and right. So you identify someone who thinks differently from you as someone who is bad and should be destroyed. We all have to ask ourselves, are we becoming so ensconced in the ideologies we believe that we're becoming terrible people? People who say 'you should get that vaccination or I hope you die.' How far is that from what happened in [Nazi] Germany? We all have to be careful about our own self-righteousness."

———

Down in Forks, seventy-five miles southwest of Sequim and just a few miles from the westernmost point of the lower forty-eight states, the rumor mill picked up pace during those first days of the racial-justice protests. The Facebook Live warnings emanating out of Sequim jumped from social media to truckers' CB radios, the remaining log haulers in the region helping to spread rumors of Antifa's march on the peninsula. A full-blown panic was born.

Outfitters store owner Bruce Paul, a tall man with a graying mustache, balding, and dressed casually in black slacks and a blue, white, and orange checked shirt, remembers watching Minneapolis burning in the wake of George Floyd's killing: "It was right when they were burning down Minneapolis. I saw it on the news. They was burning that down. A lot of the inner cities had issues, and there was the occupation of Seattle." Then Paul started hearing rumors about a "white bus on the way to burn Forks down. I heard it on social media, I guess. The white bus came to town, came to our parking lot. Anyways, they came here. Some people met the bus here and chatted with them. The lady who was in the bus came and shopped at the store. People visited with the people in the bus. The bus left here; it was followed by some vehicles. Then it was on CNN news and ABC news for way too long."

Chamber of Commerce executive director Lissy Andros was already on the edge of her seat after watching television footage of the riots in Seattle and elsewhere. From where she was sitting, it looked like a complete breakdown of all law and order. Then she heard the rumors that Antifa members were heading down the peninsula. "The prospect of bad actors coming over here and doing something was pretty threatening, because we're not that far from there [Seattle]," she recalled. "I heard the rumors. I know of the person who started the rumors in Sequim and forwarded them to people in Forks. It was very tense. We were watching live on television things you only see in the movies. It was on live TV, incredible to watch, and very scary." Fifteen years earlier the hit movie *Twilight* had been filmed in the forests surrounding Forks, resulting in a large number of fans flocking to the little town. Andros herself ran a gallery that stocked rare *Twilight* memorabilia. Now she grew increasingly anxious that her business would be gutted by looters. "I hired somebody to sit outside my business all night long," she said. "You feel vulnerable because we had one policeman at the time, maybe two. We have limited resources."

Hardware-store owner Dean Decker, a self-proclaimed conservative with a shaved head, a goatee, and a penchant for jeans, colorful shirts, and workingman's boots, had also been warned about Antifa's plans for Forks. "In my opinion, the crap-show that is Seattle kind of controls the media," he opines. "The fear of Seattle's chaos coming to a small town is always there."

For Decker, the pandemic had magnified all of the chaos, driving many people from around the political spectrum to the edge of craziness. "I put on a mask, my attitude drops," he explains. "I am a less nice person with a mask on; I feel irritated instantly. I felt like someone had a leash on me." He felt bullied into getting the vaccines, worried that unless he did, his business could be forfeited: "The pandemic made a pretty large divide in society between those who feared it and those who feared the repercussions of not following the rules—being shut down or punished for not doing what Big Brother said. The pandemic brought out the worst in society. The government has added more and more thumb, more and more control. I believe we are a less free society."

There was, that pandemic summer, more than a whiff of delusion in the air. There was a churn of chaos, a sense that the ordinary structures and limits and interactions that helped shape everyday life were breaking down. Ideas that, in calmer times, wouldn't have acquired any purchase spread like wildfire, rumors picking up where knowledge left off. Months earlier, restrictions had been put in place in Washington on travel from one county to the next, ordering nonessential workers to stay at home except for when they needed to head to the doctor or to buy food, an extraordinary intrusion into everyday life. In the Forks area, some wanted to shut down Highway 101, the only road in and out of town, in order to prevent outsiders from coming in and spreading the virus; others wanted to keep everything open, believing the outbreak to be a big fuss about nothing. Still others feared they would somehow run afoul of emergency state regulations and lose homes and businesses to ever-more-punitive fines.

In practice, people weren't prosecuted or imprisoned for violating the travel restrictions, but rumors circulated freely online about the extreme control measures being taken by the state. There were stories of military camps expected to hold huge numbers of people infected with the new virus, stories of newly activated 5G communications networks being used to track patients, stories that the vaccines in development would actually be injecting microchips into tens of millions of people to create an all-powerful surveillance network. Now, into the stew of mistrust and anger were added tales of marauding anarchists. As reported by Lauren Smiley in *Wired* magazine, white-nationalist websites, masquerading as Antifa, posted warnings about anarchists moving into the "white hoods" to "take what's ours." "In reading the history of nations, we find that, like individuals, they have their whims and their peculiarities; their seasons of excitement and recklessness, when they care not what they do," wrote the nineteenth-century historian Charles Mackay in the opening page of his book *Extraordinary Popular Delusions and the Madness of Crowds*. "We find that whole communities suddenly fix their minds upon one object, and go mad in its pursuit; that millions of people become simultaneously impressed with one delusion, and run after it, till their attention is caught by some new folly more captivating than the first." So it became on the Olympic Peninsula.

Somehow, the rumor mill managed to score a bull's-eye, focusing locals' minds on the dangers of white buses just when such a vehicle happened to pull into town. No one seems to quite know how or why or when that particular rumor took root, but within hours of Sequim's protests, Forks was rife with rumors about the white bus filled with Antifa anarchists. That, before the pandemic, white buses and camper vans and converted RVs had routinely passed through town, their drivers either looking to live off the grid or heading out for a camping holiday among the stunning forests and hiking trails of the Olympic National Park, seemed to matter not a whit. Nervous locals went on the lookout. The fact that in the past couple of weeks those buses had once more returned to town for entirely legitimate reasons, after Washington's governor suddenly reversed the rigid lockdown conditions of the first nine weeks of the pandemic and urged residents to go out into nature again to soak up the sun and warmth of the great outdoors, didn't alter the equation. If anything, it only aggravated it: the little city, which had managed to avoid any COVID infections during the first three months of the pandemic, suddenly saw its first cases, brought in when local supermarket workers came into contact with the outsiders.

"Outdoor recreation is one of the best things we can do to promote physical, mental and emotional well-being for Washingtonians during a time of great stress and isolation," Governor Inslee had announced. "And springtime in our state is Washington at its best, and people want to be out enjoying outdoor activities in a safe and responsible way." Inslee's office added a caveat: "People must recreate locally. Do not travel farther than necessary and do not stay overnight to recreate." The caveat went largely unheard. Thriftways, the only supermarket of any size in Forks, suddenly saw its shelves stripped bare as shoppers from as far away as Seattle came to try to find food staples, toilet paper, and other necessities that during the early weeks of the pandemic had fallen into short supply around the country. So acute were the shortages that store owner Bruce Paul, a conservative sort of guy who was usually loath to call on the government for help of any kind, felt compelled to reach out to the mayor's office to ask for assistance.

When, predictably, a repurposed white school bus, driven by a young African American man, Tyrone Chevall, and carrying his mixed-race family, rumbled into town the day after Larson began broadcasting his frenzied warnings and then pulled into the Outfitters parking lot, ostensibly to buy materials for a vehicle repair, many Forks residents thought that their do-or-die moment had come. Surely, this was a Trojan horse; surely, inside that innocuous-looking bus dozens of Antifa agents were hiding, waiting to spring forth, weapons loaded, to inflict mayhem on the little town. In the same ways as some of the residents of Redding, in California's Shasta County, were driven to a frenzy by rumors of a van filled with stones and bricks having been driven into town and strategically left for rioters to access, so in Forks some of the locals became convinced that the big city's social problems had finally spilled over into the remote peninsula and that a race war was about to break out at any minute.

The would-be town saviors engaged the family in conversation, trying to none-too-subtly scope out their intent. *Did the black man driving the bus, which the family affectionately called "Big Bertha," really like camping*, they wanted to know, *or was it just a cover for Chevall's true intent?* When the family left the parking lot and headed north out of town toward national forest campgrounds that were still formally closed by the federal government's lockdown requirements but where employees were letting a few campers set up camp in socially spaced ways, they were followed by a slew of pickup trucks, SUVs, and, soon after, a swarm of all-terrain vehicles. By the time that Chevall's group set up camp and realized just how squirrelly their situation had become, it was too late. They were deep in the forest, with only spotty cell-phone service, and had a convoy of gun-toting, fearful locals behind them. By the minute, more gun-carrying residents were joining the crowd.

The Olympic forest is stunningly beautiful, but in this case its beauty suddenly looked desperately dangerous. The foliage, as dense as any southern swampland, had suddenly become the grounds for a potential lynching. "A bunch of ATVs sped by and skidded sideways near Bertha, sending gravel shooting toward the bus and pelting Chevall's pant leg," Smiley wrote in her *Wired* story. "They decided to leave. As they dismantled the tent, they heard a chain saw, close, echoing around them. . . . On the far side, a thicket of cut tree trunks and branches blocked the road, and behind the barricade there was a gathering of cars and trucks. The innocent explanations they had held onto withered: This was about them, and maybe something more."

For Matthew Rendazzo V, a well-known true-crime writer originally from New Orleans, who had moved to Washington State with his fiancée in the aftermath of Hurricane Katrina and had subsequently worked a series of state jobs and held a number of positions with the state's Democratic Party, the events spoke to the rising tide of hysteria and paranoia that was surging over America. As soon as Rendazzo heard about what had gone down in Forks, a community he had spent much time in over the years, and read tweets from locals about how plucky volunteers had taken up arms and prevented an Antifa attack, he also began working social media to get out the word about what had really happened. The events made no sense to him. So far as he could tell, there was no evidence of Antifa in Forks; rather, there was just an "innocent family caught up in some shit they had no idea about." As for those plucky local volunteers, he felt they were bullies who wanted to show the strangers in town exactly who was boss.

Rendazzo's critical tweets about the hysteria went viral. He kept pushing, kept working to focus attention on what had transpired out in the forest. The situation infuriated him. He felt that many of Forks's residents, people who had nurtured a long—and, he acknowledged, justified—sense of grievance about how during the spotted owl debates of the 1990s they and their livelihoods had been cast aside by federal agencies, by people from afar, had taken up arms in order to "kick out people because, on the surface, they thought they didn't belong here."

That no blood was ultimately shed may have had more to do with blind luck than the good sense of the gun-toting mob. County sheriff's deputies soon arrived on the scene, a group of local teenagers milling around the campgrounds were corralled into removing the trees that had been cut down to prevent the white bus from leaving, and, after a while, the mob was convinced to disperse.

Chevall's family drove out of town in a hurry. Later, they would attempt to draw a line under the events of that weekend. They didn't want to talk about it and wouldn't answer most of the many requests from journalists for comment. As for Rendazzo, he woke up one day to find a rubber rat placed on the doormat outside his front door. He says it didn't scare him; after all, he had written books about mobsters and corrupt politicians, about police officers on the take and crime syndicates. "I'm a big Sicilian from New Orleans," he said defiantly. "I don't give a shit."

━━━━━━━

Around the country, the hot flames of vigilantism and paramilitarism were starting to burn bright. Over the coming months and years, several high-profile vigilantes would attract mass followings, and street-fighting groups, some formally organized like militias, others more resembling the mobs of "football hooligans" or "soccer louts" that repeatedly rioted during European soccer matches in the 1980s—their modus operandi simply violence for the sake of violence—picked up steam.

There was Rittenhouse in Kenosha. In 2021 he would stand trial for the killings and eventually be acquitted on all charges. A judge would subsequently allow him to keep nearly one million of the two million dollars that a fund-raising campaign had accumulated to pay for his bail. Authorities decided, with the support of Rittenhouse himself, to destroy the gun he had used in the killings after rumors began circulating that online buyers, eager for their piece of the vigilante pie, were willing to pay a six-figure sum for the rifle.

In Austin, Texas, in July 2020, US Army sergeant Daniel Perry shot dead a Black Lives Matter protester, a US Air Force veteran named Garrett Foster. Perry would subsequently be sentenced to twenty-five years and would become another martyr for the Right. As his fame grew, he became a political pawn as well. Even before he was sentenced, Texas governor Greg Abbott urged the state board of pardons and paroles to swiftly send him a pardon recommendation letter so that he could secure Perry's release. Abbott said that the gunman had been railroaded by Austin's "liberal" prosecutor. And when a slew of Perry's racist social media postings were released to the public, Abbott stayed silent. It would, after all, be politically inconvenient to critique a man who had become a poster child for Texas's stand-your-ground law and who was being lauded by conservative talk-radio and internet hosts for his violent actions.

Lone vigilantes weren't the only swaggering alt-right heroes of this strange moment. Paramilitary and street-fighting groups, some with tightly knit military structures, others simply loosely knit groups of individuals brought together over the internet, were also on the rise.

The Boogaloo Bois, for example, were Hawaiian shirt–wearing alt-right thugs who organized online on 4Chan and gleefully sought out street confrontations with left-wing protesters in cities across the country. They would show up in Minneapolis, Oakland, Las Vegas, and elsewhere, their weapons ostentatiously at the ready, looking for confrontations, and they didn't always seem to care about whom they fought or which side they shot at: at some protests, they turned on racial-justice demonstrators; at others, the Boogaloo Bois served more as agents provocateurs, seemingly egging on the demonstrators in attacking the police and government buildings. Some members embraced white supremacism, but others simply hated the government and were willing to ally with protesters of all races in attacking institutions of authority. Their rallying cry, "boogaloo," was, according to insiders, a call to a second civil war.

Somewhat similar to this group, but more explicitly allied with Donald Trump and the MAGA movement, were the Proud Boys, who burst onto the scene during the final months of the 2016 presidential election campaign and whose leadership proudly embraced a neo-fascist ideology. Their founder, the Canadian provocateur Gavin McInnes, regularly wrote articles for white-nationalist and virulently anti-immigrant websites. They marketed themselves as an exclusively male grouping, and their initiation ritual for new members reputedly included, according to the *Guardian* newspaper and other outlets, violent hazing. The Proud Boys were one of the groups behind the infamous and violent "Unite the Right" event in Charlottesville in 2017; were involved in bloody brawls with antifascists in Portland, New York, and several other cities; and took part in sometimes-violent protests against COVID lockdowns. In 2020 they received an overt nod from Donald Trump during a presidential debate when the president, sagging in the polls and facing demands that he denounce the white-nationalist groups that were rallying to his cause, looked into the TV cameras and defiantly told the Proud Boys to "stand back and stand by."

More formally structured paramilitary organizations were also flourishing. Groups such as the Oath Keepers, whose membership was disproportionately made up of ex-military personnel and law-enforcement officers, fashioned themselves as "guardians of the Republic" in an era in which what they viewed as liberal government overreach and moves toward one-world government were threatening the country's constitutional foundations. Critics viewed them rather differently: in 2015, six years into the group's existence, the Anti-Defamation League wrote that "with conspiratorial rhetoric as their food and drink, the Oath Keepers have several mainstay theories they repeatedly peddle to serve as proof that their 'constitutional republic' is being taken over and destroyed by evil forces. These primary beliefs, which encapsulate the one-world government conspiracy theories that underpin the anti-government movement, stoke paranoia, fan anti-government sentiment and give them purpose." On January 6, 2021, the group responded to Trump's call to travel to Washington for "wild" protests against Congress's certification of the Electoral College vote by sending hundreds of armed members to the nation's capital. The Oath Keepers' founder, Stewart Rhodes, would subsequently be sentenced to eighteen years in prison on charges of seditious conspiracy.

Around the country and in shadowy recesses of the internet, extremist organizations, some convinced that they had a unique calling to take up arms to protect the Republic, others seeking to "accelerate" the chaos that would destroy that Republic and replace it with a white ethno-nationalist state, were putting down roots. The Three Percenters. The Wolverine Watchmen. The Minutemen American Defense. The Constitutional Sheriffs and Peace Officers Association. The People's Rights Network. The Black Robed Regiment. A slew of neo-Nazi organizations such as Atomwaffen. And numerous other groups large and small. In 2022 the Southern Poverty Law Center, which tracks hate groups around the country, identified 492 antigovernment groups operating at a state level in the United States, 61 militias, 96 "sovereign citizen" organizations, 6 "constitutional sheriffs" groups, and 47 "conspiracy propagandist" organizations.

Arguably, though, what was most significant about the bloom of extremism wasn't the numbers but the impact on the political mainstream. Ideas that had for at least a half century been cast to the margins of the country's discourse were once again taking center stage, with talking heads such as Tucker Carlson and members of Congress such as Andy Biggs, Paul Gosar, and Marjorie Taylor Greene unashamedly allying with overtly racist and white-nationalist groupings. Carlson embraced the rhetoric of a "Great Replacement" displacing white Americans with immigrants of color. Biggs, Gosar, and Greene all addressed white-nationalist conferences and paid homage to the insurrectionists of January 6. In 2020, as the racial-justice protests in the wake of the killing of George Floyd gathered pace, Greene staked her position all too clearly. Black Lives Matter, she announced, "has become the most powerful domestic terrorist organization" in the country, its methodology "basically the same tactics that the Ku Klux Klan used to use." In 2022 Greene said that had she been in charge of planning the January 6 pro-Trump march on the Capitol, the protesters would have been better armed and would have won.

Such hyperbolic rhetoric from right-wing political figures and commentators went a long way to explaining the mind-set of the men of Forks, who had picked up guns that early June day and, fearful for their community's safety, followed Chevall's bus out into the forest.

———

Three years on from that surreal summer of 2020, Forks's political leaders were still embittered by how the world had reacted to the goings-on in their little town. They were shocked at the actions of the mob in following the white bus out of town, but they were also still angry at the outsized attention that these local events had received. After all, no lives had been lost. Contrast that with the violent anarchy in the Capitol Hill Occupied Protest (CHOP) district of Seattle, the police-free zone that anarchists had set up after the

George Floyd killing, in an effort to show that communities could safely self-govern without the coercive apparatus of the state behind them. It turned out they weren't so good at peaceful self-governance: in the CHOP that June, there were four shootings within ten days. Yet to the bemusement of civic leaders in Forks, the media seemed generally more interested in what had gone on in their town, population 3,385, than in the ongoing chaos in Seattle. "Was it stress of the pandemic?" Lissy Andros wondered, as she tried to piece together what had happened and why in the hamlet that she loved. "Was it fear that made people act how they acted? I was pretty traumatized on TV seeing what was happening in Seattle." Like ships in the night, the big cities and small towns of America seemed, perhaps as never before, to be heading off in their own directions, many of their residents unable to understand each other's experiences, unwilling to see the good in their neighbor.

For Mayor Tim Fletcher, a big man in his early sixties, who dressed casually in jeans and checked shirts, everything had gotten blown out of proportion during that chaotic week and its aftermath. The mayor, himself half Native American, had participated in racial-justice protests after George Floyd had been killed. It hadn't stopped the surge of emails accusing him of being a white supremacist. "Just being a mayor, I know I get death threats," he said of the fury directed his way because of the actions of men and women with whom he had nothing to do. For two months, he said, laughing bitterly, the tension surrounding his town remained high, with people from around the world emailing and phoning in messages decrying Fletcher and his colleagues. "They knew nothing about the community, and they don't care to know about the community," he argued. "They've already formed their opinion: 'We're in the middle of nowhere; we're white trash.' Not knowing how diverse the community is."

Diverse it may have been, but Forks *was* a determinedly conservative sort of place, a rural enclave surrounded by primordially dense rain forest. Geographically, it was as isolated, as hemmed in, as any Appalachian hamlet. Its denizens claimed, with good reason, that it was a warm, hospitable, tolerant town, and in the main that was true. Certainly, as the timber industry had come to be largely replaced by tourism, it had opened itself up to outsiders. But especially in the darkest days of the pandemic, it remained a place somewhat fearful of those outsiders, one primed to go off the rails during events as strange as those of the days following George Floyd's murder and the resulting explosion of racial-justice protests after months of draconian lockdowns. The pandemic, Fletcher says, "set the foundation" for all the chaos that followed. "You start restricting people and keeping them in a small area, normal people turn into something different."

In contrast to Forks, Sequim, despite the somewhat accidental mayorship of William Armacost and the presence of conservative provocateurs such as Seth Larson, was more liberal. In its support for Biden in 2020, it looked more like the progressive hub of Port Angeles, population twenty thousand, a nineteenth-century fishing port from which the ferries over to Victoria, British Columbia, departed every hour, their foghorns blaring loudly as they set off toward the north.

That wasn't enough, however, to buy immunity from the corrosive politics roiling the country. Both Sequim and Port Angeles experienced political upheavals in the Trump era. In 2021 even the usually reliably true-blue Port Angeles found itself caught up in many of the same battles around public health and around the future of the local economy that were reshaping politics in neighboring Sequim and, by extension, in the country as a whole. City council member Lindsey Schromen-Warwin, an Oberlin-educated attorney, avid hiker, and wilderness camper, had first gotten elected during a local progressive wave in 2017, but he found himself in a tough brawl for reelection against a deeply conservative candidate. Schromen-Warwin squeaked to victory with a tiny margin. "In 2017," he remembered, "I'd gotten the most votes of any city council member since 2005. In this last race, I won by 104 votes—which is way too close for comfort when your opponent is the person with a bullhorn trying to shut down the county health commissioner's forum."

For its part, Clallam's neighboring county, Jefferson, had historically been even more solidly blue. The waterfront of its one sizable city, the Victorian-era Port Townsend, was once lined with brick warehouses and canneries that in recent years had been converted into bookstores, art galleries, and restaurants; and the city itself had long been a bohemian, liberal refuge for artists escaping the crowds and prices of big West Coast cities such as Seattle and San Francisco. But Clallam County's progressives had not solidified their position in the way their Jefferson counterparts had. The QAnon movement and a variety of white-nationalist militias made inroads into Clallam County during the Trump years, and despite showing up for national elections, local Democrats were slow off the mark when it came to local politics. They didn't field comprehensive slates of candidates for city council and other regional offices, apparently not realizing until late in the day just how much of an electoral threat extremists at the local level had become.

"It does have a national ramification," argued retired elementary school teacher Bruce Cowan. Cowan lived in Port Townsend and had been involved in county politics both there and in neighboring Clallam County for more than forty years; in retirement, he did volunteer work consulting for progressive political campaigns. "Folks who don't believe in government, populists, people who don't have faith in the institutions of governance shouldn't be in charge of the government," Cowan explained. "One of the things that happened in Sequim is that people were not engaged enough to see how important it was to find candidates for city council. Now they understand the importance."

━━━━━━━

For two years, as the pandemic raged and the country fractured around public health mandates, Trump, and racial justice, William Armacost continued to outrage his opponents, at one point bouncing constituents' phone calls to a recorded message advertising herbal remedies, "in a capsule or yummy form," that he was selling on the side.

Armacost's power was magnified by a local group named the Independent Advisory Association (IAA). It was run by a couple of longtime conservative operatives, Donnie Hall and Jim McIntire, and was advised by a conservative attorney named Robert Bilow, who would show up at council meetings and, observers argued, proffer advice to Armacost as well. They claimed to be nonpartisan, but they often worked to turn local political events into a parade ground on which they could strut their particular brand of right-wing politics by red-baiting opponents and accusing critics of being outside agitators. When council seats came up for grabs, as they did three times in the early days of the Armacost mayorship, they reportedly groomed potential appointees before the mayor and his colleagues selected them. As the pandemic got under way, they sought to tap into public anger at lockdowns to Trumpify government offices along the peninsula.

Hall claimed that the IAA was just "two guys and a website" and that the organization had only ever wanted to promote independent, nonpartisan candidates for office. When I suggested in response that there was a power struggle taking place on the peninsula, of which the IAA was a part, he replied, "I can't stop laughing," asserting that "your premises are so out of alignment with reality."

Yet a power struggle there most assuredly was. Armacost's ascent to the mayorship had acted as a red flag. All around Sequim, locals, some of whom had previously been apolitical, others of whom had long been involved in political organizations and protests, reacted in horror to his bullying persona and his far-right antics. "It was so raucous, and some of the statements were so ugly," says Lisa Dekker, of the local chapter of Indivisible, a national network set up during the Trump era to respond to the administration's increasingly extreme policies. "It shocked the progressive community."

In the spring of 2021, several of these individuals came together to form what they called the Sequim Good Governance League (SGGL), with the goal of fielding qualified candidates and exorcising the QAnon demons from their midst. "It became apparent we had a city council that needed to be replaced," said Dale Jarvis, a retiree from the Seattle area who had relocated to Clallam County several years earlier. "We needed to get them out. We started organizing."

"All these conservative people snuck onto the city council when nobody opposed them," said Ron Richards, a rugged seventy-six-year-old onetime Clallam County commissioner who lived in a ranch house at the base of the Olympic Mountains and regularly hiked miles in the snow for exercise. "And then they appointed their friends to government. It resulted in the most right-wing people you could imagine running the city of Sequim." Horrified, Richards got involved in the SGGL.

Faced with the very real prospect of QAnoners consolidating power over all tiers of city and county government, the SGGL got busy. Progressive candidates were recruited to run for office; moderate Republicans, such as council member Brandon Janisse, were wooed as voices to counter the IAA; dozens of volunteers were trained to do the on-the-ground grunt work that can make the difference between a painful election loss and a head-turning win.

For concerned locals such as Lowell Rathbun, an engineer by train-ing, it had become increasingly difficult to sit on the fence during 2020 and 2021. With the city manager being forced out over the tribe's MAT clinic, with city council members waging war against the county's public health department, and with increasingly violent protests occurring against individuals in that department, this was, they felt, a fight about civic decency.

In May 2021, Rathbun filed to run for city council. And then, throughout the summer and fall, with backing from the SGGL and its growing cadre of canvassers, postcard writers, and other volun-teers, he got to work. "We organized. I broke the town down into fifty-four neighborhoods, and we worked every one of those neigh-borhoods," Rathbun recalls, over a beer and mozzarella sticks at the local Applebee's.

Volunteers would get up in the middle of the night to send out email blasts. They'd drive around town putting up scores of signs for SGGL candidates. Above all, they'd talk to people. For months on end, door knocking was the chief tool that the cash-strapped organization, known to its founders as "the little engine that could," relied on. As they talked with residents, they grew more optimis-tic: time after time, they heard on the doorstep discontent, even bemusement, at the direction that city politics had taken in recent years. There was a hunger to get back to the basics—to use the tools of city government not to litigate huge national issues but to focus on improving people's lives, on the ground, in Sequim.

On the night of the 2021 election, it became clear that all of the organizing had more than paid off. In one election after another, for city council, for the local school board, for hospital commissioners, SGGL candidates swept aside their IAA-backed opponents.

"When it turned out to be two to one," Rathbun remembered, his reaction was visceral: "Holy crap! We kicked butt."

The results were definitive: SGGL-backed candidates had ridden a wave of genuine popular fury against the faux populists centered around Armacost. In Sequim, the five SGGL candidates for city council—Kathy Downer, Vicki Lowe, Rachel Anderson, Brandon Janisse, and Lowell Rathbun—all got between 65 and 70 percent of the vote. In Port Angeles, all four SGGL-endorsed candidates won their city council races. Both hospital commissioners' positions in the county went to SGGL candidates, as did the fire commission and school district posts that were up for election.

SOS, the IAA, Armacost, and the other conservatives had, for two years, continually told everyone who would listen that they represented the ordinary, silent majority of the county, that their brand of divide-and-conquer politics was the only brand worth selling. But, said SGGL organizer Marsha McGuire somewhat giddily, "At the election we proved it: they are *not* the majority."

It wasn't so much that a given ideology triumphed—Iraq war veteran and county jail control-room technician Brandon Janisse's conservative leanings were, for example, a far cry from the liberal politics of the tattooed, head-partly-shaved Rachel Anderson, or of longtime tribal health worker Vicki Lowe—as that people's better angels burst to the surface. The electorate in Sequim finally put the kibosh on Armacost and the Trumpian, QAnon-ist threat to civic well-being that he and his colleagues embodied.

"Four of the SGGL candidates are left-leaning. I'm right-leaning," said Janisse. "But they endorsed me because of how I think government should be run at the local level. We're worried about 'Are the roads paved? Are the alleys good? Do you have sidewalks? Are the sewers not spraying leaks everywhere?'"

For Allison Berry, as the tide turned against the vocal right-wingers who had held Sequim hostage through 2020 and 2021, her correspondence with residents shifted from a daily barrage of threats to something rather different. At some point in the autumn, a contingent of elderly people had begun a letter-writing campaign to her and her colleagues, expressing how much they appreciated the public health staff. Anonymous residents would swing by the office and leave Berry and her team bouquets of flowers. "A good thing happened: there was a counter-response in the community," Berry recalled with a smile. "It was incredibly heartening."

On January 11, 2022, Armacost was voted out of the mayorship by his fellow council members, the majority of whom had been endorsed by the SGGL in the recently concluded elections. The only councillor to vote in favor of Armacost remaining as mayor was Armacost himself. The ousted mayor, his firebrand politics having been firmly rejected by the electorate, was replaced by Tom Ferrell, a somewhat conservative but non-QAnon-supporting longtime member of the council who had been nominated by both Downer and Rathbun. Brandon Janisse was elected as his deputy.

For the SGGL-backed candidates now in the majority, it represented a new beginning, a chance to restore competent, get-things-done local government. "We have issues here," said Vicki Lowe. "Housing issues. We have to work on bringing our community back together." Housing was also a key issue for Kathy Downer, a longtime nurse who had once served as a council member in the little town of Marietta, Ohio, before retiring and moving to Sequim to be near her children: "When you can't find housing for your nurses, policemen, firemen, and teachers, that's a horrific situation." Rathbun, who was suddenly widowed during the campaign and who had since thrown his heart and soul into his political work, also wanted to focus on housing. But after being the target of death threats, he was at least as desperate to restore faith in the basic workings of the democratic system and to find a way to dial down the fear and invective that saturated social media–dominated political discourse. "I would like to see a healing in this town. We can't have red and blue Sequim. We have to have Sequim Sequim.

And somehow start talking to each other about what we have in common." Janisse, with his blue-collar roots and his current job at the local jail, also wanted to focus on affordable housing as well as on changing zoning regulations in order to encourage the construction of more high-density, multiunit buildings. And longtime Head Start worker Rachel Anderson, age thirty-one, who was appointed to the council early in 2021—Armacost apparently was unaware of her liberal political leanings—wanted to place more attention on children's issues, as well as on affordable housing and local health-and-safety measures.

"I think we'll be more productive," Anderson said of the SGGL victory, "and actually make decisions that mean something, instead of saying 'We don't like this.' I feel like there's a lot more middle ground. I can only hope that with a change in local leadership, there's a change in the local political climate. I've worked with kids a lot, and a lot of the time during council meetings it felt like children throwing a tantrum. Now, with the change in leadership it feels like I'm having an adult conversation."

A week after the November 2021 election, Beth Pratt began her new job as director of Sequim's Chamber of Commerce. It was a difficult assignment: the chamber was hemorrhaging members as some businesses closed and other owners withdrew support from the chamber either because they were angry that it hadn't opposed vaccine mandates or were angry that the group hadn't been vocal enough in supporting those mandates. Many days, it seemed, you could practically reach out and touch the tension in the air. Everyone was pissed about something. Moreover, the corrosive legacy of Armacost's leadership was still playing out all too publicly. When Pratt was offered the job, a friend asked her incredulously, "Have you seen what's going on in Sequim? Are you sure you want that job?"

Pratt did. She had just turned forty-seven and was coming off years working as an administrator in a large long-term elder-care facility in Port Angeles. They had been tough years. Desperate to keep her vulnerable patients as safe as possible, she had gone into near-total lockdown in her social life. An avid amateur violinist who played for the nearly century-old Port Angeles symphony orchestra, she stopped meeting up for afternoons or evenings of music with her friends. For two years, she didn't see her family down in Oregon. When she and her fiancé got married in the fall of 2020, they invited one official, one photographer, and two witnesses to the ceremony in their greenhouse behind their home. A friend made a cake, and the wedding couple and four guests quickly downed some champagne splits. All the other guests had to attend remotely, via Facebook Live.

Everything in Pratt's life was about preventing COVID from claiming more of her elderly patients. It didn't always work. In the summer of 2021, when she was working in the memory unit of the facility, with many patients in their nineties and others who had crossed the centennial mark, an outbreak rampaged through the unit. In the space of two weeks, despite the fact that the residents were all vaccinated, eight people died. For Pratt it was devastating.

What made things worse for her was that the public health staff—those same men and women who had worked so hard to protect the community and to keep her patients safe, the people who had come into the elder-care facility in January 2021 with some of the first batches of vaccine that had been made available to the general public—were now bearing the brunt of a ferocious backlash by conservatives infuriated with Berry's proof-of-vaccination mandate. "It just struck me as so ill-informed," she said with bemusement, "as we watched our hospital system just get run over. To see the backlash, I couldn't get my head around it. What in the world is happening here? What happened in Sequim is bizarre to me—that Sequim got so divided, around the vaccine and everything else. I just don't understand it."

———

For Dominique Hall, the South African–born owner of the Rainshadow Café, those divides were on display every day. In the summer of 2021, Hall had enthusiastically supported the vaccine mandate, believing that most of her customers, who tended to be on the elderly side, wanted that extra degree of security. Many had, after all, been among that first group of locals to get inoculated in early 2021, when the Jamestown S'Klallam clinic received a few precious vials of the mRNA vaccines. Some had lined up in their cars overnight for that initial shot.

Now, seven months after the vaccine rollout, the medical professionals were recommending that indoor diners in Sequim show proof of vaccination, and, by temperament, Hall tended to follow expert advice. She instructed her staff to demand to see vaccination cards before they let customers dine inside the café.

It wasn't easy. Although most of those who stopped by the Rainshadow, unlike the younger clientele at neighboring bars, were only too happy to show their vaccine cards, and although some even thanked her for following the new regulations so scrupulously, others were less enamored: "We were called Nazis. Some people would do ridiculous things like stand in line with no mask on. This one guy was like, 'I don't need a mask. All these other people sitting down don't have a mask.' We said, 'That's because they're eating.' He sat down in the line. We said, 'You're still not eating.'" She laughed at the recollection. If customers refused to wear a mask or couldn't produce proof of vaccination, the Rainshadow employees would gently but firmly offer up alternatives: they could eat outside; they could sit in their car and order takeout; they could even order home delivery.

What they couldn't do was sit indoors at the tables reserved for those who were vaccinated.

At least twice a day, customers would get up into a staff member's face, screaming about the infringements on their liberties. Several times a month there'd be more serious blowups, where it looked like things could potentially turn violent.

But there was, at least, a silver lining. Later that fall, the more extreme voices in Sequim were given an electoral thumping. And the Rainshadow Café, despite some of Hall's more conservative friends (including a firefighter who had spent two years on the COVID front lines) telling her that she was doomed to business failure for embracing Berry's mandate, thrived during the remaining months that the mandate was in place. It turned out that many local residents felt reassured by the vaccine requirement, that they wanted to take their morning coffees and pastries at a place in which they knew their fellow diners were less likely to be bringing with them a COVID infection.

Chapter Seven

RED PILLS AND SHOCK JOCKS

Back in Shasta County, Woody Clendenen, Carlos Zapata, and Doni Chamberlain, the liberal publisher of the local online newspaper *A News Café*, agreed on almost nothing. But one thing they all were certain of was that the events that transpired in Shasta County from 2020 onward could never have happened without COVID. True, the schisms so brutally exposed by Trump and Trumpism had laid the groundwork for what came. Yet without COVID, they sensed, the county wouldn't have erupted in the way that it did. There was, for the three of them, a vision of Shasta County prior to the pandemic and an understanding of Shasta after all the chaos and heartbreak of the deadly outbreak.

"When the lockdowns happened, we expected our supervisors to interpose themselves between the state government, to not obey them.

There were a bunch of idiotic mandates," Clendenen declared. "The shop across the street with drug paraphernalia was an 'essential business,' but mine [the little barbershop] wasn't. The nudie bars were left open, but churches had to close. Locally, the health officer was trying to threaten Jeff Davis, who was putting on the Cottonwood Rodeo," which opened, to much national attention, a couple of months into the pandemic and, being one of the only shows not just in town but in the entire region, attracted thousands of visitors from around the country. "She said if anything got linked back to the rodeo, he'd be liable. But the sheriff told him to go ahead and hold it." He did, and five thousand visitors showed up from around the country to celebrate the rodeo; it made international news.

The rodeo also cemented the notion that with the politically righteous competing with one another as to who could most stringently observe the lockdown rules, as to who could have the *least* amount of social interaction, as to who could forgo the *most* amount of pleasure and still remain somewhat sane, the alt-right had somehow found a purchase on the having of fun. They had become the hedonists cavorting, carefree, while the experts and the doomsayers shouted out that the apocalypse was nigh and while the politicians in Sacramento ratcheted up the strictness of the lockdowns with each succeeding emergency declaration.

On rodeo day, Davis and his friends roped cattle from eight in the morning until midnight. For Zapata, it was revelatory. "It was like seeing people for the first time. How excited everyone was to see friends," he enthused, on a subsequent podcast with Davis. The rodeo organizer agreed. "They were just so happy to be out and be around people again and to live their life again. We took people's mental health into consideration again."

Later on in the pandemic, as they filmed *The Red White and Blueprint* episodes, Zapata and his friends would very consciously capitalize on this image. They filmed themselves drinking shots and shooting the breeze around a campfire at night. Zapata, the leader of the pack, was wearing a cowboy hat; his acolytes were toting baseball caps. They talked politics, mocked the COVID lockdowns, and ridiculed what they saw as the hysteria around the virus.

By now, increasing numbers of their neighbors in Shasta County agreed with them. Clendenen recalled how mask mandates and vaccines for kids riled up moms to argue at school board and board of supervisors meetings that schools should be immediately reopened. "Get the mama bears involved, you're in trouble," he laughed. "The kids were really damaged by the school shutdowns. It damaged their psyches."

Carlos Zapata claimed to be generally progressive on economic issues. In public he liked to distance himself from the real extremists, the people he called "crazy fuckers" who wanted to destroy everything—although that hadn't prevented him from accommodating the Proud Boys when they demonstrated in his support outside of a courtroom where he was being charged with disturbing the peace in 2022 after he and two friends got into a fracas with a liberal African American YouTuber and TikTokker named Nathan Blayze (or Blaze). He seemed to spell his name differently depending on his mood of the moment.

Blaze, who also went by the name of "Pinkney," had first encountered Zapata early on in the pandemic when the ex-marine had taken part in protests at local grocery stores, turning up to shop without wearing masks, in contravention both of state requirements and of the store's in-house policies designed to protect their cashiers and other staff. They would arrive, dozens of them, at Trader Joe's and other stores, stack their carts full of produce, and then proceed to the checkout. When the cashiers would refuse to ring up their purchases—as the protesters knew would be the case—Zapata and his crew would barrack them, live-streaming their heckling exploits for angry supporters to see. Tipped off about the protests, Blaze, who favored the public health mandates, would also show up at Trader Joe's to film the action, waiting for the police to arrive to usher the anti-maskers out. At one point he lobbed an insult Zapata's way, accusing him, in not wearing a mask, of being supportive of domestic terrorism. Zapata and his friends, Blaze said, had responded by swarming him and at close range—unmasked, of course—screaming insults back in his face. It made for great viewing and, from Blaze's perspective, helped show his audiences the dangers of the cascading opposition to public health mandates in his county. The young YouTuber subsequently made a point of turning up where the people whom he viewed as extremists were making scenes, seeking to cast a spotlight on their actions.

That first pandemic summer, Blaze made a name for himself as something of a troublemaker. Many Shasta locals were convinced that he was Antifa, certain that in the wake of George Floyd's killing and the protests and unrest that erupted in its wake, he had been involved in violent Black Lives Matter looting up north, in Portland and in Seattle—he had, in some of his videos, made satirical references to being a fellow traveler of Antifa—and several locals took it upon themselves to dox him at public meetings, to publicize some criminal convictions that he had picked up as a young man, as well as to deluge the restaurants that employed him with demands that he be fired. Some days, dozens of hate emails, filled with graphically violent fantasies against Blaze, would arrive in his inbox. He started creating folders devoted exclusively to hate mail and grabbing screenshots of the more offensive social media posts. (He was not the only target: one correspondent wrote to Blaze's girlfriend that "you looked like a crazy woman at the BOS [board of supervisors] just now. Did I get your gender right? Your bastard child is going to have one heck of a life with you and Nathan 'The Pink' Pinkney as their parents . . . they will spew Communist propaganda instead of scientific facts.")

Still, Blaze continued his campaign, generally using sarcasm and humor to try to convey to audiences what he saw as the fundamentally illogical nature of Zapata's worldview. He mocked some of Zapata's public speeches by creating a parody character named Buford White who wore plaid shirts and a large, folded-back floppy hat; talked slowly, like the stereotype of a southern yokel; tried to justify what he called "fundamental racism" to his audience; and drawled on about why it *was* a good thing to not wear masks in the face of a pandemic and also to call the police on Black people loitering in their neighborhoods. Days after the first Buford White parody hit YouTube, Zapata visited Blaze at the downtown restaurant where he was working as a cook. He confronted him, began shouting at him about the video, and then, Blaze alleged, hurled a glass of water—not just the water but the glass as well, the YouTuber claimed—at his victim's chest.

Blaze was shouting in rage. According to the records from Zapata's trial, he even threatened to get a gun and shoot Zapata. "I'm going to shoot that motherfucker," a coworker alleged that he shouted. With restaurant patrons looking on in bemusement, the furious ex-marine stormed out of the restaurant. A somewhat shocked Blaze took a break and went out back to collect his thoughts. Nine minutes after the first incident, Zapata and two of his friends—one man, one woman—returned, began screaming homophobic and racial epithets, and rushed Blaze, who was standing out back having a phone conversation with a friend. Blaze was punched in the face by one of Zapata's friends and just avoided being pummeled with a large gas canister that one of his assailants was wielding at him.

The next day, Blaze went to court to seek a restraining order against Zapata. He got the order, but over the course of the next month his attorney struggled to find anyone willing to serve it. Zapata reputedly bragged to friends that not a single person in the county would serve him with such a document. He was ultimately proved wrong. Eventually, Blaze's attorney guessed that Zapata would be attending his daughter's high school graduation one day in early June, and she corralled several friends to mill around looking like proud moms of graduating seniors. When one of them spotted Zapata, she stepped forward with a copy of the order and told him he had been served. He allegedly responded, witnesses remembered, with a string of colorful, misogynistic words, but the deed had been done.

Ultimately, none of the three attackers who had beaten Blaze went to jail. After a trial punctuated by long delays after members of the jury came down with COVID, leading to jurors being placed in a mandatory fourteen-day quarantine, Zapata was eventually convicted of disturbing the peace but acquitted on the additional assault-and-battery charges resulting from the allegation that he had thrown a glass at Blaze's chest. He was placed on probation and mandated to attend sixteen weeks of anger-management classes. He was also ordered to stay at least one hundred yards away from Blaze.

Unsurprisingly, none of this dimmed Zapata's star. During the trial, Proud Boys had congregated outside the courthouse to register their support for the anti-lockdown hero. Local denizens of the Far Right were photographed flashing white-power signs. Afterward, Zapata told any journalists who would listen that he and his buddies were simply trying to keep the country on an even keel. What was happening in Shasta, he argued, wasn't about right-wing revolution or (implausibly, given the Proud Boys' presence) street-fighting politics, but about maintaining a constitutional status quo: "COVID's what kicked off the entire movement. Nobody was very political or interested till the shutdown came." But when businesses had to close, schools were shuttered, and the public was barred from ostensibly public meetings, "There was just a boiling point. Everybody was fed up with being lied to, not being able to run your business, not being able to see your friends." The public health crowd was, Zapata felt, simply "poking the bear," and if they, or Supervisor Moty, or any of the others at the wrong end of the heated rhetoric felt intimidated, well, that was because "they're weak and feeble people who shouldn't be in the game. Why should they be intimidated by me? Shit, you name it, they've done it. I'm the one who should be intimidated. But I'm not weak." He was not averse, however, to rolling around in the mud. As the campaign against Moty heated up, at one point Zapata had even briefly posted a meme showing the supervisor's head, the top of which was adorned with a penis and the chin with a scrotum. It was beyond grotesque. Zapata removed the image soon after posting it, but not before one of the groups monitoring far-right activity in Shasta had grabbed a screenshot of the offensive image.

Once COVID lit the fuse, Zapata continued, all the other issues began to fall into place, and a worldview solidified: the presence of Black Lives Matter and Antifa, abortion, "transgenderism. Our kids started coming home and saying what was happening in the schools: boys in girls' bathrooms and vice versa. Our kids were being taught things we didn't think were appropriate." They were also being pressured to get vaccinated, and for Zapata that was a redline. At one point, when he was being interviewed for a Vice documentary as part of a series titled *Insurgency*, he blustered to the interviewers that he would shoot in the face anybody who would dare to vaccinate his children. "I don't care who you are, you're dying if you vaccinate my kids," he promised.

———

When COVID arrived on US shores in early 2020, California's state government response kicked into high gear. Seemingly overnight, daily life was upended, with unprecedented restrictions placed on residents. Those rules would stay in place for much of the next couple of years, through that first horrifying year when the populace remained unvaccinated and unprotected, and through the year following as the vaccines were rolled out and as society struggled to balance the ongoing risk of infection with the need to return to normal forms of living. The psychological, educational, and social legacy of Gavin Newsom's somewhat heavy-handed, one-size-fits-all lockdown, with its improvised rules, its color-coded grading systems for counties and for risk factors, and its precautionary principles that shut down schools and businesses and then made it very hard to reopen them in a timely manner, would last far longer than just those two years.

There was some truth in the argument that had the state and Newsom been more flexible about the rules laid out in the first horrifying weeks of the pandemic and had the public health mandates differentiated more between large, densely populated cities and smaller, more rural counties, Shasta's crisis might never have come to a head. Certainly, when Moty was chair of the board of supervisors, he hadn't been comfortable with many of the lockdown requirements. Karen Ramstrom also had strong reservations about the school-closing strategy and worked hard to keep the local schools functioning. But hindsight is, of course, twenty-twenty. At the time, everyone was operating in the dark, and the public health mandates, far from being aimed at ruining lives and communities, were desperate measures intended to keep the health system from being overwhelmed and to minimize the number of deaths from a disease that, in the early days, was thought to have a 10 percent mortality rate. (Over the following years, estimates of the mortality rate dropped. By 2023, with much of the world's population vaccinated, infectious-disease experts believed it to be well under 1 percent.)

"Like everywhere else in the world, at the beginning of 2020 we were watching to see what would happen, having our own internal conversations about what that means for us," recalled Ramstrom. She and her colleagues—who moved into a crisis-coordination office in a building that previously had served as a training center for local fire and police personnel—began holding regular conversations with the county's two infectious-disease–care providers; she was frequently on the phone with the state's health department and in regular communication with the CDC. By early March, it was clear that California was heading into a lockdown. When locals demanded to know how long the disruptions would last, how long their businesses would be closed, how long their children would be out of school, and how long their friends and relatives would be separated from them by social-distancing requirements, Ramstrom had to tell them that no one knew.

"They were pissed with the governor and his executive orders. But we were in an unprecedented event, and his priority was to keep people safe," Ramstrom, thin, her blond hair cut short and adorned with a simple hairclip, her eyes behind tortoiseshell eyeglasses, later explained. "There was this whole evolution of lack of trust in government. It made it very difficult. These groups with their issues kind of coalesced: State of Jefferson people, constitutionalists, anti-vaxxers."

As COVID spread and as local public health officials desperately tried to craft regulations to keep the populace safe, local talk-radio hosts would go on their shows and tell their audience of anti-vaxxers, anti-maskers, anti-RINOs, and anti-BLMers that it was time for blood to flow in the streets.

Doni Chamberlain, whose publication was sympathetic to the public health officials and to the board of supervisors members who were upholding state law, and whose team investigated the increasingly violent movement against these public figures, was routinely targeted by alt-right media barkers. The same shock jock who had called for Communists to have their necks stretched also urged his listeners to try under "the Nuremberg trials" the publisher of "the communist cockroach paper" and "publicly execute her." She should, he told his audience, be tied up and dragged behind a car until she was dead. "When our country collapses and you force armed conflict, you get absolutely what you deserve. If that's hooked up to a car and you get dragged down the road . . . then you get what you deserve. You truly have to understand our government has been seized by Communist trash. Propped up by trash," the broadcaster screamed, his voice rising to a crescendo. He punched the table in the broadcast booth as he raved. "They don't care why everyone's dying, because they support population control. These little Nazis within government, and Communist trash . . . they're going to continue to shove that mask and the vaccine down your throat. That's why she should be tried under the Nuremberg code and hung in the end, because it's for the greater good."

The radio show host didn't just reserve his wrath for Chamberlain and other local figures. His targets were bigger fish as well. Senator Dianne Feinstein, he continued, was a "cockroach," and Governor Newsom was a "Communist piece of trash. If the law was enforced, people like him would be in prison or executed because the death penalty does exist for treason. It's time to resist, people, resist before it is too late. I understand that the government has become lawless." A Facebook group called Open Shasta put up a posting about "taking out Dr. Ramstrom." A flood of other online threats soon followed. Anti-vaxxers picketed the public health offices. Fearing violence, the Redding Police Department ramped up patrols of Ramstrom's neighborhood. For a short time, she had a security team stationed outside her house. She put up security cameras around her home; she had to give statements to investigators from the DA's office.

With the airwaves saturated with calls to violence and noncooperation, Shasta's population resisted not only the lockdowns but also, when they became available in early 2021, the vaccinations. Only 48 percent of the population got the first two doses, and only 55 percent of those went on to get booster shots; among children in the county, the numbers fully vaccinated were vanishingly small.

Ramstrom's somber presentation to the county board of supervisors in March 2020—along with the hope that it offered of a unified response in the face of a vast crisis—now seemed an age ago. In the years since, an air of magical realism had descended on the county, fueled by the idea that the virus could be willed into the background simply by pretending that people weren't being infected and weren't dying. Perhaps, if you just laughed enough at the crazy liberals and their lockdown mandates, railed enough at Fauci and Newsom and Ramstrom and Moty, organized enough play dates for your kids, and defiantly went to enough barbecues and rodeos and family gatherings and large church services, everything would suddenly be OK again. It was a seductive vision. After all, while so much of the world was enduring soul-crushing lockdowns, while previously unthinkable isolation had become the norm for billions of people, in Shasta County and other holdouts like it, life continued pretty much as normal—even if that meant more people ended up getting infected and dying.

There was, in all of this, more than an element of the red-pill/blue-pill choice detailed in the movie *The Matrix* and turned into an article of faith by those on the conspiratorial right of American politics. Swallow the blue pill, and you would live a comfortable life swaddled in the illusions of a corrupted society. Swallow the red pill, however, and a new universe of explanations opened up. The truths you would be exposed to—be they about pedophiliac politicians or LGBTQ efforts to undermine the moral pillars of Western society, false-flag mass shootings designed by the government to discredit the gun lobby, or feminist efforts to disempower and feminize American males—would be hard, but (so went the theory) they would also set you free, allowing you to see the light through all the dust thrown up by a Big Brother state. Consider it an alt-right version of the 1960s LSD-fueled countercultural vision of tuning in, turning on, and dropping out.

In the COVID era, Shasta included, red-pill rhetoric around the disease took off. Two months into the lockdown, Elon Musk had tweeted to his thirty-four million followers that they should "take the red pill." Many, including Ivanka Trump, the president's daughter, replied that they had. It was the red-pill adherents who spoke of COVID being caused by 5G cell-phone towers. It was the red-pill adherents who talked of the virus having been created to provide politicians with the excuse to impose total control over the population. It was the red-pill adherents who spread the rumor that the vaccines were being used to install microchips in every recipient, allowing for the creation of a universal, omnipotent surveillance state.

Actual reality told a different story. As spikes in COVID infection numbers hit California, first in the late autumn of 2020, then in the summer and early fall of 2021, and finally in the winter of 2022, the deaths in the avowedly unmasked, not socially distanced, and not-locked-down Shasta County mounted. By the autumn of 2022—which was when the county website stopped posting updates on the pandemic—the little county of 185,000 residents, home to a noisy anti-vaxxer movement and street-corner orators only too keen to tell residents that the risk of COVID in a sparsely populated rural county was minimal, had posted nearly 700 deaths. That made for a death rate of 0.37 percent of the population. By contrast, California as a whole, which had a much higher overall vaccination rate—and also a slightly younger population than did Shasta County—had a death rate of just over 0.25 percent by early 2023. Although that difference might not look large, another way to understand these numbers was that three Shasta County residents were dying for every two Californians out of a comparable population sample. Older and less vaccinated than much of the rest of the state, Shasta's residents ended up peculiarly vulnerable to serious complications from COVID. Many didn't survive.

"I needed to keep the community safe," Ramstrom remembered thinking. "I didn't have time to feel scared or threatened or fearful."

But, she also recollects, things were becoming so dysfunctional nationally, with so much disinformation being thrown into the ether from Washington, DC, down to the local level, that it was getting ever harder to navigate all the cross-currents.

Seemingly on a daily basis, someone would start a Facebook or Twitter thread promising to wreak havoc on those supporting restrictions and vaccines. An email to Doni Chamberlain and several others declared that "we need to remove Doni from life as she knows it here." Another troll printed up badges with the logo "Make the Nuremberg Code Great Again" and sent the image to Chamberlain. Someone emailed her a photo, no words attached, of a group of menacing-looking men, all carrying long-arm rifles. One Facebook post fantasized about mass executions as a form of public art: "If we could turn back time to just after WWII . . . I believe the greatest generation would have filthy, vile treasonous woke liberals hanging from trees, bridges, and telephone polls [sic] all over the land. We could all appreciate it as street art." In the comments that followed the post, the fantasies built on each other, growing ever more lurid with each additional iteration.

The more *A News Café* dug in its journalistic heels and reported on what was happening in Shasta County, the more venomous and personal the attacks became. The more Chamberlain called out the far-right movements for being extremist, writing one lengthy editorial after another in which she ridiculed individuals by name and detailed their proclivities for violence, the more those at the wrong end of her pen denied that they were extreme and antidemocratic, and promised to prove her wrong through bloodshed. "She's such a lying bitch," went one Facebook post. "Her articles are always full of shit and mis-truths." When a commenter replied that it was time to kill her, another woman chimed in, "We are on board! Keep it private, keep us in the loop." One day, Chamberlain opened a private message on Facebook. It read, "I'd sure hate to be you on judgement day! You are an evil, dumb cunt!" Another told her that she was a "disgusting OLD TROLL!!! Stringy hair, no lips, stretched neck, etc . . . get a life and stop pestering people."

Chamberlain had been reporting on Shasta's underbelly for years and was used to raising the hackles of those whose misdeeds and missteps she exposed. Being insulted, she knew, came with the journalistic job description these days, and over the years she had mostly been able to shrug the attacks off. She was tough as nails, with more balls than most of the buzz-cut ranchers and farmers and faux-tough-guy militiamen around Shasta, and was determined to keep the investigative journalism flame alive, but by early 2023, even she was scared. One particularly horrifying message arrived via email on a winter's afternoon in early 2023: "All the kikes who set the arson fires are getting their arms and legs broken, and for a disgusting old frigid piece of dog shit like, I am going to smash every tooth out of your vile obsolete Marxist skull, pour gasoline down your snout, and burn you in the street like the vile, lying piece of animal shit that you are. I am watching you bitch, and I will wait for my opportunity to give you the 6 mandatory shots to the head that a disgusting fucking hag like you needs."

The publisher of *A News Café* largely retreated behind the security systems in her house, holding meetings in private rather than in public settings. Friends urged her to take self-defense classes; others suggested that she stockpile guns. When she walked to her car, she looked around, doing a quick security calculus to see if anything looked out of the ordinary.

For board of supervisors chair Patrick Jones, however, the death threats were simply blowhards letting off steam. "People that threat [*sic*] don't do anything," he said dismissively. He didn't see it as cause for concern. "I think they're inflating their death threats," Jones said of his political opponents. "Moty's an ex–police chief. He can take care of himself. They overplayed the death threats to try to make their point that recall people were violent." In fact, Jones said indignantly, it was Moty who needed to answer for his behavior. The now-deposed supervisor had, Jones argued, "a long history of being a bully, being arrogant, being a jerk, being a womanizer."

After *The Red White and Blueprint* website put up a short video edited to make it look as if Moty, newly elected as chairman of the board of supervisors, was shouting randomly at constituents, smirking at them as he silenced them—in reality, he was telling people who refused to stop talking, albeit telling them in a particularly brusque, undiplomatic manner, that their allotted three minutes of comment time were up—the comments section lit up with invective from people not just in Shasta but around the country and overseas. "He needs a dirt nap," one person posted, which apparently meant that Moty should be killed and buried. "Somebody needs a good ole cow tromping," wrote another. A woman asserted that "he won't get away with that attitude when he's before Jesus. He'll be on his knees begging for 45 minutes more." A punctuation-challenged commenter mused, "I wonder if he'll still be smiling when there's two hundred men and women in his face ready to pluck his feathers he's definitely a pedophile is he Biden's brother." Another announced, "I'm pretty sure he's not expecting a lynch mob. But I bet he's gonna get one." The comments piled up. "Time to bring back the old 'TAR and FEATHERs'!!!" "A reckoning is coming, soon hopefully! Time to dust off the old guillotine!" "Some will die a horrible death and they will see there [*sic*] wrong doings before they die."

It was as if under the austere pandemic conditions, a collective madness had been unleashed, a maleficent collective id let loose on the internet.

Karen Ramstrom was also rewarded with numerous death threats, was doxxed by those who viewed her as a mortal enemy, and was eventually fired, no cause given, by an empowered far-right majority, led by Jones, on the county board of supervisors. When asked if

Ramstrom had brought the death threats on herself by her actions during the pandemic, Jones answered disingenuously: "Well, I guess you'd have to ask the people who were upset with her." And would he condemn the death threats? "Oh, sure," he said breezily, his condemnation featherweight. "I don't like people that make threats. It's illegal." But then, once again, he couldn't resist downplaying the seriousness of the vitriol. "They rarely carry them out. I don't take them that seriously."

Chapter Eight

"IMA PLANT" AND THE RISE OF THE ELECTION DENIERS

THE NOVEMBER AFTER LEONARD MOTY WAS RECALLED, TWO MORE HARD-RIGHT CANDIDATES WERE elected to Shasta County's board of supervisors, giving them a solid majority. Depending on how Tim Garman voted, the hard-right contingent could muster either four votes or three, leaving Mary Rickert as the lone reliable moderate. In board meetings, Rickert's colleagues ostentatiously refused to ask her opinion. Frequently, she felt, they tolerated threats to her well-being. For the first time in her life, she was actively considering moving away from the county.

That same November, Authur Gorman, a local nurse with extreme hostility to the LGBTQ+ community and links to a galaxy of right-wing groups on social media, was elected to the county's board of education, which had overview responsibilities for the county's several school districts. Gorman had risen to local prominence with his relentless campaign against COVID vaccines, including his organizing of a student walkout against vaccine and mask mandates in the schools; his opposition to the teaching of "Critical Race Theory"—a university-level academic concept about the centrality of race in understanding America's history, but one that critics alleged, generally without solid evidence to back up their claims, was being shoved down the throats of young schoolkids; and his belief that sex education in schools was little more than an excuse to groom young children. On Facebook he circulated petitions with titles such as "I don't co-parent with the government." Among the groups he followed on the social media platform were the Libertarian Crusaders, Shasta County Protest Mandates, Moms for Liberty, and the John Birch Society.

Gorman didn't modify his language or his confrontational style once in office. On his county profile page he included a motivational saying from Martin Luther King Jr.: "The function of education is to teach one to think intensively and to think critically. Intelligence plus character—that is the goal of true education." In reality, however, he was a world away from the inclusive vision of MLK. On his Facebook page he posted memes mocking transgender people, including a photo of John Wayne and a young man in rainbow-colored clothing, tagged with the words "Somewhere between 1959 and 2023 things went terribly wrong." Next to it was a photograph of a T-shirt with the logo "Vote Democ" followed by a picture of a rat and the message "no borders, no walls, girls with balls." He mocked overseas aid and claimed that the American government was arming enemies abroad while seeking to disarm law-abiding Americans at home.

He posted a photo of a gun with the title "Know your gun parts" and every part labeled with "None of the government's business," and another photo, from Georgia Gun Owners, Inc., of two heavily armed young men and the words "You're hated. Train Like It." He reposted a video posted by "thatconspiracygirl" accusing Child Protective Services of trafficking in children.

At school board meetings, Gorman began picking fights with transgender parents, going out of his way to refer to them in public meetings by their birth-sex pronouns and posting deliberately confrontational Facebook messages about them. Other board members grew so irate at his behavior that they moved to censure him—a tactic that in the face of arguments that Gorman was simply exercising his free-speech rights, they ultimately didn't follow through on. At least some of his colleagues became convinced that he was more interested in pandering to his base than in shaping local education policy—that he was a performer playing to his supporters, who would come out to public meetings and bandy about allegations that the local libraries were inviting in drag queens for story hours and distributing "pornographic materials" to young children.

Gorman wasn't alone in his efforts to stamp the hard-right worldview on local education priorities. In the little town of Gateway, ten miles south of Redding, a takeover of the school board by a trio of religious hard-liners, Lindsay Haynes, Elias Haynes, and Cherrill Clifford, resulted, in quick succession, in the acrimonious firing of the superintendent and the attempted hiring in his place of a new superintendent who shared their beliefs. Clifford and the Hayneses wanted to remake the schools in their image—to promote the teaching of their version of Christianity, to oppose sex education, to end diversity curricula, to ban LGBTQ-themed books, and so on. A flurry of threatened lawsuits stopped the trio, yet even then their critics argued that they continued to violate California's Brown Act, which required open meetings, and that they were attempting to make significant hiring and firing decisions out of the public eye and without public comment. They voted to begin each meeting with a prayer—and they continued doing so despite receiving a letter from the Freedom from Religion Foundation requesting them to cease and desist the practice.

Hard-right supporters of the Gateway gang of three would routinely take to social media to denounce the teachers and parents and community members who disagreed with their policies as "libtards," triggering, in response, huge school-board–meeting turnouts by those opposed to Gateway's lurch rightward. By the winter of 2023, board meetings in the county had degenerated into hours-long shouting matches, and a coalition of irate residents and educators had grown so frustrated with the process that they were planning how to launch a recall campaign against the Christian nationalist majority.

True, the Far Right wasn't uniformly successful in Shasta in 2022. Its candidates failed to dislodge the registrar for elections, the district attorney, and several other prominent Shasta County officials during the 2022 primary season. But at the board of supervisors level, the newly emboldened conservative majority continued to consolidate its power.

Fifty-four-year-old Chris Kelstrom, who at six feet four stood out in a crowd, was one of the two newly elected supervisors. Like most conservatives in town, he had a concealed-weapons permit. He had worked as a grocery store manager for many years, then as a bread delivery driver for more than a decade. Throughout, he was getting more and more disenchanted with local and state government. He didn't like the fact that the state was building windmills in the county over local landowners' objections and that most local logging jobs had disappeared in the wake of state restrictions on the industry. He didn't trust the integrity of the voter rolls, had seen data purporting to show that numerous people had registered to vote with the dubious name of "Ima Plant," and, notwithstanding his own electoral victory, was convinced that fraud ran rampant. Kelstrom particularly didn't like the lockdowns and virtual meetings that accompanied COVID. He felt that COVID relief money had been "laundered" through the Redding Chamber of Commerce to fund Moty's efforts to beat back the recall.

Kelstrom wasn't wrong that four or five voters were registered under the name "Ima Plant." But he *was* wrong about the motives. It was, the elections clerk explained, a practice carried out by elections offices around the state: in California, businesses—or scam artists— are not allowed to use voter-registration rolls to mail out adverts and other commercial lures. To monitor this, elections offices would set up dummy voter registrations to see if they served as bait to draw in hucksters and their mailings. "Having those records use the office as a mailing address allows us to know when the file is used for commercial purposes," Shasta County registrar and county clerk Cathy Darling Allen explained. "We have referred at least one case to the Secretary of State fraud division as a result." In Shasta County, four of the five election districts had an "Ima Plant" registered, one with the middle initial A, another with S, a third with R, and a fourth with no middle initial. Come election time, the ballots would be mailed to the local elections offices and would be left unopened. Put simply, nobody was turning in filled-in ballots under the auspices of "Ima Plant." But in the heady world of conspiracy-mongering, where one rumor begets the next and one raging social media post gets reposted and reposted again until it acquires the imprimatur of truth, Kelstrom had become convinced that the Ima Plant voter registrations were the spear tip of a much broader assault on the integrity of the county's elections system. And many of the county's residents believed him.

In 2016 Donald Trump won Shasta County with 63.9 percent of the vote. In 2020, after months of COVID lockdowns and, in reaction, frequently armed citizen protests against those lockdowns, the MAGA-meister upped his share of the vote to 65.4 percent. By early 2022, more than a year after Trump's November 2020 defeat in the presidential election, as Shasta's voters prepared to send Leonard Moty packing, much of the county was in full thrall to election denialism.

———————

Eight months after Moty was kicked off the board of supervisors, the hysteria around purported endemic fraud committed by Democrats, RINOs, and other ne'er-do-wells was amplified when one of the country's leading voices challenging the legitimacy of the 2020 election results, the Ohio math teacher Doug Frank, who had long worked as a teacher at a school for exceptionally gifted children in Cincinnati, was invited into Redding by some of the supervisors to whip up the crowds. Frank, whom a National Public Radio investigation found had spoken at 138 events in 29 states in the period between January 6, 2021, and June 30, 2022 (he claimed that the number was more like 300 speeches, with a cumulative audience of 100,000), and whose speeches the John Birch Society advertised on Facebook, was a flamboyant man, bald, bespectacled, with sartorial taste running to colorful bow ties. This day, for his Shasta debut, he chose one with a Stars and Stripes design.

Frank was passionate about his findings. He was a true believer, regarding himself as being on a one-man mission to clean up a system that he had concluded was facilitating fraud—and thus the disenfranchisement of real, legitimate voters—on an epic scale. He was hell-bent on building up support for his findings, much as previous generations of John Birch speakers had traveled from one town to the next, authoritatively, in their mind conclusively, showing just how and why the US government had supposedly become riddled with agents of the international Communist conspiracy or just how and why the fluoridation of water was a plot to mind-control Americans. Like earlier generations of John Birchers, such as the organization's founder, Robert Welch, who accused both Presidents Truman and Eisenhower of being Communist sympathizers, he spun a conspiracists' web with extraordinary ease and fluency.

The math teacher arrived in town with the force of a tornado, kicking up the political dust first at a board of supervisors morning meeting, presided over by Jones, where Frank gave what was supposed to be a three-minute presentation but that, when prompted by a slew of questions from Jones, ended up lasting more than twenty minutes. He had, he announced, as he read through charts and graphs on his silver-colored laptop, been anxious to meet people in Shasta ever since he had "learned there was a group of active patriots" in the area; he was hoping that he could "coach" them on "real, actionable election fraud. Fraud they can take to their sheriff, elections officials, and local courts. . . . Local citizens will bring to you hundreds of cases of fraud, documented frauds." He turned and addressed the supervisors solicitously: "I don't see you as the enemy; I see you as our most important allies. Once we prove to you there is fraud, then you're going to have to do something about it."

It was a modus operandi that Frank had perfected over the previous months. He would trawl through local elections records, pinpoint what he saw as inaccuracies in the voter rolls—systemic inaccuracies that, somehow, all the elections clerks and other officials had missed—do some back-of-the-envelope calculations ostensibly showing there were large numbers of dead people or out-of-towners voting, and then present a bundle of information to the local sheriffs and political leaders. Those officials, often unschooled in the minutiae of how voter rolls were compiled, frequently took all of Frank's claims at face value. When most of the mainstream media ignored his findings—or conducted their own research, which debunked the notion of a mass conspiracy to commit voter fraud—Frank simply doubled down. "The rolls are full of people who aren't real voters," he insisted. "Twenty to twenty-five percent. Thirty percent in some places." It was, he argued, not simply a result of incompetence or of the slow pace at which voter rolls were updated; rather, it was malicious. "It's systemic fraud. The system enables people to cheat." It was, he said, a problem that transcended red and blue states. He had found that the red state of Kentucky's voter rolls were utterly riddled with errors; similarly, he had found that deep-blue states such as Oregon and California also suffered from "very dirty" rolls. "They don't clean them. When people die, they remain on the rolls."

For Cathy Darling Allen, this represented a fundamental mis-understanding of how voter rolls work. California, like other states, the Shasta County clerk explained, had three categories of voters: "active" voters who vote on a regular basis and thus are automatically enrolled on the voter rolls and in California's case are sent ballots in the mail; "inactive" voters, who haven't voted in recent elections and haven't accepted ballots delivered by the postal service; and "canceled" voters, who have moved out of state or who, according to the county or state public health departments, have died. Add all those three categories together, and, yes, it was possible that voter rolls seemed abnormally large. But, she stressed, the canceled voters couldn't vote, and the inactive voters had to prove to their local elections office that they were indeed residents in order to be reinstated as active voters and thus be able to vote again. In Allen's office, there was a full-time worker whose sole duty was to work on maintaining the voter-registration rolls. That employee received information from the post office when people filed a change-of-address form, from the DMV when they registered to vote upon receiving or renewing their driver's license, from the public health department, and so on. If the voter rolls really were bloated by upward of 20 percent, Allen said, it would have been discovered in short order and remedied.

Kim Alexander, president and founder of the Sacramento-based California Voter Foundation, was even more scathing. Alexander had worked on election issues for more than thirty years, twenty-five of which had been spent studying the ins and outs of voting technology. She was one of the country's foremost experts in how elections systems and voter-registration records worked. When she heard Frank's allegations, red flags went up. Yes, California had more "inactive" voters than many other states, but that was because it had strict laws, designed to protect voters, that limited the ability of the state or of counties to purge the voter rolls. Therefore, when people stopped voting, rather than being scrubbed from the lists they were merely listed as "inactive." But that didn't mean that all those inactive voters were illegally receiving ballots or that other people were nefariously filling in those ballots in their names. Yes, she acknowledged, if a person moved without telling the elections office of the county in which they had previously resided, it was possible that they might receive a ballot at more than one location; but were they to fill multiple ballots in, they would be committing fraud and perjury, and would be exposing themselves to significant sanction. *Did it ever happen?* Possibly. *Did it happen on the system-wide scale that Frank said was occurring, at a level large enough to swing elections in county after county and in state after state?* Absolutely not. "Just because the system isn't perfect isn't evidence there is fraud," she insisted. "It's evidence there is a *risk* of fraud. And there's a big difference. It doesn't mean people are voting in multiple places in an election."

But the push-back from elections officials and voting-systems experts didn't carry water with the Ohioan. He was convinced that with his data on voter rolls and his information on the vulnerability of electronic voting systems, with his discovery of secret algorithms

ostensibly used to rig elections, he was in a fight for America's survival. He was adamant that if political leaders didn't respond to his
arguments, he would build a movement, an unstoppable ground-
swell of citizen outrage, to take them down. "If we bring the fraud
and they're not willing to do anything, wc start campaigning
against them," he explained. "We'll sue them for their surety bonds
and picket them at their homes." His testimony had, he estimated,
led to political leaders being picketed in at least twenty counties
around the country. "[Critics] like to criticize the methodology, but
nobody talks about the evidence I bring forward. The statistics are
the smoke that leads to the fire. I actually go into counties, teach
people to find actual fraud, get it validated by the sheriff, and that
allows them to go to their leadership and say they don't want to use
that system [electronic voting machines] anymore because it disem-
powers us."

Frank's critics weren't convinced. Although the Ohioan shied
away from pointing his finger at individual election workers, to
believe in the level of voter-roll manipulation that he was positing in
his speeches clearly suggested human agency. Yet such a coordinated
assault on the voting process was hard to fathom: in a decentralized
system such as America's, where not only each state had its own rules
and regulations surrounding voting, but each county within each
state bought its own vote-counting machines and county officials
presided over the vote count, the idea of a meta-conspiracy somehow
swamping the entire country made precious little sense. It implied a
level of coordination over years among hundreds, if not thousands,
of local elections officials, all in the shadows, all without error, that
implied almost superhuman powers. To believe in such a coordinated conspiracy, Justin Grimmer, a political science professor who
divided his time between Stanford University and the Hoover Institute, where he studied—and worked to debunk—election conspiracy
theories, involved a vast leap of faith, an assumption that "a network

of unnamed elites" was able to shamelessly pull the strings in every county in every state in the country.

In Shasta County, however, despite Grimmer repeatedly emailing the supervisors to warn them that he believed the Ohioan was peddling bad information, Frank needn't have worried about how the commissioners would receive him. With Jones and his allies in charge, it was, after all, a place primed to believe that Trump had had the 2020 election stolen right out from under him. When Grimmer contacted Jones about his concerns, Jones emailed back, "Yore [*sic*] flawed. Get some help."

Frank's presentation to the commissioners was compelling, his command of data and of detail impressive. He had his sales pitch down pat, and for a conservative audience, primed by an ex-president to believe in conspiracies aimed at rendering their votes meaningless, it was a startlingly effective message. He talked authoritatively of California's electoral machinery as "being one of the most vulnerable in the country." He had, he said, studied every precinct in California—"a lot of work, that was a month of my life"—and found elections were in reality being "centrally controlled at the state level, not at the county level." He argued that Shasta was "definitely regulated down to the precinct level" and talked about anomalies in his graphs that showed "a symptom of manipulation." He told his audience, in his authoritative, rat-a-tat professorial voice, that "there was a lot of hacking." And he claimed that he carried a sensor with him that would allow him to check whether voting machines were illicitly connected to the internet but that when he offered elections clerks his services, they refused to let him near the machines.

Jones intervened with softball questions every few minutes. He said that he had "a feeling, it's just a feeling . . . I never had this feeling years ago, it's a feeling I've had more recently, along with half the population of the entire country," that elections were no longer free and fair. Based on this hunch, he asked the so-called expert, how could trust be restored in the system? Frank answered with more authoritative pronouncements. "Many of them know they have fraud," he said of local elections officials, "but they're afraid to speak out. . . . If you step out, the whole infrastructure comes down on you." In the audience, one could hear rumblings of dismay. Their hunches were right, the scientist was telling them: things had indeed gone squirrelly.

Mary Rickert, the one board of supervisors member to approach Frank with even a whiff of cynicism, finally got a word in. She noted that she'd been Googling Frank during his presentation and found a statement by Justin Grimmer arguing that Frank's ideas were beyond the pale and lent themselves to conspiracy theorists. "To be fair and balanced, not everyone in this country is supporting you," Rickert concluded dryly.

It was too much for Jones. Unable to sit silently as Frank's work, his proof-positive that Trump had had the election yanked out from under him, was disparaged, he jumped in. "And we know that Google is 100 percent accurate," he said, his voice dripping with sarcasm, as if Google had literally conjured up this Stanford counter-"expert" out of thin air. The audience, filled with Jones's supporters, began whooping and laughing. *Atta boy, Jones!* they seemed to be saying. *You sure showed her!*

The video of the meeting, posted on Rumble, as well as Jones's shutting down of Rickert, all meticulously chronicled by Doni Chamberlain in *A News Café*, prompted one reader from the neighboring county of Tehama to comment pithily: "Your board of supervisors have broken the crazy meter. It's amazing that any actual business of the county is taken care of at these meetings. Tehama's board is frustrating and mean, but don't hold a candle to the shitnado to the north."

That evening Doug Frank continued to peddle his pseudo-statistical wares, this time in a sell-out, twenty-dollar-a-ticket lecture at a local church. Among his claims that night was that "eight US states have more people on the voter rolls than they had voting age people," an assertion that voting-rights scholars such as Kim Alexander were quick to dismiss as nonsense. The Ohioan also argued that increased numbers of actual votes cast were similar proof of machine totals being tampered with.

Frank's ideas, said Justin Grimmer, revolved around the idea of "a network of unnamed elites" manipulating vote totals around the country. "It's all totally ridiculous, bunk. But he's an incredible organizer. He gives these talks, then recruits people to knock on doors."

As Grimmer understood it, Frank was relying on findings that deliberately conflated active voters with inactive or canceled voters—in some states, the preferred label was "deactivated" voters. As Cathy Darling Allen had also pointed out, that was disingenuous, to say the least. In Wisconsin, for example, the House Republicans had, after the 2020 election, hired a onetime State Supreme Court justice to compile a report on the state's voter-registration system. He had come back with findings that Wisconsin, a state with roughly 4.5 million eligible voters, had more than 7 million names on its voter rolls. On the surface, of course, that was horrifying, grist to every conspiracist's mill. In reality, however, upward of 3 million of those voters were listed as being either "inactive" or "deactivated." In short, they weren't voting, and they couldn't vote; their names were simply part of the paper trail that all states kept so that they had good statistical records of who had voted, who was still voting, who was alive, and who was dead. To Frank and other election conspiracists, however, this exercise in record keeping was evidence of a dastardly plot, continental in scale, traitorous in its implications, to flood elections with illegitimate ballots. It was a plot that, in Frank's telling, was made even worse by the hacking of vote-counting machines to tip the scales even further against candidates such as Donald J. Trump.

––––

In Mesa County, Colorado, a local county clerk named Tina Peters had also become convinced that voting machines had been compromised. In May 2021, she met with Frank in her office to get a briefing from him on how he thought the 2020 election had been stolen, and a month later she allegedly helped an activist copy sensitive election files—thus putting her on the FBI radar. When Bureau agents dug into the case, Frank's name came up, as did that of My Pillow CEO Mike Lindell. More than a year later, in September 2022, when searching for evidence in the case the FBI seized the cell phones of both Frank and Lindell, although neither was charged in the case.

None of that was enough to discredit Doug Frank and his arguments among those in Shasta who had decided that the elections weren't legitimate. In the aftermath of Frank's speech, right-wing vigilantes wearing orange vests and "voter taskforce" badges could be found banging on doors in Shasta County and asking residents about their voting history in a nefarious effort to root out supposedly rampant electoral fraud, presumably among the one-third of the electorate who *didn't* cast their ballots for Donald Trump when presented with the opportunity to do so. Armed men and women even forced their way into the electoral count during the primaries on the night of June 7, 2022, as "observers," setting off a flurry of concern among elections officials and ordinary citizens in the county. "I certainly had unpleasant interactions with folk," registrar of voters and county clerk Cathy Darling Allen recalled of this period. "They came in and made poll workers feel very unsafe. The physical presence and the intimidatory attitudes. Three different people were live-streaming from my office on the night of June 7th, 2022."

In 2022 the county clerk had beaten back a primary challenge from a far-right opponent. Since then, she had been focused on simply trying to keep the electoral system functioning in the face of escalating attacks from MAGA proponents and personal threats leveled against election workers. "We are the moderators," she explained. "Referees are the moderators for any sports match. That's how it works. We're accustomed to some hotheadedness, but what's happened in our community in the last few years. . . ." She stopped and tried to gather her thoughts. "The idea that any person would [have to] feel grateful that they're *not* afraid at work, it's an interesting thing. There are many of us who are still very surprised and dismayed that this seems to be our new normal."

Chapter Nine

CHAOS

For Shasta County's ascendant chaos-mongers, suspicion of the electoral process was but one of their gripes. Other issues also got under Chris Kelstrom's skin: he intensely disliked the direction that California's schools were heading in. "The boys and girls bathrooms thing is not very popular here. They recently put tampon machines in the boys' bathrooms," he alleged. He was horrified by what he saw as the spread of "Critical Race Theory" into the classrooms. And he was dismayed by the media criticism leveled at militia groups and at street-fighting outfits such as the Proud Boys. From what he had seen, the Proud Boys, in taking the battle to Antifa, were doing a damn fine job. Moreover, he supported them in their efforts to prevent Confederate and other statues from being torn down. "They are proud of their country," he asserted, "proud of the history of their country." Kelstrom was also generally infuriated by the liberal arc of California politics, and he had long ago decided to support the secessionist movement that favored carving out a new, conservative State of Jefferson from California's rural north. "We love where we live," he explained tersely. "We don't like the state we live in."

Finally, in 2022, wanting to do his local part in clearing the swamp, Kelstrom ran for and won a seat on the board of supervisors.

In that same election, in one small-town school district after another in the county, "parents' choice" advocates, opposed to mask and vaccine mandates, hostile to lockdowns, and dismayed at what they saw as "woke" curricula on race, gender, and other lightning-rod issues, swept into power. They were, Kelstrom enthused, "conservative patriots" taking back control of their children's destiny from an out-of-control liberal elite. Others were less enthusiastic. For Jessica French, who worked for a nonprofit cultural-exchange program bringing teens from around the world to study in the Shasta region, the new school board members were hitting the ground running. They were making "crazy, outlandish decisions very quickly."

Kelstrom's "conservative patriots" were backed by moms such as Patty Plumb, an ordained minister at a church that had refused to shut its doors during the lockdown and instead had gone underground, its members meeting for services in private homes. Over the years of the pandemic, Plumb had become somewhat obsessed with the urgency of reclaiming the political system, from the most mundane of local positions on up to the most powerful, for those who resisted what she saw as tyrannical pandemic-era restrictions. She would regularly go out and canvass communities, collect petitions, give public speeches, and urge her audiences to "follow the money" and see in whose pockets all the COVID dollars had ended up.

Plumb had begun reading voraciously, as well as watching right-wing documentaries by Dinesh D'Souza, *Fox News* host Peter Hudspeth, and others on everything from COVID vaccines to electoral fraud, and thinking through the ways that the schools and the political system more generally had let her children down.

Plumb was in many ways a dyed-in-the-wool conservative, yet her politics couldn't simply be reduced to labeling her as being monolithically right-wing: a longtime fan of the German dissident priest Dietrich Bonhoeffer, who had resisted Nazi rule and ultimately paid for his resistance with his life, Plumb viewed herself as a fighter for individuals' rights. She had convinced herself that the American political elites, the schools, and the medical establishment had all thrown in their lot with deeply authoritarian thinking, that they were all sacrificing the rights of the individual for the needs of their collective, and thus merited resistance. In another world or another time, had she come of age in a different environment, had she not been so anchored by a particularly conservative strain of Christianity, Plumb's innate suspicions of authority might have taken her down a very different path—her rhetoric had more than a passing similarity to that of various anarchist groupings on the left. Had she been a generation older, and had the critiques she was exposed to been new left instead of alt-right, she might even have found herself a sympathizer of the Black Panthers or of Students for a Democratic Society. There was, in much of Plumb's rhetoric, as with that of Zapata and others who were reshaping Shasta in their hard-right image, a stick-it-to-the-Man quality, a delight in pushing the boundaries of the politically palatable, that 1960s-era rebels such as Abbie Hoffman would have understood all too well.

"Opening a can of worms suddenly became a ball of snakes," Plumb explained somewhat cryptically, as she pondered how the public health emergency affected ordinary people. The more she thought about the political situation in 2020 and 2021, the angrier she got. She found the COVID pandemic to be deeply "suspicious," viewing it as a "circus" that was used by political elites to undermine the Constitution. She was still "pulling the thread on that sweater" about whether or not the virus was even real. Many people, when they crunched the numbers, had concluded that deaths were being attributed to the new virus that actually had a variety of different causes—this was a common complaint heard in the circles that Woody Clendenen, Carlos Zapata, and others ran in. Either way, the social-distancing rules were, Plumb argued, so onerous that "you can't even get together and sing in church because you might spit on somebody." Plumb, her husband, Ronald, and their friends began researching—usually on websites and via those documentaries that were tailored to the Hard Right—and the more they researched, the more they became convinced that the whole thing was being foisted on them by political leaders who in theory had been duly elected but in practice had actually been "selected" by elites such as George Soros, hot to trot to use voter fraud to secure their nefarious ends. This endemic voter fraud had, she concluded as a result of her readings, been going on for decades, and a blind eye was turned to it by election officials such as County Clerk Cathy Darling Allen, who Plumb believed had received a nearly $50,000-per-year pay raise as an incentive to help manipulate district boundaries to try to protect Moty's position. She feared that vaccines, supported by the uncritical likes of Moty and Rickert, were leading to an epidemic of deaths and talked of embalmers and coroners whom she knew who were "seeing things they've never seen before—in terms of blood clotting, because of the vaccines apparently."

Plumb was also a firm believer in the fundamentalist "Seven Mountain Mandate." Capture all seven commanding heights of society (family, church, education, government, business and the economy, the media, and arts and entertainment), Dominionists believed, and you could trigger the end-times or, at the very least, gain control over your government and your community. Unfortunately, she had discovered, Karl Marx had beaten them to it, targeting all seven of those mountains back in 1848, the year of workers' revolts and of the publishing of the *Communist Manifesto*, and had "done a pretty good job of taking over, causing damage to families, corrupting government and education curricula in schools." Ever since then, the Marxists had been in the driver's seat when it came to educating America's children. "We just didn't realize it; we'd been asleep. Oh my gosh, Karl Marx was addressing the Seven Mountains back in the day! Who knew?!"

Finally, the COVID pandemic had exposed all of this, and as a result the people had risen up in revolt. "The people are making the changes," Plumb claimed. "We didn't realize how bad it's been for so long. Now we've passed the point of no return." In her mind, in liberating the school boards they were performing a divine mission similar to the one carried out by the brave anti-Nazi priest Bonhoeffer eighty years before.

———

By early 2023, Patrick Jones, the new board chair—who spent much of each workday serving as general manager at his brother Marshall's Jones Fort, a sprawling gun mart in a low-end strip mall a couple miles from the county building, which had been in the Jones family since the early 1970s and in which Jones says he first did chores as a four-year-old—was attempting to declare Shasta a "Second Amendment Sanctuary County." The idea was to make county employees swear an oath specifically to defend the Second Amendment and to expand local open-carry ordinances. His efforts included helping raise money for a lawsuit challenging the state of California's open-carry restrictions. The new board was committing the county to a multi-hundred-million-dollar project to build a huge new county jail, despite the fact it struggled to staff its existing jail and two of the four floors of the facility were currently closed. To make matters worse, the county had fired the original architects for a sally port connecting the jail and courthouse and had replaced them with another company, whose bid was said by Rickert to be favored by Jones, despite the fact that its design would likely cost millions of dollars more than the original proposal would. "I've been here my entire life, I've been in county government twenty-seven years, and I've never seen it like this," Eric Magrini, the salt-and-pepper-haired onetime sheriff and now assistant county executive officer, said angrily.

The new board of supervisors had also set about banning Dominion voting machines. These machines, used by many counties around the United States, had become the target of election deniers' wrath, with Trump, Mike Lindell, and others arguing that they were inherently unreliable and prone to being hacked. The board's move garnered praise in February 2023 from Trump, Steve Bannon, and Lindell, the last of whom checked into a late February board meeting via cell phone after being wooed by Supervisor Kevin Crye. Lindell promised to help defray the legal expenses should the county be sued by the state. Darling Allen, the county registrar, calculated that the move would ultimately cost Shasta's taxpayers several million dollars. "It's a spectacularly ill-advised decision," she said of the county's decision to change voting systems in the immediate run-up to a presidential election.

The board's upending of the status quo hadn't stopped with the Dominion decision. On an array of different fronts, Jones and his colleagues had quickly made their mark. In early May 2022 the majority had fired Dr. Ramstrom and had dismissed without cause the director of the Department of Housing and Community Action Programs.

That majority was, it seemed clear, looking to remake the entire county in the image of Carlos Zapata's *The Red White and Blueprint*, which had ultimately generated several hours' worth of slickly produced local "documentaries" that were available to viewers on YouTube and then later on Amazon Prime, as well as an ongoing series of podcasts—at which groups of hard-right talking heads sat around a table, their guns frequently placed in front of them for effect, and talked revolution for a half hour at a time. In episode 1, titled "We the People," a folksy Patrick Jones is featured sitting on the steps of the county offices and explaining what had happened since the revolt against pandemic restrictions. "Correction needed to happen, and that's what we did," he says. His words cut out, and a song starts playing. "There is a heaven," the performer sings. On the screen, a forest of US flags flutters breezily. The documentary cuts to Zapata and his viral board of supervisors tirade against masks and lockdowns and social distancing. "It's not going to be peaceful much longer . . . good citizens are going to turn to real concerned and revolutionary citizens real soon." The camera cuts afresh to Zapata, this time donning a cowboy hat, narrating this apex moment in his life. "I was born to fight," he tells the audience. "I love fighting. There's nothing I love more than a good fight. . . . If punching the occasional person in the face to move the ball forward is what I have to do, then I'm going to have to do that." The episode mixes threats with kitsch, fury with bromides about nationalism and the American spirit. "Some of us have stood up in this fight and kept our businesses open," the ex-marine explains, discussing the local opposition to lockdowns. "We refused to give up on our hopes and dreams. We simply chose to be American. It is this pioneer spirit that won the West." And true to the American spirit they admired, Zapata and his crew hawked T-shirts and baseball caps, the former starting at $21.35 and ranging up to $50, the latter a cool $30.

By 2023, there was an omnipresent background hum of extremism and a growing presence both of disinformation and of paranoia in everyday life. Most residents weren't political fanatics, but too many had chosen to sit this fight out, and with too few people voting in local elections to counter the militias, the QAnoners, the Christian nationalists, and the Second Amendment absolutists, those extremists were now running the show.

the Christian nationalists, and the Second Amendment absolutists, those extremists were now running the show.

Back before COVID, Mary Rickert had taken great joy in bringing her young grandchildren with her to the board meetings. It was, she thought, democracy in action, a way to give the children a real-life lesson in civics. Now, however, she was terrified of letting them anywhere near a board meeting, panicked that they might hear all the coarse insults leveled at their grandmother or—God forbid—might even see someone try to physically attack her. "It's a constant barrage of intimidation," Rickert explained, sitting in her office in the county building. "It's wearing. It's hard on staff. We've lost a lot of employees. Our county counsel is leaving in April [2023]. For three years, it's just been nothing but insanity. I've had people standing in our driveway, stalking our place. It's not January 6th; it's a different version of it—except they're succeeding. I don't understand why someone hasn't stepped in—the attorney general's office—to say this has gotten out of hand. They've intimidated and bullied enough that people are afraid enough that they can do anything they want. It's pretty unsettling." When Rickert went to a local supermarket or restaurant, the first thing she did was to glance quickly around at all the customers. It wasn't exactly that she was expecting trouble—in fact, people often came up to her to tell her to keep up the good fight—it was just that you never knew anymore: "I've had enough threats. I'm trying to be prudent."

Rickert's brother, a psychologist, was convinced that the board of supervisors member was suffering from PTSD. A clinician friend of hers was also convinced. When she talked to military veterans about what she had undergone since 2020 and how her mind and body were reacting to the ongoing stream of threats, they agreed. On a near-nightly basis she had nightmares, and often she would wake up screaming. In her sleep she saw attackers prowling on the edge of her property. She couldn't shake the feeling that her county had lost itself in extremism; moreover, she couldn't see a way out of this maze. Sure, it was possible that moderates would regain the initiative electorally, but the venom had been unleashed, the routinization of physical threats, the sense of menace: "It's very disturbing. It's a movement that is having far-reaching and long-term consequences, and teaching our young people all the wrong values," Rickert said as she drove around her ranch one sunny afternoon in May 2023. "That really bothers me a lot."

Not surprisingly, Chairman Jones disagreed with Rickert's thoughts on the state of the county. "You have to understand *real* northern California," he explained. "These are smaller, conservative counties. People are conservative, self-reliant; we believe in strict constitutional government. Over the last two years, a lot of people rose up and said they're tired of what's happening in local government. That's what's happening in Shasta County today. It's a course correction. It's long overdue." In other words, *keep going—there's nothing to see here.*

But, in fact, there *was* plenty to see in Shasta.

By the spring of 2023, a growing number of Shasta's residents were beginning to think their county had jumped the shark. Despite Shasta's seemingly unstoppable slide rightward, on the ground, especially in the city of Redding, the antics of the board of supervisors had led to a growing chorus of unease. A number of residents banded together to form a group that they called Shasta County Citizens for Stable Government and—after documenting how Supervisor Kevin Crye, who represented the most liberal (or rather least conservative) district in the county, had used what they claimed were taxpayer dollars to travel to meet with Mike Lindell in Minnesota—launched a recall campaign against the supervisor. They were infuriated that he had voted with the majority to scrap the Dominion voting machines contract at a likely cost to Shasta of millions of dollars. They were enraged, too, by the fact that he had then compounded the insult of meeting with Lindell by accepting his promise that he would personally pony up the cash to defend the county in the lawsuits that seemed all but certain to follow. Throughout that spring, as the recall effort picked up steam, Crye would appear on podcasts with Lindell and other conservative commentators, ratcheting up the rhetoric on stolen elections and compromised voting systems, stressing his bona fides as the sort of supervisor that Jones's *real* northern Californians could trust; he would barnstorm northern California's swath of conservative rural counties, hopscotching from one event to the next, fund-raising against the recall movement against him that, he claimed, was being paid for by liberal Bay Area types and backed by Governor Newsom. The governor was, in Crye's opinion, champing at the bit to appoint a liberal replacement were Crye to be pushed out, this despite the recall campaign having sent a letter to Newsom stating that they preferred an election to replace the supervisor rather than a gubernatorial appointment.

The recall's proponents were realists. They knew that even if their effort succeeded, even if they could raise thousands of signatures in forty days, it wouldn't, of itself, undo the far-right tilt of county politics. Their hope was that it might at least put the brakes on the continued lurch into conspiracist thinking and policies. "We've been reaching out to as many of our Republican and independent friends as we can," said attorney Jeff Gorder, one of the architects of the new good-governance organization. "Ideology is not an issue here. It's about poor decision making, bad management, wasting money. Highly qualified people are leaving county government." Above all, Gorder argued, it was about restoring a sense of local dignity. He was tired of hearing news reports about Shasta County that made it sound like "we're just the crazy uncle up here in northern California."

Crye responded to the notice of recall by putting out a statement that he was elected "fairly and freely." This was grist to his opponents' mill. The recall committee immediately put out a gleeful retort: "We agree. That is why it was so irresponsible of Supervisor Crye to put his name to the destruction of the very voting system that provided that free and fair election. Rather than support the voting system that has proven to be reliable, trustworthy, and cost-effective, Supervisor Crye instead chose to support an untested, extremely costly, and error-prone hand-count voting system promoted by a discredited pitchman."

More than a year after Karen Ramstrom had been fired, the top public health job in the county still remained open. In the late spring of 2023 the county finally seemed near to hiring a replacement for Ramstrom—it had been more than four hundred days since she was fired, and in the meantime several potential replacements had withdrawn their applications once they did a bit of internet research and realized how hostile the county was to the work of public health officials. With the fentanyl epidemic running rampant and the health woes associated with high rates of poverty on the increase, Shasta's public health system was rudderless. "It's a real shame," noted Roxanne Burke, who had worked with the county's health and human services administration for the better part of three decades. "There are a lot of health issues, beyond COVID, affecting this county. I worry for the clients we serve, who are some of the most vulnerable, marginalized in our community and rely on us for food, housing, employment, mental health services."

The holes were everywhere. The county CEO, Matt Pontes, had been forced out, and the man the conservative majority had hoped to bring in to replace him had, after the board members perused the results of a background check, been deemed unsuitable for the job.

The county attorney had quit after a series of increasingly acrimonious interactions with board members about, for example, whether it was constitutional to force all employees, per Jones's initiative, to swear an oath specifically to the Second Amendment. And his deputy, who replaced him, was, according to Rickert, growing increasingly nervous about the actions of the board. Every day, Rickert said, she worried that he would jump ship. Her worries were merited: later on, he did indeed choose to depart. So, too, did those who briefly followed in his footsteps.

In April roughly a thousand unionized county employees, members of the United Public Employees of California, which represented many of the lowest-paid county staff, went on strike after the board's majority failed to come up with adequate cost-of-living pay increases. That spring, they could be seen picketing the county offices in Redding, holding up placards denouncing Jones for being unable to do the basic math that would allow the board to increase salaries to reflect cost-of-living increases caused by inflation.

Meanwhile, Chairman Jones was working on getting his colleagues on the board to approve a huge outdoor gun range on 155 acres of scrubby land, reachable only by a particularly bone-jolting, unpaved road, that he owned on the outskirts of Anderson, complete with a five-thousand-square-foot clubhouse. This struck many constituents as a blatant conflict of interest, given that Jones's family had owned a large gun store in town for half a century. Despite the fact that Jones presented the board a slickly produced, thick report designed to show how economically beneficial the range would be, local residents, worried about noise from the shooting, about increased risks of brush fires, and about stray bullets peppering nearby properties, protested vocally enough to convince the board to kick the vote on the range down the road. Jones hadn't given up on the idea, however. He was still hoping, Rickert believed, to bring the issue up for a vote later that year.

No matter how much they attempted to sanitize their beliefs, no matter how many times they accused the *mainstream media* of distorting their positions, in the end Jones, Zapata, and their Shasta County allies kept undermining their own efforts at appearing moderate.

Although Jones wanted the media to simply move on and ignore the goings-on in Shasta, it was hard to avoid the sense that things were askew, that *weird* was pervading the land on a daily basis. In March, according to Doni Chamberlain's reporting, Patty Plumb turned up at a board of supervisors meeting to discuss whether to remove Dominion voting machines from the county. The event turned into a free-for-all, with thirteen hours of angry back-and-forth. At one point, according to reports published in *A News Café*, Plumb could be heard shouting during a public comments period that her critics were "uncircumcised Philistines."

Deep into one of our conversations at his gun store, Jones, who proudly asserted that he never read newspapers, that they "aren't worth piss," and that he got his news mainly from "search engines I do use—won't name any names," started talking about LGBTQ+ rights. Prior to his election, the previous board had each year passed a symbolic resolution supporting gay rights. Jones said that under his chairmanship, those supportive resolutions would now stop: "Their lifestyle, I don't believe in that. I don't think it's acceptable." Civil rights in general were, it could be said, not exactly up his alley. "BLM is a form of racism," Jones opined. "Everybody should be treated equal and the same." It wasn't just BLM that he didn't like. "I don't believe in the NAACP," he explained. "Most people here didn't appreciate any of that."

That sour view of civil rights may have had something to do with how the weekly board of supervisors meeting unfolded later that spring, on the evening of May 30, when a member of the public, one Alex Bielecki, got up to make his comments.

Bielecki was bald and squat, with a trimmed white goatee and a green T-shirt. His face seemed to wear a perpetual snarl; there was nothing gentle or calm about his demeanor, nothing soothing in his tone of voice. At some point during his allotted three minutes, in which he rambled indignantly about tiny houses being built in the county—Bielecki had a reputation for coming to board meetings and making what Doni Chamberlain would describe as "unhinged, disjointed statements"—he went off on a racist jag. "I am not a fool; I am not a *nigger*," he shouted into his microphone. From the audience came an audible, collective gasp, an intake of breath as Bielecki's vile language hung like a stench over the crowd.

It would have been easy for Jones to intervene, to say something—*anything*—or in some other way to register his disapproval. He, for example, could have turned away in horror at the verbal diatribe, showing through his mannerisms that he had no time or patience for such bigotry. The week before, at a meeting of the Sacramento City Council, two and a half hours south of Redding, a local provocateur named Ryan Messano had spewed bilious anti-Semitic language around the room. Mayor Darrell Steinberg, himself Jewish, had pointedly turned his chair around so that he had his back to Messano and could refuse to acknowledge his presence. As soon as Messano's allotted time was up, the mayor shouted out words of contempt at him, told him in no uncertain terms that no one wanted to hear his ugly diatribes, and ordered him to leave the building pronto. Jones did none of this during the Bielecki incident. In fact, nothing in his demeanor suggested that he was particularly horrified by what he was hearing.

Into the moral void stepped Nathan Blaze, who by mid-2023 had emerged as something of the voice of conscience for many frustrated Shasta County residents. Sitting in the front row, Blaze began shouting at Bielecki. He told him to shut up. Not mincing his words, he called him a "racist piece of shit." He asked Jones to turn Bielecki's microphone off. Jones didn't. Bielecki gave as good as he got. He screamed back at Blaze, gave him the middle finger, dared Blaze to *make him* shut up. For a minute, it looked like the two men were about to come to blows. Jones continued to sit passively.

Later, after his colleagues Mary Rickert and Tim Garman made statements from the supervisors' platform against Bielecki's abhorrent behavior, the chairman would say that Bielecki had an absolute First Amendment right to say whatever he wanted. (Civil rights experts weren't impressed; in disputing this, they would subsequently roll out several provisions of the California penal code that limit the ability of a speaker to use offensive words in a public venue in a way likely to trigger a violent reaction.) When Blaze refused to stop heckling Bielecki, the chairman of the board—who in a previous meeting had, according to Doni Chamberlain's reporting, called Blaze out as a domestic terrorist—decided to use his powers of the gavel against him. Jones demanded that Blaze, the African American Air Force veteran-cum-provocateur, be silent, and when Blaze refused, he ordered a sheriff's deputy to remove him from the room. When that deputy told Jones he could not carry out the order, the supervisor then brought a private security guard into the fray. The guard was only too happy to escort Blaze from the premises. And Blaze, in turn, was only too happy to send a letter to the ACLU, the NAACP, and everyone else he could think of, protesting the county's treatment of him and threatening to bring a lawsuit against Jones.

Of course, it was all there on the internet for easy viewing. The chaos that now passed for Shasta County politics was yet again on vivid display.

———

Six weeks after Jones allowed Bielecki to go off on his racist tirade, on Thursday, July 6, two of Jones's colleagues, Kevin Crye and Chris

Kelstrom, attended the inaugural meeting of a new group, Citizens for Freedom (CFF).

The brainchild of Jesse Lane—who had acquired something of a reputation in Shasta County as a take-no-shit conservative—Citizens for Freedom was being established, its splashy social media announcement noted, to unify all the disparate far-right groups percolating around the county. The invite for that inaugural meeting called on self-described patriots, concerned citizens, and other conservatives to show up at the Cottonwood Community Center to strategize about how to consolidate their gains and how to make further inroads in Shasta County.

In their droves, conservatives answered. There was Woody Clendenen, Crye, and Kelstrom. (Patrick Jones didn't show up because California law prohibits a majority of a body of elected officials from attending an event in which political pressure will likely be put on those officials regarding their official business.) Lane, the convener of the group, was there. Mark Kent, a local accountant who was the host of a right-wing radio show on KCNR and who served as treasurer on the conservative political action committee known as the Water Users' Committee, was also there. In the past he had been known to go on angry social media tirades against progressive critics of the Jones-dominated board of supervisors. Blaze was, he wrote, an "out of work activist commie cook." All told, roughly two hundred people showed up at the little community center. There wasn't an empty seat in the house.

Because the event had been advertised on social media as open to anyone who identified as a patriot, a concerned citizen, or several other generic categories, Doni Chamberlain, publisher of *A News Café*, figured she had a perfect right to attend. She did, after all, consider herself a patriot and a concerned citizen. And she was pretty sure that the First Amendment was on her side.

The journalist, who had spent the last several years arousing the wrath of many of the people in this crowd, confidently walked through the doors of the community center and into the crowd, her cell phone dangling from a strap around her neck. She turned on the Facebook Live streaming function on her phone and, once she was sure the camera was recording, made her way to the back of the room, scouting out a place where she could stand, rest against the wall, and record the proceedings. It was the sort of mildly gutsy, in-your-face journalism that she had done year in, year out as she chronicled her county's slide rightward. Although she was used to verbal abuse, now, within moments of entering the room, she suddenly got that spidery feeling that things were different.

First, she recalled, Jesse Lane confronted her, accused her of trespassing, and shouted at her that she was a liar, that she published dishonest articles, that she was a horrible person, and that she needed to leave the meeting. Chamberlain refused; she told him that the invite had been generic, allowing anyone to attend, and that as a journalist she had a First Amendment right to be there and to cover a newsworthy event.

Instantly, it seemed, she was surrounded. People came at her from all directions, screaming abuse, getting in her face, blocking her camera, demanding that she leave. "It was like a receiving line of assholes coming up and berating me," Chamberlain remembered. Even had she wanted to bolt for the exits, she probably wouldn't have been able to. On all sides, there were infuriated Citizens for Freedom attendees, pressing in on her, getting in their two cents against this woman who had been a thorn in their sides for so long: "I was totally surrounded. I couldn't see. They put their hands in front of my face. I was a little nucleus, the hole in the middle of a donut. I thought it was so ridiculous—I couldn't believe a journalist could be detained like that. I made a break to the left, and they ran after me and scooted me off to the door. I guess at some level I must have been afraid, because I didn't push it. I felt myself going into this adaptive mode where you're under a huge trauma. I just kept trying to talk to them; I felt like I was a hostage negotiator."

She says that she heard a young woman, Rebecca Walker, calling 911, where the emergency dispatch operator took her statement that Chamberlain was trespassing at a private event and was assaulting attendees, and then routed her to the California Highway Patrol, which promised to send out some officers.

While the crowd waited for the CHP to arrive, the barracking continued. Finally, Mark Kent made a beeline for the journalist. He ordered her out, and then, Chamberlain subsequently alleged, he grabbed the neck strap on which hung her phone. Kent was a large man, on the heavy side and tall, and Chamberlain was a petite woman in her late sixties. It wasn't exactly an equal fight. He pulled at the strap violently, Chamberlain told the personal injury lawyers whom she consulted in the wake of the event—so violently that she was yanked up off the balls of her feet and onto her tiptoes, and suddenly the journalist felt like she was being strangled. The strap lacerated and twisted her neck. She felt a surge of pain and fear, and knew that for the first time in her career she was suffering physical injuries for her reporting.

Soon afterward, three CHP squad cars arrived, and four officers descended on Chamberlain. When she told them that she had a First Amendment right to be at the event and also alleged that she had been attacked, they insisted that it was a private meeting and that she was behaving like an uninvited guest at a wedding. In such a situation, one of the officers told her, if the gate-crasher refused the officers' friendly advice to leave voluntarily, the CHP would have no choice but to cart that unwelcome intruder off to jail.

Chamberlain reluctantly accepted that her time at the CFF event was over, and she allowed the officers to walk her out to her car, a brown Kia Sol. They stood there while she drove off—the journalist was shaking with sobs as she clutched the steering wheel—making sure that she wouldn't simply turn around and return a few minutes later. Woody Clendenen watched her go, then strutted back into the meeting room and grabbed a portable microphone: "Just to let you know, Doni Chamberlain has left the building." He might just as well have been Donald Trump at one of his mega-rallies, haranguing the journalists who were penned into small areas off to the side as enemies of the people. The crowd erupted in cheers.

Over the coming days, the extent of Chamberlain's injuries from her manhandling became apparent. She was diagnosed with a concussion, a CT scan showed damage to two of the vertebrae in her neck, she had suffered a whiplash, and the event had so traumatized her, reminding her of moments of violence from far back in her childhood—her mother had killed herself when Doni and her twin were twelve years old, and she had spent much of her childhood in what she remembered as being abusive foster-care homes—that she had to seek out a therapist. Weeks later, Doni Chamberlain's brain still felt like it was in a fog; she'd lose words mid-sentence, leave her car running when she parked it and came in the house, put food that she had no intention of freezing in the freezer. She left her garden hose running all day, got confused over her bank account details, stumbled over word games that she used to complete with ease. When she sat down at her computer to write, she could feel her neck spasm, and her left hand would begin to tingle.

"This was a turning point," Chamberlain explained a month later. "We walked through a door July 6th. Not only was I assaulted and treated horribly, but those guys were celebrated and treated as heroes. I used to feel so brave—with my notebook and my pen and my phone. I don't think I'll ever be the same." She spent $4,000 installing a high-security gate in her driveway, added another gate to her backyard, put in even more cameras around her house, and largely stopped going out to cover events in her county. A group of retired female teachers, many of whom had taught the young men and women now barracking Doni when she ventured out in public, offered to accompany her on her outings, betting that their ex-students would be shamed into civility if they saw who was accompanying the journalist on her rounds. Doni refused the offer. A local karate instructor offered to serve as her bodyguard; again, thinking it would only inflame an already dangerous situation, she thanked him but said no. When she needed to meet up with someone, rather than go out she would invite them to her home. And when the weather was nice, they would head into her garden, climb the steps to the large tree house in her fruitless mulberry tree, its platform and side rails hewn out of twisted branches rescued from one of the local wildfires, sit on the chairs she had lugged up there, and talk. The elevation and the view of all potential entry points to her property calmed Doni down, gave her some sense of security.

Nearly three months after the altercation, Doni Chamberlain received the officer's report. Despite her testimony, despite her video footage—she had been live-streaming the event when she was surrounded and manhandled—and despite the fact she had, unbeknownst to those who attacked her, been wearing a wire at the time for a videographer who was surreptitiously recording political gatherings in Shasta County for a documentary that he was making, the sheriff recommended that no charges be filed against any of the participants. Notwithstanding the documented injuries, the officer who wrote up the report all but accused her of malingering. "I felt Chamberlain was exaggerating the amount of discomfort she was in at that time in order to convince me she was suffering severe injuries," wrote Officer Quintan Ortega. Kent had denied, to Ortega, that he had grabbed Chamberlain's cell phone and tried to pull it off of her, and none of the other witnesses would corroborate the journalist's story. At the end of his thirteen-page report, Ortega wrote, "CASE STATUS: Closed." Dismayed, Chamberlain fired off a long letter to Sheriff Johnson. "I was assaulted," she wrote. "I was falsely imprisoned. I am a 67-year-old senior citizen. I am a journalist who was injured while doing my job, covering a public meeting. Sheriff Johnson, I hope you can see what's happened here. Mark Kent lied. Rebecca Walker lied. Jesse Lane and others lied. They're protecting each other and sticking to their collective lies to avoid getting in trouble." Page by page and paragraph by paragraph she detailed what she saw as flaws in Ortega's report—erroneous information, misinterpretation of the facts, neglect of all the audio and video files that she had provided. Her protests were to no avail. The case remained closed. In the eyes of Shasta County's law, nothing wrong had befallen the publisher of *A News Café*.

———

Meanwhile, even as the fire that he had helped to ignite in Shasta grew seemingly hotter by the day, Carlos Zapata himself sought to convey a newly minted image of mellowness. Months after the COVID public health emergency was declared over and the mandates around vaccines and masks ended, he had stopped showing up to board of supervisors meetings on a regular basis and had toned down his inflammatory remarks at the meetings that he did attend. He had made his peace with Nathan Blaze and had even invited him for drinks at the Palameno Room, the bar that Zapata ran in Red Bluff. When a Blaze critic emailed the YouTuber to say that he was going to rape his girlfriend in front of him and then boasted to Zapata about what he had done, the ex-marine took pride in making the man phone Blaze to personally apologize.

Yet under the newly mellow surface, a bubbling hostility still lay. After a week in which Zapata kept texting me messages about how we would agree on an array of economic issues, such as the scandal of poverty in America or the vileness of people being denied health care because they lacked resources, late one night, apropos of nothing, he suddenly sent me a couple of text messages with a distinctly different tone. Zapata informed me that "many Latinos complain that the Jews are horrible people. They don't tip worth a shit." Then he concluded that "I was raised not to trust a Jew but I'm open to hear what you have to say since you're one of them."

That "you're one of them" summed it all up. In the minds of the people who had successfully orchestrated a political revolution in Shasta County, you were either with them or against them, either one of them or forever an untrusted, unwanted outsider. The word "Jews" was, it seemed to me, almost an afterthought. It could just as well have been "gays" or "public health officers," "transgender people" or "liberals." It could have been, in short, anyone who didn't agree with *The Red White and Blueprint*, anyone who wasn't entirely on board with its efforts to reshape the picturesque county in its my-way-or-the-highway image.

Chapter Ten

THE CULTURE WARS
COME TO TOWN

MORE THAN THREE YEARS AFTER MAYOR WILLIAM ARMACOST AND THE PANDEMIC UNLEASHED chaos on Sequim, things had begun to calm down again on the Olympic Peninsula. Starting with a run of election wins in late 2021, the Good Governance League had recaptured most city government positions from Armacost and his allies, and the business of local politics was, once more, tackling genuinely local issues such as zoning ordinances and affordable-housing developments. The city was now permitting the building of larger multiunit buildings instead of just single-family homes, and Habitat for Humanity had come into town to build two affordable-housing developments for low-income residents.

Perhaps most surprisingly, after the November 2021 elections Armacost himself, no longer in command of a right-wing council, had started voting with the majority on important local policy priorities. His was one of the votes cast for increasing access to affordable housing. He spoke in support of investments such as purchasing a fleet of hydrogen-fueled buses aimed at greening the county's public-transit system. At policy forums, he even began speaking somewhat favorably about the MAT clinic that he had been so adamantly opposed to during the Charlie Bush controversy. And Seth Larson, who had stirred up so much fear during the demonstrations following the George Floyd killing, was no longer running a gun store; instead, he was reputedly in charge of a tiny-house company situated near a local elementary school. Meanwhile, the Washington legislature, at least partially in response to the events in Sequim and in Forks, had passed a law banning the carrying of weapons within fifty feet of a political protest.

Charlie Bush, after eight months out of work, had found a job as a city administrator in the town of Sedro Wooley, across the water from the peninsula and nestled near the spectacular glacial wildernesses of North Cascades National Park. He hadn't returned to Sequim since he and his wife moved away in October 2021. Instead, he was hiking more than ever and had begun to reflect on the craziness of the past three years. "It left a lot of people scarred," he concluded. "A lot of rippling impacts: impacts on families, people turning to substances, a lot of different impacts." The pandemic had also taught him not to sweat the small stuff. "Here we are, and life goes on," he said philosophically. "We've come out the other side, and life's too short to be upset by these things. Yeah, I'm thankful for everything."

Even Jodi Wilke was telling anyone who would listen that the country was riven by too many divides and needed to find common ground. The MAT clinic, which had stirred up so many heated emotions back before the pandemic, had been up and running for years—and despite the warnings from Save Our Sequim that it would result in an invasion of seriously mentally ill, addicted, homeless residents from Seattle, the sky hadn't fallen in, and the peninsula hadn't been inundated.

Allison Berry had, after three years, managed to get back to the work she loved: planning out strategies for combating tough social issues, from drug addiction to teen pregnancies. One day a week, she worked with patients at the MAT clinic. "It's great," she said, perhaps thinking back to the work she had done with the homeless and the mentally ill in Seattle when she was just starting out in medicine. "They're getting new patients every day and having a lot of success getting people off of opioids. Almost all of my patients have pretty significant mental health trauma—and we can treat them for that. People have gotten so used to feeling terrible they don't know there's another way. And they're super grateful for whatever you do that makes them feel better."

Yet underneath the surface, things still hadn't entirely returned to normal. Lowell Rathbun, one of the Sequim Good Governance League candidates who won office during the 2021 sweep, worried that the toxic politics of the Armacost era had turned off a critical mass of people from participating in local politics. Fewer people were attending council meetings these days, he estimated. Bruce Cowan talked of "the commons being poisoned." And P. J. Harris, one of the architects of the Good Governance League, pondered aloud about how hard it still was for the community to heal. "It is so important," she pled. "We are so suspicious of each other. We are so nervous of each other."

For Berry, life in late 2023 was a whole lot better than it had been during the pandemic. In her more optimistic moments, she even dared to hope that a new generation of younger residents were pushing back against the political divisions of the recent past and that

this generation would corral the chaos. "Some of the most thought-
ful correspondence I get is from high school students," Berry stated.
But then she immediately tempered that observation, saying that
many of the local teachers she interacted with worried that since the
pandemic, at least some of the children had gotten ever more unruly
and ever more distrustful of any and all sources of authority: "They
say the students say the most wild, outlandish things to them. Some
of them, their dads are the ones who came to the courthouse and
wanted me hung. So I'm not surprised their children now feel they
can shout at teachers. If there's enough distrust sown in all forms of
expertise, it's hard to see how we get out of this."

New fronts in the culture wars had also opened up during those
last three years.

As the pandemic ceased to dominate public discourse, Berry noted
a shift in the attacks leveled against her. These days, the online trolls
and senders of crude emails who had spent 2020 and 2021 accusing
her of having committed crimes against humanity by implementing
vaccine and mask mandates had taken to accusing her of being a transgender man pretending to be a woman. On Facebook, in particular,
the vitriol flowed freely. In response to one person complimenting the
public health officer with the words "Dr. Berry is amazing," another
replied, "Really? He is? How many vaccines injuries and deaths is
he responsible for???? Do you have a total?????" To which another
replied with, "Glad I'm not the only one that recognizes a biological
male when I see one." The "really?" woman replied with a succinct
"Yup." This apparently passed for sophisticated political debate and
discourse in the social media–meets–COVID era.

For Berry, it was a disheartening continuum of the vitriolic
discourse unleashed during the pandemic. "A lot of the same people who comment on COVID will comment in our posts about
gender-affirming care and abortions. It's the same crew. There's a lot
of cross-pollination."

In March 2023 a purported well-wisher sent her a note warning her that members of the community were planning to "Benghazi" the public health office—a new verb, based on the events in Benghazi, Libya, several years earlier, in which four US embassy personnel, including the ambassador, had been killed by insurgents during attacks on a diplomatic outpost and a CIA compound. "Just doing a nice low and loud flypast of the Brotherton Bunker also known as the Jefferson County Board of Health," the warning note stated, referring to public health workers in the neighboring county of Jefferson. The author was ostensibly on Berry's side and said that he simply wanted to warn her of things he had heard on the grapevine around town: "Understand we have enemy forces closing in on Dr. Berry ready to Benghazi her, and understand there are some complaining about masking." The email concluded with "No way in hell am I gonna Benghazi my public health doctor. One low, loud, effing flyover delivered."

Now, however, Berry was feeling too angry at all the hate directed at her to be really threatened by it. True, her sleep was still pocked by nightmares from her experiences in 2020 and 2021, but during the daylight hours she felt in control again: almost, at times, above the fray. "I'm like, 'Oh my goodness, try me. You have no idea what I've been through. You're going to have to do better than that if you want to scare me.'"

Just up the peninsula, a forty-five-minute drive from Sequim, Port Townsend was immersed in its own culture-war battles around transgender issues.

In August 2022, when a young transgender individual on staff at the Port Townsend YMCA went into the girls' locker room at the pool to help some of the younger children, an elderly woman, Julie Jaman, who was showering at the gym after her daily swim, began screaming at her, accusing the nineteen-year-old of inappropriate behavior with the children and asking intimate questions about the staffer's genitalia. "Do you have a penis?" Jaman asked the person who, based on their voice, she had identified as being male; as she waited for an answer, Jaman stood, naked and on edge, in the shower cubicle.

Jaman was eighty-one years old and had spent much of the previous sixty years protesting for one cause or another. She had been in the anti–Vietnam War movement as a young woman in the 1960s, turning up at demonstrations in California, Oregon, and Washington— she had lived in each of these states before stumbling upon Port Townsend in the 1970s as a young single mother of two children, and settling there. She had been active in the women's liberation movement and had worked with victims of domestic violence and sexual assault. Creating "safe spaces" for women, places where they wouldn't feel that they were vulnerable in the presence of males, had long been one of her passions. Some of her fellow townspeople described her as a hippie, a granola personality. If she was, it made her a good fit on the peninsula, where back-to-landers who had come of age during the counterculture had for decades sought to remake themselves away from the corrupting influences of the big city.

Over the decades, to pay her bills, Jaman had taken a variety of jobs—working on a farm for many years, putting in hours at the local food co-op, and so on. Recently, with the country ravaged by the COVID epidemic, she had become increasingly anti-vaccine, believing that Big Pharma and the government were conspiring to expose people around the world to inherently unsafe and experimental new vaccines.

Jaman's politics were difficult to categorize. In 1964, the first presidential election for which she had been old enough to vote, she hadn't cast a ballot for either Lyndon Johnson or Barry Goldwater. She couldn't exactly remember whom she *had* voted for but thought it was likely a write-in candidate. She did recall voting for Jimmy Carter and, in the year 2000, for Ralph Nader. More recently, she had been disgusted by the candidates for both the main parties and had avoided casting a ballot for anyone during the Trump years. Now, with another presidential election looming, she had gotten interested in the message, especially the opposition to vaccinations, being put out by Robert Kennedy Jr., although she didn't have opinions on Kennedy's adherence to increasingly outlandish conspiracy theories, including the notion that COVID was a bespoke virus designed so that Jewish and Chinese people wouldn't become infected and that the side effects from the vaccine were also experienced less frequently and less seriously by these groups.

After Jaman intemperately requested intimate details about the transgender employee's private parts, she was told by the YMCA's aquatics manager, Rowan DeLuna, to leave the gym and never come back. Port Townsend, DeLuna declared, wouldn't tolerate bigotry. Complying with Washington State law, the YMCA allowed trans individuals to choose which bathroom they wanted to use; it also hewed to a Washington law that barred the harassment of individuals through asking them invasive questions. As for Jaman's allegations about abusive behavior in the changing room, several YMCA staff who were present all denied that anything untoward had occurred between the staffer and the girls. It was Jaman's line of questioning, the staff felt, that was inappropriate.

Jaman did indeed get dressed in a hurry and leave, but a few days later she showed up with friends, among them Jodi Wilke, to picket the facility, arguing that the rules surrounding bathroom access were so incoherent that they produced an unsafe environment for young girls. Activists from the transgender community responded by aggressively heckling her, rushing the platform, and ripping up the suffragette flags that formed the backdrop to her speech. Some of the protesters held up signs that read "Die Nazi TERFS," TERF being an acronym for Trans Exclusionary Radical Feminists. The chants progressed from "Trans rights are human rights" to "Women's rights are human rights" to "Trans women are women." They blew whistles, blared horns, and played loud music from their cell phones. "Gosh, it was ear-splitting," Jaman recalled. "I've never experienced anything like that. It was as if they didn't want anybody to hear what I was reporting, what happened to me."

At one point, as the crowd, determined to stop Jaman from speaking, began to rush her, she got so scared for her personal safety that she began calling out for police intervention. Wilke, standing next to her, was pushed roughly to the ground and reactivated an old knee injury as she fell.

In some ways, Jaman was an uncomfortable mix of New Left and New Right, her suspicions of state power that were nurtured in the 1960s in a world of left-wing activism having morphed into a suspicion of state power in the era of COVID that often adopted the language of right-wing activism. However, what Jaman knew she wasn't was what she called "woke," a worldview that in her mind embraced gender fluidity and one that she firmly believed was poisoning hearts and minds throughout the country. The more she read about it, the angrier she got. That was why, even though she certainly didn't identify as a Republican, she leaped at the chance to talk about Port Townsend, the YMCA, and the transgender employee who had seen her naked when local Republican groups contacted her, when Tucker Carlson's people reached out to her and asked if she would come on his show, and when a slew of other right-wing media outlets picked up the story. For a few weeks in the summer of 2022, the octogenarian was the darling of the right-wing media ecosystem.

While Jaman was being feted by Carlson and other conservatives, all too happy to have another example of leftist ideology run amok to use in their burgeoning culture war around transgender issues, Port Townsend's self-proclaimed progressive mayor, David Faber, was doing his side no favors.

As mayor, Faber was immersed in the nitty-gritty of an array of causes dear to progressives' hearts. He understood the ins and outs of housing policy and the reasons why the West Coast was in the midst of a housing and homelessness crisis, he could—and did—tweet intelligently on everything from environmental policy to human rights, and he was nothing if not entirely confident that on these issues he was on the right side of history. At the same time, however, nuance wasn't his strong suit. Faber believed that Jaman's arguments were entirely meritless, and he felt strongly that right-wing agitators were trying to pour fuel on the flames of what should have been just a local issue, simply a clash of personalities at the local Y: "When given the opportunity to calm down, and understanding YMCA policy and Washington law, she refused. So ultimately, Julie was in the wrong," the mayor said. That she was also an octogenarian and had been put into what for her was an intensely awkward personal situation, that the event could plausibly have been mediated without her being forever banned from the swimming pool at which she had swum for decades, didn't carry weight for the mayor.

Faber didn't like to hold back, whether it was critiquing his political opponents or letting his id hang loose on social media. He felt compelled to take to Twitter multiple times a day to comment on everything from his bowel movements after jogging to his sexual preferences. These tweets had more than a little too much information (TMI), as older political advisers, such as Bruce Cowan, had at times pointed out to him. "Never great to discover you have to use the bathroom (and not the good kind) halfway into a 2.5 mile run," Faber tweeted one day. And then, a couple hours later, he decided to tell his audience how the story ended: "Two follow-ups: 1) I made it home without incident, and 2) which is the 'good kind' very much depends upon what you're into." On Mother's Day, 2023, he tweeted out, "can't forget the MILFs [Mothers I'd Like to Fuck]."

"We have a basic disagreement about what is appropriate for him to share on his social media feed," Cowan acknowledged. "I've counseled restraint; he's disagreed." Cowan felt that there was a risk that social media simply whipped up emotions without contributing much to underlying debates, and he worried that one outrageous post simply led to an outrageous response, creating a never-ending circle of coarseness. The result, he feared, would be a country permanently tearing itself apart.

Faber vehemently disagreed. The mayor dismissed the allegations against him as fearmongering and argued that if he couldn't tweet freely about whatever came into his mind at any given moment, "it'd take all the joy out of life." Pausing before tweeting and reflecting on how his social media presence might be interpreted by the broader populace given that he was now a public figure would reduce him to being a "mindless automaton." He was, he explained, often simply being ironic—mocking the conspiratorial worldview of adherents to QAnon when, for example, he tweeted that his position as an elected official compelled him to be a pervert and a deviant—or just having a bit of fun.

Immediately after Jaman and her friends—including Jodi Wilke, who had recently gotten into a fierce disagreement with members of her own family after an adult relative had decided he was a woman and she had refused to address her relative by their new female name—had been swarmed and their suffragette flags ripped up, the thirty-nine-year-old mayor took to Twitter to proclaim his unadulterated support for those in Port Townsend who were standing up for transgender rights. "What an incredible night," Faber wrote of a subsequent city council meeting in which he read out a proclamation in support of LGBTQ rights. "The Port Townsend community showed up in huge and peaceful fashion to say that hate has no place here. Trans and cis-allies alike spoke love & support, and the only TERF speaker was from out of town. Tonight reminded me why Port Townsend is home."

Faber's tweet, including his use of the derogatory term "TERF" against women who argued that there was a biological basis for womanhood, was guaranteed to stoke outrage among his opponents. For Wilke, it was simply disingenuous: "In an age where people are told you can't appropriate another person's culture—dress like a Mexican on Halloween, or whatever—it's weird that female appropriation is totally acceptable. A woman is a total life lived. You can't just call yourself one and just be one." Wilke realized that she was treading on toes, but she was beyond caring. "I'll be called a TERF for sure. But XX chromosomes make a woman; that is the most basic biological truth. So if a person wants to adopt a persona of a woman, they can adopt it and dress like a woman and act like a woman, and think they'll feel like a woman. That's their reality. But I'm not obligated to participate in anything but objective reality to the best of my ability."

In an era in which social media amplified political and cultural tensions and stoked the flames of chaos, Faber was as proficient a provocateur as any of those on the right of the political spectrum whom he abhorred. His use of the term "TERF," as Wilke realized, was meant to shut down debate, to demonstrate that anyone who disagreed with him on this issue was worthy only of an insult. Moreover, in true social media fashion, his interventions were limned with exaggeration. He was undoubtedly stretching the bounds of credibility when he argued that the counterprotesters coming out against Julie Jaman, some of whom had showed up at meetings and protests with signs comparing her and her supporters to Nazis and had swarmed Jaman while she tried to speak, were preaching only love.

Faber, an estates and trust attorney, loved the provocative nature of Twitter and the ability to play devil's advocate with a large audience. He, for example, had gotten into public debates online about bestiality and had at one point argued that, ethically, it was OK to have sex with a chicken so long as the chicken was already dead before the act began.*

Predictably, conservative media on the peninsula loathed the mayor and relished every chance they got to highlight his foibles. Opponents within Port Townsend also took to printing out stickers, adorned with his more outré Twitter statements, and plastering them to lampposts and street signs all over town. Nevertheless, the often-inane Twitter stream continued. Faber had, his critics claimed, even liked an incel tweet in which the author had announced that unless a woman had sex with him, he would kill himself. As a result of all this, Faber was hardly on the moral high ground when it came to denouncing for her insensitive comments an elderly, somewhat fragile-looking woman who had spent years working with sexual-violence victims.

In the wake of this confrontation, the YMCA began getting threatening phone calls; patrons were approached by protesters who shouted out to them that there were men using the women's bathrooms. When conservative media outlets picked up on the story—Tucker Carlson's interview with Jaman turbocharged the conflict—the threats escalated. Now they weren't just coming from locals; they were flooding in from around the country. At one point the YMCA staff was so scared that the facility had to be closed down for several days.

---

* When I asked him about this, the mayor said that he was particularly "proud" of that tweet: "It was in response to someone posting the question, 'Is it better to have sex with a live chicken or a dead chicken?' The answer is obviously a dead chicken. It's morally better." Why the mayor of Port Townsend felt compelled to intervene in this particular debate or what he hoped to accomplish with his public intervention was never really explained.

As for Faber, the young mayor was barraged with increasingly vicious hate mail and voicemails, some coming from as far as North Carolina, then the UK, New Zealand, Spain, and even Azerbaijan. And although his social media presence might have been inane, it was milquetoast compared to the absolute venom that now came his way. "Let me tell you something, David, you motherfucking piece of shit," one snarling, nearly two-minute-long voicemail began. "You're a fucking cocksucker, you faggot son of a bitch." The man went on to elaborate his sick fantasy, screaming into the voicemail recording that "they're probably having orgies at your house, fucking your wife up the ass, while you're sucking someone's dick. Your dad probably fucked you in the ass when you were a kid while your mother was fucking whoring on the street." There was a bloodcurdling timbre of hatred in his voice. The would-be savior of Port Townsend's elderly ladies and young children continued: "You and the whole fucking city council, you're going to ban a grandmother from the YMCA for wanting a man out of the locker room for showing a dick to people."

Faber began having nightmares. For the month that the hate onslaught continued, he found it hard to sleep. He installed a security-camera doorbell at his home, and after his wife pleaded with him to not engage with these purveyors of violence, he stopped answering phone calls from unknown numbers. When he worked out of his law offices, a tastefully decorated suite of rooms on the ground floor of an old building on one of the hilly side streets near the small downtown, he now made sure to lock the door so that uninvited visitors couldn't surprise him.

None of the security measures really helped against the onslaught of hatred: the crude and threatening voicemail messages and emails continued to pile up. "Congrats for being a left wing scumbag," one email opined. "America is baffled that a supposedly educated person can't grasp that a pedophile in a woman's swimsuit staring at innocent young girls undressing is sick. Children need to be protected.

You took an oath to protect them. I invite you to stop by my neighborhood in St. Louis. We'd be glad to pummel you bloody. Maybe then you would get it."

Not to be outdone, a correspondent from Texas wrote to the city council members that "I loved seeing your feminine masked mayor making the case for stroking it to 5 year olds in the women's locker room." Of course, he continued, in part Julie Jaman got what she deserved since she, too, was a left-winger. "I have no dog in this fight," he wrote; "that 80 year old woman is a life long democrat. She got what she deserved, deranged man meat in the ladies locker room."

On August 11, 2022, the deputy mayor, Amy Howard, received a voicemail that delivered what seemed to her to be a death threat against Faber: "I have a feeling you'll be in there before the month is over, because the current mayor will not survive this month." She reported it to the police. Faber, who prided himself on his tough skin and who had previously thought the whole thing would just blow over, began to wonder whether his next city council meeting would become a "Pizzagate" thing, whether some nut job high on too much social media exposure and too much rage would try to shoot the place up.

Chapter Eleven

BOOK BANS, FLAT-EARTHERS, AND DEATH THREATS AGAINST THE WEATHERMAN

B Y LATE 2022, HYSTERIA OVER TRANS ISSUES HAD BUMPED OUT MOST OTHER CULTURE-WAR issues as the manufactured crisis du jour. Hard-right politicians who in 2020 or 2021 had spent precious hours attacking Dr. Anthony Fauci and his public health pronouncements were now ready to take to the barricades to defend America's elderly women and innocent children from transgender people who were apparently set on flashing old-timers and "grooming" youngsters wherever and whenever the opportunity arose, be it in swimming-pool locker rooms or the reading rooms at local libraries.

Not just in Clallam County but around the country, seemingly by osmosis many of those who had spent the pandemic years railing against vaccine mandates, masking, and social-distancing requirements, who had honed the fine arts of social media trolling by mocking or threatening doctors and public health workers, politicians in favor of COVID restrictions, and ordinary citizens who lined up for vaccinations, were now turning their attention to the new hot-button issue of LGBTQ books available to children in schools and in libraries, and to health services provided to transgender teens. In numerous communities and states, librarians reported upticks in censorship movements, noting that many of the same people who had shown up at library board meetings in outrage at the pandemic restrictions were now turning up at board meetings in outrage at books like *What's the T?* and *Gender Queer* being held in the library stacks.

Take, for example, the fast-growing suburb of Meridian, Idaho, just west of Boise. Library director Nick Grove was a trim African American man who showed up at work each day in a well-cut suit and pressed, formal shirts. His office was in the sprawling brick building on Cherry Lane that was the main library in the system. Grove presided over four libraries, a mobile facility, and several home-delivery book vans, but he faced a furious campaign by conservative parents and activists over his refusal to remove books that they deemed offensive from the kids' shelves in his library system. "It seemed to escalate as they coordinated after COVID happened," Grove explained, "after the battles over the library shutting down and then [when it finally reopened] requiring masks." Groups such as the Concerned Citizens of Meridian, the Sons of Liberty 1776, and the Idaho Liberty Dogs turned their political energies toward the library.

The tactics that Grove's opponents deployed were often deeply personal. "They sent letters to my neighbors with pictures [from the books] and information they don't like," the library director recalled in amazement. "With my picture, my address, and phone number." When library board of trustees chair Megan Larsen refused to bow to their demands—"Restricting other people's access to materials is censorship; that's a nonstarter for us," she explained—the activists threatened to hold "prayer vigils" outside both her home and Grove's. When the library's leadership explained to the activists that they believed putting books on trans issues behind a curtain and demanding library patrons show ID before being allowed to view them was unconstitutional and wouldn't withstand a court challenge, the activists grew more agitated. They expanded their list of books they deemed objectionable, returning to the library lists with dozens of LGBTQ-themed books, books on race, and books on Islam. The titles, said Grove, seemed to have been "cut and pasted off the internet." Some of the books weren't even in the Meridian library's collection. Others looked to have been chosen almost randomly, as if the people objecting to them hadn't even bothered to read them first.

Eighteen hundred miles east, in Ottawa County, western Michigan, a landscape peopled in the nineteenth century by Dutch immigrants and today speckled with stunning tulip fields, an even messier battle was unfolding. The affluent, fast-growing, but still largely rural county was historically as deeply conservative as any region in America. It had not once voted for a Democratic presidential candidate since 1864 (when its residents came out against Abraham Lincoln's reelection), it voted overwhelmingly for Trump, and, like so many small counties in pandemic-era America, it had in recent years been roiled by increasingly vitriolic protests against mask mandates and school shutdowns. Ottawa County had an outsized evangelical influence and a large number of residents who saw the world in starkly Manichean terms: heaven versus hell, good versus evil. The gray areas of modern life, the contested areas of moral and material ambiguity, didn't hold for many of these men and women.

When the Ottawa County Health Department issued a mask mandate for students in local public schools in August 2021, and the county commissioners, all but one of them Republicans, told critics that they didn't have the power to overturn this mandate, the commissioners' email inboxes were flooded with hundreds of messages per day. According to reporting done by the local *Bridge Michigan* publication, one of these emails, quoting a passage from Matthew 18:6, warned that failed leaders could have millstones wrapped around their necks and be dropped into the sea. Other emails were more personal, one even threatening to kill a commissioner's wife by injecting her with a poisonous serum in retaliation for the mask mandate. Protesters flocked to county meetings to cite biblical scripture in their opposition to the masking requirements. Local Christian schools sued to try to block the mandate from kicking in.

Now, in 2022, with the pandemic emergency fading into the background, groups like Ottawa Impact—which fully embraced Trump's MAGA movement and would endorse only political candidates who signed a nationalist contract recognizing America's "Judeo-Christian heritage"—had begun shifting their emphasis away from the public health response and toward "parents' rights." By 2022, they were targeting rural libraries, hoping to force the removal of books with LGBTQ themes.

In the small community of Jamestown Township, campaigners identified roughly ninety books out of the sixty-seven thousand items in the library's collection that they deemed offensive; the books had been bought, and displayed, to celebrate Pride Month in 2022. At a meeting about the library's future, one opponent of the books stated that the volumes sympathetically represented "lifestyle choices that are destructive and wrong." In the *Bridge Michigan*, another resident was quoted as saying that "they are trying to groom our children to believe that it's OK to have these sinful desires."

The book banners peremptorily ordered the library to remove the books they deemed offensive. When the library director, backed by the library board, refused to do so, the censors, organized by Ottawa Impact, as well as by a group named Jefferson Conservatives, responded with a defund-the-library campaign, urging residents to vote against the renewal of a small local property tax, known as a millage, that generated the hundreds of thousands of dollars a year the library needed to continue operations. On Facebook they strategized about how to target the librarians. They put out flyers and put up yard signs accusing the librarians of grooming kids. Some opponents directly accused the librarians of being pedophiles. Others flat-out stated that the librarians were demons and that the good citizens of Jamestown Township were involved in a biblical struggle against evil.

In quick succession, two attempts to fund the library were voted down by huge margins. And although a Go Fund Me campaign organized by a local software engineer, Jesse Dillman, whose young children were regular users of the library, quickly raised more than a quarter of a million dollars, including a $50,000 donation from romance author Nora Roberts and a $100,000 check cut by a businessman in a neighboring town, the damage was largely done: the library director, Amber McLain, resigned after months of harassment; the interim director who followed her, Matthew Lawrence, quit soon after; and the library, perhaps not surprisingly, struggled to find a librarian willing to replace him.

Around the country, variants on this censorious theme began to accelerate, with laws passed in seven states between 2021 and the spring of 2023 restricting what sorts of books could be checked out by children in schools and in public libraries, and with more than a dozen other states preparing to follow suit in legislative sessions later in 2023 and 2024. These laws were generally written in such a vague manner regarding which books would be banned that they served as catchalls, the chilling effect of the legislation mattering more than the nitty-gritty of the language. After all, with teachers being threatened with a revocation of their teaching licenses or even prison terms for lending out the "wrong" sort of book to students, it took a brave educator to take the risk of keeping a controversial volume on the shelves.

Arkansas's new law specified that teachers could be sentenced to six years in prison for distributing "harmful" texts. In Indiana, school staffers could now face up to thirty months behind bars for providing "obscene" material to students. Legislators in Missouri, North Dakota, and Oklahoma also passed laws mandating fines or imprisonment for school employees and librarians engaged in distributing the wrong sorts of books. And a proposed bill in Idaho, which the governor ultimately vetoed, would have allowed parents to sue school districts for $2,500 for every instance of "explicit" material loaned out to students, creating a form of bounty hunting, akin to Texas's bounty law allowing any private citizen to sue anyone who aided and abetted a woman in securing an abortion.

In Georgia in 2022, Governor Brian Kemp signed a raft of bills into law that were aimed at banishing "divisive concepts" from school classrooms. The language in this legislation was left so vague as to be almost impossible to interpret. Critics said that this was the point— that it was aimed at stifling debate on anything remotely controversial, that it was intended to scare educators away from talking about systemic racism or about issues of sexuality, or teaching any sort of history that might be deemed critical of the United States.

In Florida, Governor Ron DeSantis, with the enthusiastic support of his GOP base, embarked on wholesale assaults on the state's school curricula and higher education system. Gone was the ability to talk about issues of sexuality in the classroom. Gone was the ability for school districts to consider "diversity" in their decision-making processes. Gone as well was the ability to teach controversial subjects that might make students feel uncomfortable, meaning that discussions of America's often ugly racial history were suddenly deemed out of bounds. So nervous did this new law make textbook publishers that one went so far as to produce a version of Rosa Parks's story which explained that the civil rights icon was told to move to the back of the bus but neglected to mention that the reason she was ordered to move was the color of her skin.

Conservatives in Florida and many other states organized feverishly against antiracism efforts in classrooms and in workplaces, setting up political action committees, heckling school board members for being "Marxist," accusing nonwhite members of "reverse racism," and declaring that schools were infringing on Christian values because of the nod toward teaching about issues affecting gay and transgender children. In town after town, especially in states that had voted for Trump, voters elected slates of hard-right members to school boards and city councils. For these activists, it was a new battle against a familiar enemy: Big Brother and his elitist, anti-Christian, nonwhite, antigun, antifreedom, anti-*real*-American election-stealing army.

Indeed, with the COVID pandemic easing up and emergency public health measures a thing of the past, conspiracy buffs, many deeply immersed in the MAGA movement, turned their attention to a slew of increasingly bizarre notions, looking to park their post-COVID energies wherever an audience could be generated. Every day, it seemed, another conspiracist idea blossomed. InfoWars propagandist Alex Jones might have been ordered to pay more than a billion dollars to the parents of murdered children of Sandy Hook for his heinous lies that the school shooting was somehow a false-flag operation conducted by the gun-control lobby or the feds, but in many ways 2023 was turning out to be Jones's moment: in a world of massive disinformation, more and more people—including a shocking number of elected officials—were looking to the notion of bizarre conspiracies as an explanatory force for the social chaos surrounding them. *Global warming?* A con. *Pandemic?* A meta-conspiracy involving the Chinese, Big Pharma, the CDC, and miscellaneous other government agencies. *January 6, 2021?* A false-flag operation carried out by a nefarious alliance of government agencies and Antifa activists, designed to embarrass the MAGA movement. *Mass shootings?* Similarly false flag in nature. In May 2023 CNN reported that meteorologists were receiving death threats for their reporting: apparently, a growing body of conspiracists now believed that weathermen and weatherwomen were themselves either responsible for generating the bad weather or were hyping storms and droughts and heat waves to benefit some faceless but all-powerful environmentalist world-controlling cabal.

In 2021 researchers at the University of New Hampshire found that about 10 percent of Americans, spread across all age groups, were literally flat-earthers, inclined to disregard evidence that the Earth was a sphere rotating in space; a slightly larger number believed that the 1969 moon landings were faked. During the COVID pandemic, activists began parodying the mushrooming conspiracy culture by putting up signs around the country saying, "Birds aren't real." Unfortunately, at least some observers missed the satirical intent, and a movement developed around the idea that birds had gone extinct and been replaced by government-operated drones that could spy on the entire human population. In 2022 researchers with the Public Religion Research Institute found that one in four Republicans identified with the bizarre package of conspiracy theories, many of them involving ideas of a pedophiliac political elite, loosely spun together as QAnon.

Nothing, however, was guaranteed to ruffle the feathers of the post-COVID Right as much as the issue of how and whether schoolkids would be exposed to literature and teachings on transgender themes. Even "Critical Race Theory" and whether parents had a right to prevent their children from being exposed to teachings on America's history that might make them feel guilty or uncomfortable paled beside this front-burner culture-wars issue, the ginned-up emergency of the moment, of kids choosing their own personal pronouns, of onetime boys wandering into girls' bathrooms, of transgender competitors competing in girls' and women's sports events, of youngsters reading about people with marginalized sexual identities.

Despite the free-speech protections embodied in the First Amendment, book-banning movements and general censorship campaigns have a long and dishonorable history in the United States. Take the Espionage Act, which allowed the postmaster general to deny mailing privileges to radical magazines and newspapers during and after World War I. Take the Scopes Monkey Trial or the burning of Beatles albums in the Deep South. Take the attacks from the Left in recent years against authors like Mark Twain and the efforts to ban books such as his *Tom Sawyer* because of the use of racially offensive language, or attacks from the Right against William Burroughs's *Naked Lunch* or Anaïs Nin's sexually explicit diaries.

In the 2020s, with the country riven by political and cultural conflicts, the grim voices attacking literary freedom were coming at libraries from myriad political directions. They were all wrong. Yet they weren't all equivalent. Censorship from the Left might be entirely misguided, but it wasn't generally backed up by major legislative effort. By contrast, censorship from the Right now had a vast political infrastructure behind it, all aimed at further marginalizing vulnerable people already living, all too often, on a knife-edge.

Throughout 2022 and 2023, organized campaigns against writings with LGBTQ and racial-justice themes picked up legislative steam in GOP-controlled states around the country. And in their smaller, more conservative counties, even liberal states such as California and Washington saw escalating challenges to the books that libraries stocked.

Dayton, Washington, was a good example of this. The tiny town (Dayton's population was barely 2,400 people) lay in the heart of southeast Washington's lush farm country on the other side of the state from Sequim. Nearly 300 miles southeast of Seattle, 270 miles east of Portland, Oregon (for much of the way, the road east follows the spectacular Columbia River, which serves as a natural barrier between Washington and Oregon), and 125 miles south of Spokane, it was about as far from the region's big cities as it is possible to be in Washington State. It was also nearly an hour's drive from the closest interstate, giving it a particularly insular feel. The overwhelming majority of its residents were white, and most were conservative; in recent elections, upward of 70 percent had cast their vote for GOP candidates. The little town's Main Street was lined with cutesy old stores and cafés; the historic Weinhard Hotel, complete with a Victorian-era parlor and piano room; and a drugstore that still had its original soda fountain, decked out with red swivel stools and prices—$1 coffees, $3 small milkshakes—seemingly out of a long-gone decade.

In the early nineteenth century, Lewis and Clark's exploratory expedition went through this region. Seventy years later, following the routes of the new cross-country railroads, pioneers began settling small communities like Dayton. The town itself was founded in 1871; the heavy Victorian-style courthouse that dominates the eastern end of Main Street was built sixteen years later. By the early twentieth century, townsfolk and nearby farmers, many of them growing red apples and Bartlett pears on their sprawling orchards that relied on water out of the Touchet River, were pitching in to fund a library. They would donate dollars from bake sales, from the selling of scrap metal, and from miscellaneous other fund-raisers. In the 1930s, Governor Clarence Daniel Martin reputedly donated $5,000 of his own money toward the library fund. And in 1937, at the heart of the Great Depression, Works Progress Administration crews set to work to construct a little brick library on South 3rd Street, finally making that hope a reality.

For three-quarters of a century, the library was run by the little city. But in the early 2000s, when the lending center faced insolvency, three-quarters of county residents voted to end the freebie that they were getting—until then, only the city residents were paying taxes for the library, whereas all county residents qualified for free lending privileges—and to set up a library district that would tax all county residents so that the institution could survive and flourish.

One could go to the library to access computers, to copy documents, to fax paperwork; one could use its seed bank to accumulate seeds for a garden; one could borrow everything from books to state-park passes, movies to cooking equipment. Families could attend story hours; residents could use rooms off the main reading areas to hold group meetings. It was a sort of jack-of-all-trades institution, filling in crucial gaps that in a town as small as Dayton would otherwise remain unfilled.

By 2023, however, it was also at the center of a fierce local firestorm, with a young mother named Jessica Ruffcorn (who had once worked in a nearby town's library) pushing a ballot initiative to defund the library in the wake of the librarians' decision to place books such as *Gender Queer* and *What's the T?* in the kids' section of the lending institution.

"I'm a conservative Christian. I've been in church leadership for twenty years," said local special-education teacher Tanya Patton, who led the campaign for the library district in the early years of the century. But, she said, "I support 100 percent the freedom to read. I believe passionately in libraries and the value of libraries." Criticizing Ruffcorn's efforts, Patton declared, "It doesn't make sense to me. I have the right to take the books out or not take them out. If there's a movie on TV, I have the right to watch it or not watch it. But I don't have the right to tell others what to watch or read. It doesn't seem right to me that one person or group of people is making moral or ethical judgments about certain content, and saying it needs to be singled out and labeled as dangerous." Moreover, she argued, the whole thing was a red herring: if kids wanted to find certain material, all they had to do these days was whip out their cell phones and do a Google search. To Patton's mind, removing books from libraries simply made them desirable contraband.

———

With receding curly hair, a slight paunch, and a mildly ruddy face, Todd Vandenbark, who bore more than a passing resemblance to the actor Geoffrey Rush, was an unlikely local hero. When he talked, his voice was gentle, more that of an academic than of a fighter. His Dayton library office was adorned not with fiery posters advocating free speech but with haphazard piles of folders, with a stash of red Folgers instant-coffee containers, and with some of the electronic devices—including those providing WiFi hotspots—that the library lent out to patrons. Yet circumstance had placed the librarian at the fore of the messy culture-war battle around "parents' rights" and who should decide what children can and can't be exposed to in public institutions such as schools and libraries.

So far, Vandenbark had stood firm. It was, the librarian said, a slippery slope once you ceded the principle that individual complainants could serve as arbiters of taste and morality for an entire town.

Vandenbark had also faced down critics from a group called Conservatives of Columbia County (CCC) who argued that the library, and the books that it chose to purchase, were a waste of taxpayer dollars. Members of CCC had in the recent past also opposed the building of a child-care center—one member spoke out at a public meeting to say the center was unnecessary because women should stay home and look after their kids.

Throughout the long battles of 2022 and early 2023, the library's five-person board of directors backed Vandenbark up, this despite the conservative county commissioners having recently appointed a member of Conservatives of Columbia County to the board. "Nothing got banned," said Jay Ball, a book-loving auto mechanic who moved to Dayton in the early 2000s and is currently chair of the library board. "We're in the middle of it. It's not that much fun. But we stick with it."

"There are a lot of people upset about the books and budget, and a lot of people not happy with our director," Jessica Ruffcorn stated. "We've asked to have a few books moved and a policy to protect our kids. We've been shot down every time." A diminutive, soft-spoken young mother who headed the local Little League and, when she wasn't organizing around the library, obsessively posted about the Little League and its young denizens' achievements, Ruffcorn didn't see this as censorship but rather as a fight for individual freedom.

Standing on her front porch and wearing blue plaid pants and a T-shirt with the logo "adulting requires alcohol," her dark brown hair hanging loosely down over her shoulders, Ruffcorn—whose Facebook page had until recently been adorned with the motto "Let men be masculine again. Let women be feminine again. Let kids be innocent again"—argued that the books "involved sexually explicit material, sexual material involving minors, abuse against minors, racial topics—basically, racist books." In keeping these books at the eye level of young children, Ruffcorn felt that ideas she found offensive were being pushed onto kids against their will and against the wishes of their parents: "My eight-year-old, looking for a dinosaur book, doesn't need to come upon a sex book instead."

———

Throughout the spring and summer of 2023, Dayton continued to be roiled by the controversy. *Would the initiative to defund the library pass?* Back in the spring, Ruffcorn thought the odds were 50/50. That seemed wildly optimistic, the product more of a social media echo chamber than of detailed polling. Around town, even among deeply conservative individuals who loathed the books that had been displayed in the kids' section of the library, there was growing anger about Ruffcorn's efforts.

The local prosecutor sent a letter to Washington State's attorney general asking for an informal opinion on whether the dissolution petition was even constitutional. There was, it seemed, a pretty strong legal argument to be made against putting such a ballot measure to voters. Then followed a series of court battles—over the validity of the signatures that Ruffcorn had gathered, over the constitutionality of the initiative, over the legitimacy of a process that allowed unincorporated county residents to vote but not residents of the city of Dayton itself, where the library was actually located. Finally, in late September, the opponents of the defund-the-library effort won. They secured an injunction against the initiative. There would be no November vote; the library would survive.

But that didn't mean the danger was over. Amid all the fury, Vandenbark had stepped down, letting it be known that he could no longer work in a city in which he was routinely harassed and threatened. He accepted a new job, far away—he wouldn't tell locals where—and asserted that he had no intention of ever visiting Dayton again. The interim director who replaced him was seeking to dodge a fight and had promptly removed some of the "offensive" books from the kids' section of the library. Ruffcorn might have lost her defund-the-library battle, but she seemed to be winning her war, setting a precedent where a few angry citizens were effectively able to dictate to librarians which books should be issued with warning labels or placed on the top shelf of the adult section, and which books should be deemed so risqué that parents would have to sign off on having their kids borrow them from the library.

Chapter Twelve

"WE WANT TO KILL YOU"

L OUD AND OFTEN UGLY DRAMAS HAVE BEEN PLAYING OUT ON LOCAL STAGES WITH INCREASING frequency in recent years. There is, in modern America, a soundtrack of extremism and often irrationalism, transforming even the most obscure corners of the body politic into potential battlegrounds.

Pick pretty much any state in modern-day America, and chances are that in some community, somewhere, QAnon supporters, election deniers, militia members, or fervent anti-vaccine, anti-science advocates have taken the political initiative. That demagogues have seized their moment and whipped up the crowd through ginning up fear and flirting with violence. Pick pretty much any state, and odds are that one or more political figures have had barrages of death threats leveled against them recently. Pick pretty much any state, and it's likely that armed men and women have brought their weapons to a political protest or counterprotest at some point in the not-too-distant past and that armed men and women will continue to bring their weapons to protests in the months and years ahead.

Sheriffs with QAnon sympathies have been elected in many counties. So, too, a growing number of school boards have been taken over by those with QAnon leanings. In border communities in Arizona, far-right militias with names such as Border Angels and Veterans on Patrol have put down roots in several towns, intimidating opponents who don't support their demonization of anyone and everyone trying to cross the border with Mexico in order to claim asylum. The QAnon-supporting Marjorie Taylor Greene was elected to Congress in 2020 to represent a district in Georgia despite—or maybe because of—her calls to violence against Democratic politicians, her beliefs in a pedophilic conspiracy at the highest levels of government, and her bizarre anti-Semitic claims that "Jewish space lasers" were responsible for setting California's recent million-acre wildfires. In Michigan, armed militia members plotted the kidnapping and execution of the state's governor.

Meanwhile, in Arizona defeated gubernatorial candidate and ex-anchor on the local Fox station Kari Lake perhaps went furthest in wrapping herself in the Trumpian mantle. Before the election, she warned there *would* be fraud. After the election, she declared there *had* been fraud. She claimed, despite a paucity of any evidence to back up her allegations, that this rampant fraud at the ballot box had robbed her of her win, and she ostentatiously refused to concede defeat. Lake went to court to try to stop her opponent's win from being certified, and when the court threw out her case, she accused the judge of bias.

Six months after Lake's opponent, Katie Hobbs, was inaugurated, the defeated gubernatorial hopeful traveled to Georgia, this time to address a gathering of Republicans and to ramp up her verbal assaults against the president, the attorney general, and the special counsel who had recently indicted Donald Trump on charges resulting from his having kept top-secret documents in his estate at Mar-a-Lago. "I have a message tonight for Merrick Garland, and Jack Smith, and Joe Biden," she declaimed. "If you want to get to President Trump, you're going to have to go through me, and you're going to have to go through 75 million Americans just like me. And I'm going to tell you, most of us are card-carrying members of the NRA." Lake added, perhaps as a legal disclaimer, "That's not a threat, that's a public service announcement." If it was, it was a particularly intimidating version of a PSA.

By the summer of 2023, Donald Trump was facing more than ninety criminal charges in four separate trials—one in New York, another in Georgia, a third in Florida, and a fourth in Washington, DC. At least some of those trials, in which Trump was accused of everything from illegal hush payments to conspiracy against the American people to hoarding top-secret documents in violation of the Espionage Act to racketeering, would likely begin during primary season, while the GOP front-runner was hoping to lock down his delegates for the 2024 nominating convention.

None of that had dampened the enthusiasm of Trump's most fervent fans. Around the country, his legal travails were resulting in a torrent of threats from loyalists against public officials and private citizens alike. Trumpists were bombarding the prosecutors and judges in these cases with threats. Grand-jury members were trolled. Potential witnesses were threatened. Despite being theoretically bound by terms of release that prohibited the ex-president from using social media to intimidate people involved in the trials, Trump himself was repeatedly using his Truth Social and other accounts, as well as his speaker platforms, to lambaste the district attorneys and special counsel who had brought cases against him. "IF YOU GO AFTER ME, I'M COMING AFTER YOU!" he wrote on Truth Social against US District Judge Tanya Chutkan, who was presiding over the ex-president's trial for conspiring against the people of the United States and not accepting the peaceful transfer of power. Throughout that summer and into the fall, Trump kept up a barrage against the prosecutors who were bringing him to trial, training much of his wrath on Fulton County (Georgia) district attorney Fani Willis. He labeled the African American prosecutor a racist, claimed—without evidence—that she had had an affair with a gang leader, and said she was head of the "fraud squad." On pro-Trump internet forums and social media, Trump's supporters responded—as the indicted ex-president surely knew they would—with a slew of threats against the DA and her family. In response, law enforcement felt compelled to throw up a ring of high security around the prosecutor. A similar story unfolded with Judge Chutkan, with Manhattan DA Alvin Bragg, with New York attorney general Letitia James, as well as with the lawyers involved in the civil lawsuit brought against Trump alleging that he had sexually abused author E. Jean Carroll. All reported receiving death threats; all ended up with extraordinary security protocols being implemented to protect them and their loved ones. In New York, Judge Juan Merchan, presiding over the hush-money case brought against Trump by Alvin Bragg, received dozens of death threats after the ex-president announced that he was "Trump-hating."

As the ex-president amped up the rhetoric, the response from Trump's followers was all-too-predictably violent. In Houston a woman was arrested and held in detention pending trial after allegedly leaving a phone message for Judge Chutkan threatening to kill anyone involved in prosecuting and trying Trump. "You are in our sights; we want to kill you," Abigail Jo Shry was alleged to have said. "Trump doesn't get elected in 2024, we are coming to kill you, so tread lightly, bitch."

Rachel Kleinfeld, a political-violence expert with the Carnegie Endowment for International Peace, told *Time* magazine that "these threats look more like those in gang cases or organized criminal cases. In organized criminal conspiracy, the person at the top rarely is a trigger-puller." Kleinfeld continued: "It seems to me that what's going on here is [Trump] calling on a much larger network that perpetrates violence, and our justice system isn't very well equipped to handle it."

Throughout 2022 and 2023, Trump leaned into ever-more-extreme rhetoric and borrowed ever more extensively from QAnon iconography. At rallies, his supporters often used what seemed to be hand gestures associated with QAnon symbolism. In September 2022 he appeared at a campaign rally in Youngstown, Ohio, with an instrumental song that sounded remarkably similar to "WWG1WGA"—the QAnon decal and anthem—playing in the background. Trump disingenuously claimed that it was just a royalty-free song his crew had picked up on the internet; his crowd, many of them giving the one-fingered QAnon salute, weren't fooled. "We are Americans, and Americans kneel to God alone . . . we are one people, one family, and one glorious American nation," he announced. The dulcet string tones of the QAnon anthem played on, making it sound as if his sentences were being melded to the music, as if the music had been written to accompany his prophetic words. On his Truth Social account, Trump menacingly wrote, in QAnon-speak, about a "coming storm." Time and again in 2022 and 2023 he reposted QAnon-affiliated messages. In March 2023 he took to telling his audiences that he would be both their vengeance and their retribution. At a Conservative Political Action Committee event in Maryland, he told the crowd, "I am your warrior. I am your justice. And for those who have been wronged and betrayed: I am your retribution." In darkly messianic terms, he declared that 2024 would represent "the final battle" for America.

In September 2023, as he ramped up his reelection bid and sought to shore up his extremist base, Trump implicitly called for the execution of Chief of Staff general Mark Milley because of a phone call to his Chinese counterparts after the January 6, 2021, uprising, in which Milley sought to reassure China that an unstable president wasn't about to launch a war as an excuse to try to remain in power. Milley had also taken secret steps to secure the country's nuclear weapons in the event that a rogue president decided to create a nuclear emergency. All this was, Trump opined on Truth Social, "an act so egregious that, in times gone by, the punishment would have been DEATH." Not to be outdone, Arizona's extremist congressman Paul Gosar opined in his newsletter to constituents that "in a better society, quislings like the strange sodomy-promoting General Milley would be hung." In what risked becoming a game of endless fascist one-upmanship, Trump then announced that Comcast, the company that owns NBC and MSNBC, should also be found guilty of treason for its negative coverage of him during his presidency. Days later, he urged an audience in California to encourage the police to simply shoot shoplifters on sight. Such summary justice, he claimed, would solve the crime problem instantly.

These weren't isolated rants or social media missteps. Nor were they simply the stuff of an ornery old man whose self-control left something to be desired. Taken as a whole, Trump's repeated calls to violence were a calculated assault on the very concept of political pluralism, on the notion that disagreements could, and should, be dealt with via the ballot box rather than the gun or the hangman's noose.

For the political strategist Steve Bannon, still looking for that epoch-making burst of alt-right energy that would forever break apart the administrative state and replace it with a government and a bureaucracy marching lockstep in pursuit of American nationalist goals, all of this was music to his ears. It represented, in real time, a startling zag rightward in the politics of the country: an institutionalization of attacks on the judiciary, on the notion of a separation of church and state, and on the professional, nonpartisan civil service and military leadership. He cultivated far-right candidates to run for political office, and he urged the creation of a right-wing popular front that would destroy the Democratic Party and secure a century of undiluted right-wing rule. As George Black wrote in a lengthy essay in the *Washington Spectator* published in late 2022, what made Bannon stand out was "the breadth of his ambition, the sweeping nature of his vision, and the extent of his influence. His plans for a hostile takeover of the Republican Party are quite explicit."

The rise of the ideologues of Shasta County in California and Clallam County in Washington were indications, if any more were needed, that the populist takeover, larded with violent rhetoric, of the Republican Party that Bannon had so long dreamed of was in many locales already a fait accompli. In Shasta County, in particular, Patrick Jones was telling anyone who would listen that the county was suing California to overturn its open-carry gun ban and that he and his allies on the board were also planning to sue the state to nullify the recently passed AB 969, which, in response to Shasta County's efforts to eliminate machine counts, required all counties in the state with more than one thousand voters—which, in practice, meant all counties in the state—to use some form of machine counting of ballots to determine election results.

Meanwhile, the county was still struggling to fill the public health officer's job, which had been vacant for more than five hundred days since the Jones-led majority on the board of supervisors had ousted Dr. Karen Ramstrom. The county had also gone through five county attorneys in the span of a few months—after the board repeatedly refused to listen to legal advice given by its own counsels and repeatedly put forward policies that those counsels viewed as being illegal. "No attorney wants to lose their license over doing something illegal," Mary Rickert noted. "You can't make this stuff up. It's just absolute chaos. There are the conservatives in Shasta County, there are the MAGA people, and then there are these people. They're off the charts."

In late September 2023, Cathy Darling Allen, the Shasta County clerk and registrar of voters, announced that the campaign to recall Supervisor Kevin Crye had qualified for the ballot, having submitted nearly five thousand signatures that were deemed to be valid signatures of District One voters. That was nearly one thousand more than the required number. Recall supporters had organized strategy meetings in the lounge area of the Axiom Hotel, which was on the east side of the Sacramento River from downtown Redding. They had spent the previous months knocking on doors and gathering signatures at tables set up outside of local supermarkets (during one such event outside of the Raleys market, an elderly signature-gathering couple had inadvertently tried to get Crye himself to sign the recall petition; the unrecognized supervisor wasn't amused). Now, the recall supporters sent out a giddy press release predicting that the vote would be held in early March of 2024, on the date of the California primary, and that they would send Crye packing. The campaign immediately set about organizing rallies as well as town-hall meetings to explain to voters just why they were so angry at Crye's dealings with Mike Lindell, at his vote to cancel the Dominion contract without having an alternative form of voting ready to go, at his refusal to abide by the county attorney's finding that a resolution making Shasta a Second Amendment sanctuary county would likely be illegal, and why all of this was, to their way of thinking, such a betrayal of the public trust.

Increasingly, mainstream Republicans were expressing their opposition to Crye—and, by extension, his political cohorts, Patrick Jones and Chris Kelstrom. Tim Garman had been elected in Moty's place back in 2021 as a firm ally of Jones, but he had long since grown disgusted with the showboating antics of the Hard Right and had modified his positions and begun voting with Rickert against the extremist proposals. He was particularly scathing of the efforts to get rid of machine counting at elections, realizing that to hand-count the ballots of more than a hundred thousand voters would take local volunteers weeks. One evening, to the delight of the recall's organizers, he showed up at a board meeting ostentatiously sporting a "Recall Crye" shirt.

Opponents muttered about electoral fraud, claiming without evidence that Allen had approved signatures that weren't valid and had somehow tipped the scales against Crye. Jones talked of "red flags" that pointed to the likelihood that Cathy Darling Allen was working to undermine the beleaguered politician. Reluctantly, however, when he was unable to prove these allegations, Jones joined with Garman and Mary Rickert in voting to schedule a recall election. As Jeff Gorder and the other recall advocates had predicted, it was to be held on Primary Day, March 5, 2024.

———

Crye himself barnstormed the county and the Central Valley to the south, denouncing the recall effort as a sham and alleging it was all part of a plot to allow Governor Newsom to appoint a liberal replacement.* His supporters printed out glossy leaflets warning voters against letting "a small group of noisy, ultra liberals take control of your board room."

The hard-right supervisor didn't mince his words. Those who opposed him, he repeatedly declared in interviews with the local press and in "Freedom Fest" gatherings farther south in the Central Valley, were showing their hostility to "faith, family, country, duty." He accused his adversaries of trying to extort him and painted himself as standing tall in the face of a ruthless intimidation campaign. At these events, he routinely received standing ovations.

Crye's opponents weren't buying it. After all, he had done nothing to moderate his tone in the past few months. He was fully backing Jones in his efforts to ban machine counts even in the face of state law. And he was supporting Jones in the most extreme of his hiring decisions. Recently, the chairman had picked a fight over an obscure volunteer position, that of membership on the local Mosquito Vector Board. Although one of the candidates for the position was an epidemiologist with more than two decades of public health work for the county under his belt, the other, Jon Knight, was a fervent MAGA loyalist with a long track record of hard-right activism. He had used some of the profits from his hydroponic-supply business to help fund *The Red White and Blueprint* docuseries, and on January 6, 2021, he had posted photos of himself, clad in camo gear, outside the Capitol in Washington, DC. He also subscribed to bizarre conspiracy theories, including a belief that Bill Gates was planning to use mosquitoes to mass-vaccinate Americans against COVID. When it

---

* Unlike when Supervisor Leonard Moty was recalled and the successor was selected on the same ballot, the rules were now different: after Newsom himself had beaten back a recall effort against him in 2021, California's legislators amended the recall process, through passage of AB 2582, separating out recall votes from the replacement contest. Now if Crye were to be recalled, the election for his replacement would occur only months later. In the interim the governor had the authority to step in and choose a temporary member for the board of supervisors.

came to the Mosquito Vector Board position, Jones had no doubts: he would, he stated, trust his health in the hands of Knight over the epidemiologist any day of the week. The board majority agreed, and Knight, the hydroponic-supply businessman without significant medical training, found himself shaping responses to the county's mosquito problem.

All of this was very much in keeping with other decisions that were being made. After a year and a half in which the public health officer's position had been left vacant, the supervisors were finally getting serious about finding a replacement. Their lead candidate was a doctor who was against the COVID vaccine, was an anti-masker, and was opposed by the county's scientific advisers. "These guys are choosing the least educated, least informed people to be in key positions that are really important," Doni Chamberlain bemoaned. She reserved particular disdain for Crye, who had recently pushed a resolution declaring that were the state to ever again introduce vaccine and masking mandates, Shasta County would refuse to enforce them, no matter how urgent the public health emergency might be.

———

For voters in Redding, which formed the bulk of Crye's district, the rolling chaos was starting to grate. Three years after Zapata, Jones, Clendenen, and their allies had turned on Moty, Rickert, and Chimenti, with Shasta County's far-right board of supervisors leaping from one extreme to the next, at least in Redding's District One a critical number of voters finally seemed to have woken up.

Outside of the urban hub of Redding, however, the red tide showed no sign of ebbing, and the county's politics remained on a fiercely conservative trajectory.

Jones's store was doing a roaring trade. When I visited in the autumn, an elderly man came in to discuss with Jones what sort of gun and ammunition he should be buying. "I haven't had a gun in

forty years," he confided in Jones, as if it were a guilty secret. "But
the shit's going down." Jones, standing behind the cash register and
next to a half-eaten cup of coffee ice cream and several piles of leaflets opposing the Kevin Crye recall, agreed and began telling him
exactly what sort of firepower he could purchase for only $399; the
board chair then promised his customer that within the year Shasta
County would win its lawsuit versus California and the entire state
would become open carry.

If Jones was worried that the recall campaign would succeed and
that he'd lose the majority that gave him such a stranglehold on the
county, he was hiding it well. He probably believed that with the culture wars in full bloom, and teachers and librarians replacing public
health officers as bugaboos for conservatives, his brand of right-wing,
burn-it-all-down politics still had tremendous wind in its sails. A
local Moms for Liberty chapter had recently been set up in Shasta
County and was pushing the county's school board and the Gateway
Unified School District to implement ever-more-conservative policies around LGBTQ issues in particular.

Nathan Blaze had taken to TikTok, where he'd become something of an influencer, to call the moms "assholes with casseroles,"
"minivan Taliban," and "Moms for Bigotry." In response, his local
enemies had set up a number of fake Facebook accounts with photos
of Blaze and his girlfriend, Lisa Jensen. They showed images of the
couple's home, despite the precautions taken to keep their address
private. Others featured doctored photos showing a monkey shit-
ting on Lisa's face. They posted insults about Nathan's race and
about Lisa's physical appearance. They even included insults about
Lisa's mother's looks. More worryingly, the TikTokking activist had
noticed a few times that they were being followed by strange cars.
So rattled were the couple that they had, like Doni Chamberlain,
turned their home into a high-security fortress. They also, like the
customer at Jones's gun store, were of the opinion that the shit was

starting to go down, and they had bought a Mossberg 500 shotgun in response.

In the early fall, the board of supervisors moved toward establishing a committee, handpicked by Jones and his colleagues, to "oversee" elections. The county counsel told board members that such a committee, usurping the role of the registrar of voters, would likely be "legally insufficient and unenforceable." The majority on the board decided to push ahead regardless. It would, they argued, help voters once more feel confident about an electoral process that many were convinced had become riddled with fraud.

Leonard Moty saw it rather differently. The ousted supervisor, who was now dividing his time between political consultancy work, some long-deferred home repairs and yard work, trips east to his alma mater of Notre Dame to see college football games, and rounds of golf with friends at the local country club—his handicap, he sheepishly admitted, still ranged from 14 to 18—viewed the new committee as nothing short of "election interference."

Moty had, in his enforced retirement, grown more and more suspicious of the motivations animating those now running the county that he called home. He didn't think they were capable of much other than burning everything down, and he was particularly scathing about their ability to run county government effectively and honestly. They were quick to use the language of "We the People" in pushing all their changes, he said, but they didn't really mean *all* the people. "They mean, 'We, the certain people,' 'We, the people who think like us.' It's very disingenuous. It's nothing more than grandstanding—following in the footsteps of the national 'election fraud' stuff." When he tuned in to watch board proceedings or when he read about them in the local newspaper—which he tried to do only sparingly these days—he was struck by what he called the "circus" atmosphere, the endless meetings during which Jones and his allies went down one alt-right pathway after the next.

Above all, the deposed ex-chair of the board of supervisors was horrified by the ways in which local politics, which had traditionally been a relatively low-key, civilized affair, was increasingly mimicking the angry, irrational, violent tones of national politics. He was, he said, continually amazed at Trump's and Trumpism's persistent looming presence over the body politic: "What bothers me is how many people are still blinded by their willingness to follow their leader, no matter what he says or does. It's scary to me that our country could be like this. Unfortunately, there aren't enough people who know how Hitler came to power."

Every so often, Moty contemplated attempting a return to the political arena. But he had decided against it. There was just too much vitriol these days, too much rage. "You've got extremists holding up a whole party," he had concluded. "It's so frustrating to see what these people are doing to my hometown, my county."

By the fall of 2023, Mary Rickert was contemplating her political future. Some days, as the endless misogyny and casual insults hurled her way by some of her colleagues rained down, she told Moty and other friends that she was planning to retire at the end of her current term, in 2024; other days, she seemed ready to fight another election battle. She was cautiously optimistic that Crye would be recalled and hoped against hope that this would lead to a gradual recalibration of Shasta County's politics back toward the political center. But realistically she feared that the impact of years of extremist government would be felt in the county for many election cycles to come.

In Sequim, as the warm summer days gave way to the autumn chill, William Armacost was in the political fight of his life, campaigning for reelection against Councilwoman Kathy Downer, one of the Good Governance League's most recognizable figures. Downer, who was elected in 2021 in the first wave of popular reaction against the QAnon-sympathizing council majority, had switched districts specifically so that she could take on the ex-mayor, and as the November 2023 election neared, she was coming out swinging.

At candidate forums, the Good Governance League candidate lost no opportunity to remind her audiences of Armacost's past comments regarding QAnon and to explain why she had switched districts in order to take him on. "Even though these seats are nonpartisan," she told a meeting hosted by the county chapter of the League of Women Voters, "I really feel like we should not let someone who has QAnon ideologies run unopposed." Armacost would try to sidestep the issue. On radio shows, as well, he refused to take the bait when asked about conspiracy theories. In fact, since 2021 he had studiously avoided issuing full-throated public homages to QAnon. Now he was campaigning on many of the same issues that animated Downer's political work: expanding the city's affordable-housing stock, encouraging investments in technical-training programs for non-college-bound teenagers, protecting the environment. At gatherings of local voters, the hairdresser stressed his business experience rather than his conservative politics as the main reason he should be entrusted with another term in office.

———

Armacost's tamping down of his more firebrand tendencies didn't surprise Vicki Lowe. The executive director of the American Indian Health Commission for Washington State and city councilwoman for the Third District had noticed a distinct cooling of the political fires in Sequim over the previous year. It was as if all of that furious passion unleashed in 2020 and 2021 had, in her city at any rate, somewhat burned itself out.

Day to day, fireworks became rarer; since the November 2021 elections, the city council had, absent a QAnon-supporting majority, moved back toward civility and collegiality. And with less posturing about national issues over which the city council had no control, things were at last getting done again. "We've been really focused on things that impact our city," she explained. It might not be hugely sexy, but spending time on working out how to address the fact that local sidewalks weren't ADA-compliant, leading to wheelchair-bound residents having to head out into the street in order to get from place to place, was important to locals. So, too, was promoting zoning reforms to allow for the building of more affordable housing.

Lowe no longer felt like she was dealing with a continual five-alarm fire: "I wouldn't say it's like before. Because we're a little bit wiser. We're more focused on the people who are here, more focused on local—and on being a caring community. People are proud that we've pulled it together and are doing a lot better." She was spending more time with her five children and seven grandchildren, was cherishing visits with her elderly mother, and for the first time since the pandemic was taking the time to go on local First Friday art walks. She had begun attending the local theater again. One evening she even went to a poetry slam. And, for the first time since 2019, she was a participant in her tribe's organized canoe journey, paddling from Sequim south one hundred miles to the Muckelshoot tribal lands near the town of Auburn. Each evening, the participants shared songs and danced, and when they finally reached their destination, where they stayed for a week, they gave gifts to members of the host tribe.

Lowe's colleague Brandon Janisse, who was gearing up to put his hat into the ring in January 2024 to be the city's next mayor, agreed with her. Though temperamentally more conservative than many of the other six councillors, he had found over the nearly two years since the November 2021 elections that they had managed to put ideology to one side and knuckle down to tackle the hard work of local government. They had worked out, he said, "that to find common ground is to the benefit of those you serve. At this level of government, it's essential to put partisanship aside and not think in black and white—but in seven shades of gray. Low-income housing transcends ideology. Yes, there may be differences in how you achieve those goals; as long as you address them in an adult fashion it's OK to have these differences. Instead of dealing with partisan politics, it's grassroots, baseline, everyday 'what do our constituents need to live their fullest lives?'"

Habitat for Humanity had recently come to an agreement with the city to build more than fifty affordable-housing units in town, and zoning changes that the seven council members were pushing through meant that more multiunit, affordable-housing buildings would soon be added into the local mix. Two economic-opportunity zones were bringing in new jobs. And Janisse was working with colleagues in Sequim and beyond to lobby the state legislature to create more equitable funding models for the state's K–12 school systems.

He was also spending more time with his family, and he was finally able to indulge in his hidden passion—writing about missing people's cases to make sure that these victims of unsolved kidnappings or murders weren't "lost to time." He had been fascinated by such cases ever since 2009, when he had first read about a young girl snatched from off the street in the rural town in which her family lived, west of Olympia. Now he was hoping to fine-tune his writings and actually begin publishing books about these lost souls; maybe one day, he thought, he could even become a private investigator following up leads on cold cases.

Janisse hadn't realized until after the fact just how exhausting the fissuring politics of the Armacost mayorship were. Now, though, with the turbulence from that perfect storm easing up, he was starting to feel optimistic again. Sequim's golden days, he believed, could be in the future. "I think Sequim is going to surpass a lot of cities in the peninsula and in Washington State," he confided. "You're going to see Sequim take off in a way I don't think it has in a long time."

———

Lowell Rathbun agreed. After years in which he had so feared for his city's future that he felt compelled to jump back into the political fray to help save it, he now felt that in Sequim, at least, the spell of irrationalism and extremism had been broken.

Confident that "the reactionaries have been pushed out," Rathbun was getting ready to quit the city council. He wanted to spend time reading and writing about what he called "human overshoot," the overuse of resources that was pushing the planet into a climate emergency and creating a host of political and societal crises in its wake. After the November elections, he would put his home on the market, pack his bags, and head east to Minnesota. His son and grandson lived there, in the Twin Cities area, and he felt it was time to nurture his relationships with them.

Decades earlier, Rathbun had spent several years in a conservative Lutheran cult—a life choice perhaps born, he thought, out of having been repeatedly told by his mother as a young child that if he misbehaved, God would throw him into a fiery hell for all eternity. It had taken him more than a decade to fully extricate himself from the cult, to reassert the primacy of the values that, he knew in his heart, gave his life meaning.

Now seventy-five years old, when he looked at QAnon, when he looked at the MAGA movement, he saw cult followers, people who were in "an altered state of consciousness" and who would fight like hell to maintain the illusions that glued them to the cult. Nationally, he feared, the cultist fever hadn't yet broken. Certainly, it hadn't broken in places like Shasta County, California. In Sequim, by contrast, to his delight he saw people who were growing tired of all the craziness, who were ready to return to a more reasonable mode of discourse.

———

Four years after the first COVID cases surfaced in Wuhan, China, a prologue to events that would quickly transform the world, Allison Berry was still trying to understand all that had happened. For a while during the pandemic, she had been convinced that somebody would kill her, and she had been tormented by nightmares on a near-nightly basis. At the same time, however, she had also watched with great hope as America rolled out a vastly expanded social safety net to protect the vulnerable from the worst impacts of the pandemic: COVID testing was made free, as was treatment for the disease; unemployment benefits were expanded; eviction moratoria were put into place; and child tax credits were enacted that resulted in a huge drop-off in child poverty. Not least, for the first time that she could remember, public health departments were being adequately funded. She talked about how in her department she had tried to ensure that she and her colleagues held to "a moral compass. People should be allowed to live, and the vulnerable should be protected. These are your community members; they're vulnerable. People got on board, recognizing the general humanity of everyone."

Now, with the worst of the pandemic in the rearview mirror, America seemed to be reverting to "normal" again. Berry was watching, in frustration, as the safety-net programs created in 2020 and 2021 ended and child poverty began once more to soar. She was attending meetings with county commissioners who were determined to claw back much of the temporary funding that had been sent the way of her public health department; by the autumn of 2023, despite the rearguard action that Berry was fighting, more than $700,000 of the roughly one million dollars provided her department annually from the county's general fund during the pandemic had been withdrawn. And whereas during the pandemic nonviolent offenders were being released from the county's jail, now low-end offenders were once again finding themselves behind bars. In the conservative town of Forks, city officials were balking at allowing a state-funded mobile addiction-treatment van to park in town to provide services to local opioid addicts. "It's hard to see the missed opportunities to help people get better," Berry observed. The public health officer was also watching with growing alarm as at the national level people continued to isolate themselves into fortified political camps, seemingly getting more accepting by the day of the notion of political violence as a means to solve disputes.

Yet at the same time that she feared for the country's future, the relationships that Berry had nurtured with county and city officials—with the sheriff, with the fire chief, with the head of the Sequim Police Department—all gave her cause for hope at a local level. The fire chief, a conservative Christian, was working with her to set up a "leave behind buprenorphine" program so that residents addicted to opioids could have ready supplies of emergency medicines to use in case of an overdose. Even the sheriff, who came from Forks and shared many of its populace's conservative beliefs, trusted her—because he had seen how hard she had worked and how closely she had been guided by the medical data during the pandemic. She and her team were focused now on lowering the local infant-mortality rate and on raising the availability of lead testing to protect children from exposure to the toxic metal.

But the biggest change for Allison Berry wasn't in the workplace; it was in the home. In the spring of 2024 the doctor was getting married—to a man she had met during the pandemic response when he had come out to volunteer with her department at an event held in a local park to vaccinate and feed homeless residents. They had hung out afterward and then, when they found out they shared a love of running, had begun jogging together. Now, two years on, Paul and Allison were planning their nuptials on the shores of Lake Crescent.

For Berry, her upcoming marriage was part of a larger post-pandemic reset. For years, she had been too spooked by the gun-toting men and women who wanted her dead to dare to jog alone. Now, with the political temperature finally cooling in Clallam County, she had regained the confidence to go off solo into the woods. She had begun tending her garden once more, growing vegetables and fruit—her four-year-old daughter was a particular fan of currants—and "flowers that make me happy." And she had started playing music in her spare time: her French horn as well as the piano that she had inherited from her grandmother. After school and on weekends, she would sit with her daughter, teaching her to pick out notes.

"It feels like a fog has lifted and everything is a little clearer," the doctor said, her voice soft, as if she were afraid that speaking too loudly would break the spell. "And it's really nice."

Epilogue

O N November 7, 2023, William Armacost, onetime mayor of Sequim, lost his bid for reelection. The result wasn't even close. Kathy Downer, the Sequim Good Governance League candidate who had resigned from the seat that she had been elected to in 2021 specifically so she could take on the QAnon-supporting councilman, got well over 70 percent of the vote. For the political strategist Bruce Cowan, the vote represented a climactic moment at the tail end of two years of backlash against the corrosive leadership style the hair-salon owner had unleashed on the little Olympic Peninsula town. In 2021 voters had given the thumbs-down to most of Armacost's allies on the city council. Now, two years later, they had delivered the coup de grace, with fewer than nine hundred residents backing Armacost himself in his reelection bid. "Today the voters had a chance to tell him what they really think of him," Cowan declared. "They sent him packing."

All around Sequim, voters delivered similar verdicts. Every candidate backed by the Sequim Good Governance League won, be they contending for seats on the city council or on the local school board. In Port Angeles, progressive candidates also won their city council races. In the lone county commissioner's race held that November, Clallam County's bellwether voters returned a Democrat by a nearly two-to-one margin.

After years of rolling culture wars and years of bitter fights about how best to respond to the COVID pandemic, Clallam County's voters were sending a message. The majority wanted to move on. They wanted a restoration of normalcy, of competence in government, and of civility in discourse. They wanted their local public officials to be laser-focused on issues such as housing rather than going down rabbit holes about QAnon, about the evils of public health responses to a once-in-a-century pandemic, about stolen elections.

———

Four months later, on March 5, 2024, Californians went to the polls. At the state level, it was primary day, with voters choosing the top two US Senate candidates to go forward to the general election in November, as well as having their say in a slew of other races, from US House representatives to local mayors.

In Shasta County, with the rain falling steadily and the weather chilly, residents finally got to weigh in on recalling Supervisor Kevin Crye. They also got to vote on whether or not to give Patrick Jones and Mary Rickert another term in office.

Over the previous months, the political rhetoric around the recall vote had gotten ever more heated. Each side accused the other of accepting copious amounts of funds from outsiders, although, according to an analysis by the online publication *Shasta Scout*, the "No" campaign was far more reliant on outsiders' dollars. Much of the money opposing the recall came from the Water Users Committee, a political action committee that was funded in large part by the wealthy Connecticut resident Reverge Anselmo, who had played such an outsized role in the campaign against Leonard

Moty more than two years earlier. At the same time, many donors, both for and against the recall, were locals, including some who had been embroiled in the conflicts of the previous years: Carlos Zapata was listed as a donor to the "No" campaign, as was Mosquito Control Board member Jon Knight; Dr. Karen Ramstrom was listed as having given money to the proponents of the recall, as were several high-profile, locally based Democratic political operatives.

When the board of supervisors met, recall supporters would line the steps leading up to the county's administration building clad in colorful T-shirts bearing "Recall Kevin Crye" logos and holding banners that read "Cronyism," "Millions of dollars wasted," "Outside money means no local control." Some days, in a mirror image of the disruptive right-wing protests of the COVID era, the anti-Crye organizers would head into the supervisors meeting en masse to make their displeasure known.

Within a few hours of the polls closing, it was beginning to look like Shasta's voters—or at least the relatively low percentage that cast votes in the March election—had soured on Crye. By one in the morning, with the early ballots and most of the in-person precinct votes already having been counted, the recall campaign was a few hundred votes ahead. Given that mail-in ballots would still be accepted for the next week—the day after the election, county elections officials estimated as many as thirty thousand ballots countywide remained to be counted—the results wouldn't be known for several weeks to come, but at least some of the recall proponents were already popping the champagne. "We're very optimistic. We don't want to jinx anything, but it looks good so far," Nathan Blaze reported, having just returned from an election-night party at the Axiom Repertory Theater. "Based on these numbers, it seems very possible. It means we get to bring our county back to sanity." What made Blaze even happier was that Rickert was way out in front of her two opponents in her reelection bid, although she would, it seemed, fall short of the 50 percent needed to avoid a November runoff. By contrast, Jones, long the scourge of progressives and moderates in the county, was trailing far behind his only opponent; if those results held up as more votes came in over the next weeks, come the end of the year he would no longer be sitting on the board of supervisors. And in District Two, as well, the MAGA candidates—one of whom had publicly accused Rickert of being a satanist because one of her vehicles had the number 666 on its license plates—were also losing to a moderate Republican.

It all looked like it was adding up to what Jeff Gorder, one of the organizers of the recall campaign, called a "huge victory," a somewhat improbable recalibration back toward the political middle for a county that had in recent years become a byword for political extremism in California. Gorder was experienced enough to know that things could change on a dime as the late votes came in, but his instincts told him that a corner was finally being turned. For the first time since the pandemic and the turbocharging of the Hard Right in Shasta County, the retired attorney was beginning to think that there might be light at the end of the tunnel. And, he said, it felt good: "It's nice to see a pushback; it's very gratifying."

For Doni Chamberlain, too, the moment felt sweet. The day of the election, she had written an article for *A News Café* referring to the vote as "a life-and-death election tug of war; a battle for Shasta County's heart, soul, viability and reputation." Now, as the ballot count proceeded and as the numbers started to trend against Crye and Jones, she was daring to hope that maybe, just maybe, the brakes were being pumped on the seemingly endless lurch rightward that she had chronicled in her county for so long. At the same time, however, she felt that she wouldn't be able to fully exhale until the election was certified and, even then, wouldn't be completely at ease until the new board members were sworn in ten months later, in

January 2025. "It's been a stressful four years since the extremists got a death grip on Shasta County to turn it into the MAGA promised land. They had so much power for these four years," she explained. "And they caused so much damage. It will take a long time before I can trust that the worst is over."

———

Chamberlain's wariness at exhaling too soon was soon validated. As the early April vote certification date approached, more late-arriving ballots kept being added into the totals. By March 22, Jones was still trailing by huge margins; his time as a Board of Supervisors member was, it now seemed clear, ending. So, too, Rickert had held onto her lead, although her margin of victory had declined significantly, and it looked at least possible that in the November runoff, she could lose to a hard-right opponent. As worryingly for the reformers, by the smallest of margins Kevin Crye now stood posed to remain in power. The vote stood at 4,612 in favor of recalling the Supervisor and 4,660 opposed.

There would be, over the coming days, a mandatory recount, including a hand-tally of the recall ballots. But at the end of the day, Supervisor Crye would emerge the winner by fifty votes, and thus remain in his job.

True, with Jones on the way out, come 2025 Crye would have fewer allies on the Board and that, for the supporters of the recall, was a saving grace. Yet Shasta's voters had indeed sent a message: In the roiling political battles and culture wars ravaging the country, it appeared that by the slimmest of margins they weren't yet ready to return to the political middle. Chamberlain was distraught. As she pondered the implications of a failed recall effort, her bemusement grew. It would, she feared, lead to "a slash-and-burn alt-right destructive derby" and presage yet more chaos in the county that she loved and still considered her home.

ACKNOWLEDGMENTS

As with my other books, *Chaos Comes Calling* would not have been possible without the assistance, encouragement, and emotional support of dozens of people.

To my family—my wife, Marissa, who has made my middle age feel like youth again and who lightens my days; my extraordinary children, Sofia and Leo, for whom I hope the world offers up many adventures in the years to come; my parents, Jack and Lenore, who raised me to care and taught me that my voice matters; and my siblings, Kolya and Tanya, who have always, always had my back, and their partners Dottie and Carl; to Tanya's daughters Izzy and Molly—thank you all for being you. And an additional thank-you, Marissa, Sofia, and Leo, for your patience at my often-long work hours as I reported this book, for your pep talks during dark moments, for your enthusiastic belief that I was capable of bringing to life this sprawling project. To my aunt Jenny, thank you for introducing me to the world of journalism and helping me become aware of the power of the pen. To my cousins Rob, Maia, and Lauren, thank you for sharing laughs and memories. I desperately wish that my grandparents, Chimen and Mimi, and Mim and Bob, were still alive—but to them as well, I owe huge debts of gratitude: you helped shape me into the person I am today.

To my brains trust, I cannot say enough how much your insights and your observations over the past several years of reporting on

America's slide into chaos have meant to me. You know who you are, but a particular shout-out to Adam Shatz, Eyal Press, Carolyn Juris, David Yaseen, Anders Krab-Johansen, Malou Deichmann, Jason Ziedenberg, Theo Emery, and Audie Cornish; to Sameera Khan, George Lerner, Alyson Shotz, Maura McDermott, Kim Gilmore, Chris Stamos, Rocky Anderson, and Eric Klinenberg; to Sam Freedman and Michael Shapiro at the Columbia University Graduate School of Journalism; to my colleagues and friends at *The Nation*—in particular to Elie Mystal, Joan Walsh, John Nichols, Katha Pollitt, Katrina vanden Heuvel, Don Guttenplan, and Shuja Haider; to my Sacramento and Davis crew: Steve Magagnini, Edith Shanta Crawford, Glenn Backes, Joe Rubin, Lara Downes, Rick Grosberg, Gina Ayon, A. G. Block, Jessica Bartholow, Shawn Hubler, Karma Waltonen, John Hill, Anci Titus, Simon Sadler, and Bruce Haynes, as well as all of my colleagues and friends in the University Writing Program at UC Davis; to Vicki Colliver, Andrew Moss, Jesse Moss, and Amanda McBaine in the Bay Area; to Jerry Singleton and Seth Hettena, who have served as my southern California sounding boards for the past couple of years; to my old friends in the UK, Jon Wedderburn, Ben Caplin, Clive Swillman, Pete Sarris, Kitty Ussher, Pete Colley, Kitty Stewart, Jim Driscoll, Kate Raworth, Roman Krznaric; and, of course, to Andrew Graham, my Balliol College, Oxford, mentor in Politics, Philosophy and Economics. Without the hours of stimulating conversation and good cheer that you all provided, in different cities and continents, in homes, in restaurants, in cafés, and in bars, I doubt very much whether I would have had the stamina to bring this book to completion.

I owe my agent, Victoria Skurnick, my publisher, Clive Priddle, and my editors, Jeffrey Kusama-Hinte and Geoffrey Shandler, an immense debt of gratitude for seeing the value of a work such as

Chaos Comes Calling and for realizing the larger American story that such a book could tell.

Finally, to my many sources—both those with whom I agreed as well as those with whom I didn't—thank you for spending the time to tell me your stories and for sharing your worldviews and observations about this stranger-than-strange political moment.

INDEX

265

Credit: Gabriel Teague

Sasha Abramsky is a veteran political journalist and book author who has spent the past thirty years exploring the American political and social justice landscape; he is currently the West Coast correspondent for *The Nation*. He has written extensively on poverty, criminal justice, immigration, and the rise of hard-right and alt-right political movements. He makes regular media appearances on outlets such as MSNBC, NPR, Pacifica Radio, and various popular podcasts.